The Readers' Advisor's Companion

The Readers' Advisor's Companion

Kenneth D. Shearer
and
Robert Burgin
Editors

2001
Libraries Unlimited
A Division of Greenwood Publishing Group, Inc.
Englewood, Colorado

LIBRARIES UNLIMITED
A Division of Greenwood Publishing Group, Inc.
P.O. Box 6633
Englewood, CO 80155-6633
1-800-237-6124
www.lu.com

Library of Congress Cataloging-in-Publication Data

The readers' advisor's companion / [edited by] Kenneth D. Shearer, Robert Burgin.
    p. cm.
  Includes bibliographical references and index.
  ISBN: 1-56308-880-0
  1. Readers' advisory services--United States. 2. Public libraries--Reference
services--United States. 3. School libraries--Reference services--United States.
4. Library education--United States. I. Shearer, Kenneth D. II. Burgin, Robert.

Z711.55 .R43 2001
028.5--dc21

                                            2001054374

Contents

Part II: Advisory Services in Public and School Libraries Today: The State of the Art

Part III: Envisioning an Expanded Advisory Services Role in Libraries

PREFACE

I find television very educational. Every time someone turns it on, I go in the other room and read a book.

Groucho Marx

Writing is play in the same way that playing the piano is "play" or putting on a theatrical "play" is play. Just because something is fun doesn't mean it isn't serious.

Margaret Atwood

What to Expect from This Book

The Readers' Advisor's Companion

- Identifies the aspects of readers' advisory services that need more attention: What gaps need to be filled? Where is weakness evident?

- Depicts the state of the art of readers' advisory in school and public libraries: How well developed is readers' advisory today? What are the best tools to use, including those on the Internet and those designed for multicultural audiences? How does an advisor best put them to use?

- Suggests where librarians may find appropriate educational foundations: How can readers' advisory take its rightful place in LIS education? What is readers' advisory practiced at a professional level? How can readers' advisory be taught at the graduate professional level?

- Presents rich insights from research findings: What do we know about the way experienced readers perceive reading? What is the trancelike state we enter when we are engrossed in a book or a story that someone is reading to us?

- Sets forth a vision of a future in which advisory services thrive and achieve their potential: How do librarians integrate print nonfiction and audio and visual story formats into an advisory service that is broader than one that focuses almost exclusively on print fiction? And what will a Center for the Reader look like (i.e., a library branch location that exists solely to encourage quality recreation for a diverse population)?

- Endorses Margaret Atwood's view that "[j]ust because something is fun does not mean it isn't serious." Just because advising readers, auditors, and viewers involves recreational materials and people enjoying themselves does not imply that there is not much to learn and master before one achieves a degree of professional skill.

Perspective

The Readers' Advisor's Companion assumes that public and school librarians address a wide range of human needs: emotional, spiritual, intellectual, physical, and work-related. Quality of life, the quest for meaning, and the urge to find satisfying interpersonal relationships are major concerns of all clients. They are therefore the business of the public and school librarian. Just as we ought to pay attention to the reference and research requirement of users, so ought we to pay attention to the formation of their values, recreational interests, and social lives. This attention is expressed indirectly through steps such as the development of collections responsive to individuals' interests and attractive displays. It is expressed directly by discussing reading, listening, and viewing preferences with users and providing opportunities to explore the creative process and to discuss materials with others in the community.

Novels and recreational materials are as important to people as facts and knowledge (Smith 1998). The youngster who is finding a direction in life is far more likely to find it in a novel or a biography than in a textbook, research report, or Web site. A sensitive librarian can recognize and meet that youngster's need. Long before scientists, medical personnel, and entrepreneurs undertake their useful work, they are youngsters choosing their fields. Inspiration precedes perspiration; stories precede work. People find role models in books and carry them in memory throughout their lives. The work of Mother Teresa or even the little engine that could inspires an untold number of people to keep on trying.

The right story at the right time can facilitate finding out how to deal with challenges in interpersonal relations and how to find a productive place in society. For many, the right book or film can ameliorate the trauma of severe illness, divorce, or the death of a loved one. Integrating one's sexual needs into a meaningful relationship may be approached in part by exploring strategies that the characters in stories employ. Stories also offer us depictions of successful parents, friends, and partners to guide our behavior (Saricks 2001).

Entering the spell of a tale that grabs our attention is one of the great satisfactions of life for most people and has always been so. Perhaps this universal phenomenon explains why fiction accounts for more than 61 to 70 percent of circulation from the public libraries in Kentucky, New York, and North Carolina. Unfortunately, these three states are the only ones known to measure fiction versus nonfiction circulation in public libraries at this time (Kentucky Department for Libraries and Archives 2000, Lynch 2000, State Library of North Carolina 1999, Peters 2000). Oddly, there appears to be resistance to collecting these data. Although the effort to do so for all fifty states would be considerable, it would provide important evidence that fiction is a major reason for public library use, a fact that would be valuable in monitoring library users' interests. The failure to measure the most common use of public libraries suggests that most state library policymakers either have not considered collecting this information or are avoiding compiling evidence because at some level they question the value of circulating fiction. Readers' advisory appears to be a core business even though it is treated shabbily by great numbers of librarians and by most designers of library and information science curricula. Borrowers have expressed their preference for fiction in all the figures I have seen since public libraries began. In Chapter 1 of this book, historian Wayne Wiegand writes with regard to public libraries, "And for decades now…fiction has consistently accounted for 65 to 75% of the circulation."

The Readers' Advisor's Companion assembles the work of many of the field's established leaders and pioneers as well as several new ones. Contributors are drawn both from those in practice and those in graduate professional education. This book should, as its title suggests, become a companion and a handy reference for the school or public librarian who deals with students and the general public. Although an anthology, it also works as a single integrated text. Indeed, it can serve as a textbook for a graduate course in readers' advisory. It focuses on advisory services and the needs of multidimensional people in a multicultural society.

One of the premises of this book is that most people who use school and public libraries experience stress and are busy trying to live life as well as they can. We believe that they will benefit from apt recommendations and appropriate displays. We encourage a highly visible commitment to advisory services both in the library building and at the library's Web site. We recommend a variety of discussion groups in every library and advisors who know which tools are best, how best to use them, and how to handle advisory transactions.

The Readers' Advisor's Companion advocates full equality for readers' advisory and reference services. The efforts of a librarian spent on finding a good book, an audiocassette, or a video to fill recreational time enjoyably is at least as likely to add value to user experience as the effort to find a fact, a Web site, or a commentary. I admire John Milton's enduring defense of the freedom to disseminate thought, *Aeropagitica*. However, on rereading the famous passage, "A good book is the precious lifeblood of a master spirit, embalmed and treasured up on a purpose to a life beyond life," I became aware that there is, in a normally censored corner of my mind, a voice I cannot still. It suggests, "John, you need to get a life!" A few classics deserve his accolade, to be sure. But we all know that many good books are good fun; maybe they will not endure forever but they are very good nonetheless. Good books can afford deeply satisfying recreation. They can bring on a good night's sleep. They can reward by offering diversion. They can decorate one's interior life in attractive colors and appealing textures. The same is true of the spoken word and film. A good book for me may not be a good book for you. A book just right for you now may have been wrong for you earlier and may be boring at a time later in life. A book's "goodness" is not a property of the text but is rather a property of a reader's response to a text. A major goal of librarians must be to increase the number of these positive responses to text.

Milton lived when books were expensive and rare. We live when books are relatively affordable and plentiful. And all those books are supplemented by stories in video and sound formats. The information explosion and the entertainment glut are but two sides of the same coin. Librarians' advisory skills must match their reference skills in order to serve the needs of students and the general public in the twenty-first century. Librarians must successfully locate the right needle in the right haystack. The needles can be publicly accepted truths or private stories with the power to motivate. The haystacks can be reference books or Web sites; they may be bookshelves or video collections.

Many librarians have allowed baggage from a time of book scarcity, male denigration of women's enjoyment of novels, and relentless puritanical pursuit of "virtuous living" to lead them to anachronistic behavior with regard to the recreational interests of clients (Shearer 2001). Many librarians have, publicly at least, valued fact over fiction; reference over advice; and computer technology over audiovisual and print technologies. State libraries have collected statistics on many aspects of public library use but appear generally to avoid reporting the circulation of fiction. Many librarians have deployed financial and professional resources in an unbalanced way, a way that shortchanges the emotional, spiritual, and imaginative lives of their clients. Many library educators neglect education for readers' advisory services.

The Readers' Advisor's Companion, along with offering outstanding models of readers' advisory practice and presentation of the tools of the trade, challenges this state of affairs and sets forth an agenda for change in library priorities.

—K.D.S.

References

Kentucky Department for Libraries and Archives. 2000. Statistical Report of Kentucky Public Libraries. Fiscal Year 1998–1999. Frankfurt, KY: Department for Libraries and Archives.

See page 4 for figures. Adult fiction circulation is 60 percent of total circulation; for children, the fiction circulation is 76 percent. The total is 70 percent of circulation accounted for by fiction.

Lynch, Mary Jo. 2000. Several personal e-mail messages sent during the fall.

I wish to thank Mary Jo Lynch, who e-mailed state librarians asking them to help me determine the percentage of book circulation accounted for by fiction versus nonfiction; she received replies from about half. Several correspondents suggested ways that I might begin to answer the question, but they had not gathered the data themselves. So far, only Kentucky, North Carolina, and New York are known to collect statewide data. I have not yet pursued the leads that might produce more evidence of the preponderance of fiction over nonfiction circulation in public libraries in the United States. But it may be of interest to note that the figures I have seen for other countries mimic those in the United States.

My colleague Robert Burgin points out that interested readers can keep up to date on recent state statistics by checking the site "Public Library Statistics on the Web" (URL: http://www.lrs.org/html/library_statistics_ on_the_ web.html [accessed January 26, 2001]).

Peters, Judy G., Education Program Assistant, New York State Public Library Data Coordinator. Personal correspondence dated October 10, 2000, and forwarded to me by Mary Jo Lynch.

Peters reports that the circulation statistics for New York state in 1998 were as follows:

Adult fiction: 28,389,692
Adult nonfiction: 22,116,997
Children's fiction: 23,257,141
Children's nonfiction: 11,126,991

These figures work out, after rounding off, to a fiction total of 61 percent and a nonfiction total of 39 percent.

Saricks, Joyce. 2001. Reading the Future of the Public Library. In *Readers, Reading and Librarians*, ed. Bill Katz, 113–21. [Copublished as *Acquisitions Librarian* no.25]

Shearer, Kenneth. 2001. The Book's Remarkable Longevity in the Face of New Communications Technologies—Past, Present, and Future. In *Readers, Reading and Librarians*, ed. Bill Katz, 23–33. [Copublished as *Acquisitions Librarian* no. 25]

Smith, Duncan. 1998. Valuing Fiction. *Booklist* 94, no. 13: 1094–95.

State Library of North Carolina. 1999. Statistics and Directory of North Carolina Public Libraries, July 1, 1998–June 30, 1999. Raleigh: State Library of North Carolina.
    See tables on pp. 20–21. The figures are given in percentages. Fiction
totals 69 percent and nonfiction totals 31 percent.

CONTRIBUTORS

Nora Armstrong is the Information and Referral Supervisor at the Cumberland County Public Library and Information Center in Fayetteville, North Carolina, where she has worked for four years. After earning a BA from Rosary College in 1980, she enlisted in the U.S. Army. She served in the MP Corps for two years before marriage and children distracted her. When her youngest child entered kindergarten, Armstrong enrolled in the School of Information and Library Science at the University or North Carolina at Chapel Hill, graduating in 1997 and receiving the Dean's Award for one of the two best Master's papers presented that year. In her first year as a librarian, she stumbled across Duncan Smith's "Valuing Fiction" (*Booklist* 94 [March 1, 1998]: 1094–95), which converted her to the gospel of readers' advisory. She has designed and conducted staff training in readers' advisory and genre fiction and has presented nationally on the subject of adult summer reading programs.

Angelina Benedetti is a full-time Young Adult Librarian with the King County Library System, located in the Puget Sound area of Washington State. In her job she works every day to bring teens and books together. Her MLS is from the University of Washington's Graduate School of Library and Information Science. She has served, and continues to serve, on ALA committees in both ALSC and YALSA, and she presents programs on the best in new young adult literature for a number of local professional groups each year. She serves on the boards of both the Washington Library Association and the Puget Sound Council, one of the largest book review organizations of its kind.

Robert Burgin is Professor at North Carolina Central University's School of Library and Information Sciences. He holds a BA from Duke University and a Masters and Ph.D. from the University of North Carolina at Chapel Hill. He worked in public libraries for ten years and taught for fifteen years at NCCU before serving as Assistant State Librarian for Information Technology with the State Library of North Carolina for two years. He recently returned to teaching at North Carolina Central University. His publications include articles on readers' advisory, management, and information retrieval. He contributed two chapters to *Guiding the Reader to the Next Book* (1996): "Readers' Advisory in Public Libraries: An Overview of Current Practice" and "Readers' Advisory Resources for Adults on the Internet."

Bill Crowley worked for twenty-three years in New York, Alabama, Indiana, and Ohio in many capacities. He earned a BA in history from Hunter College of the City University of New York, an MA in English from The Ohio State University with a thesis in occupational folklore, an MS in library service from Columbia University, and a Ph.D. in higher education at Ohio University in Athens. Crowley has published in both the higher education and library and information science literatures, addressing diverse topics, including the competition between "library" and "information" in graduate education. He served as chair of the State Library Agency Section of ALA's Association of Specialized and Cooperative Library Agencies. In 1996 Crowley joined the faculty of Dominican University's Graduate School of Library and Information Science, where he is now an Associate Professor.

Alma Dawson is an Assistant Professor in the School of Library and Information Science at Louisiana State University, where she teaches courses including collection management, library user instruction, and foundations of library and information science. She also has worked in school and academic libraries in Louisiana and Texas. She is an active member of ALA, the Association for Library and Information Science Education, and the Louisiana Library Association. A graduate of Grambling State University, she received her MLS from the University of Michigan and her Ph.D. from Texas Woman's University. Dawson's contributions to the library and information science literature include two publications related to readers' advisory services: *African American Readers' Advisory* (with Connie Van Fleet) and a special issue of *Louisiana Libraries* on "Enhancing Information Literacy for Diverse Populations."

Carol A. Doll is a Professor in the Library and Information Science Program at Wayne State University, where she teaches courses on youth services in both public libraries and school library media centers. She has taught in library and information science education since earning her doctorate at the University of Illinois in 1980. She is a member of the American Library Association, active primarily in the Association for Library Service to Children and the American Association of School Libraries. She is the author of many articles, including several dealing with school library media collections. She is coauthor of several books, including *Collection Analysis* *for the School Library Media Center: A Practical Approach* (1991) and *Bibliotherapy with Young People: Librarians and Mental Health Professionals Working Together* (1997).

Frank Exner, Little Bear, is a Squamish Indian from British Columbia, Canada. With articles and book reviews in *Journal of the American Society for Information Science* and *Bulletin of the American Society for Information Science,* he has indexed *Guiding the Reader to the Next Book* and created a master index for twenty years of the State Library of North Carolina's summer reading program manuals. Exner, Little Bear, is currently a doctoral student at South Africa's University of Pretoria Department of Information Science by distance education, having received MIS and MLS degrees from North Carolina Central University's School of Library and Information Sciences. His current research focuses on the authority control of Native American personal names. Exner, Little Bear, completed the index for this publication.

Glen Holt is the Executive Director of the St. Louis Public Library (SLPL) and holds Master's and Doctorate degrees in history and urban studies from the University of Chicago. Before coming to SLPL, he taught at Washington University and directed the honors program in the College of Liberal Arts at the University of Minnesota. At various times Holt has served as a consultant to libraries, museums, historical societies, city governments, and foundations. He publishes and speaks extensively and is the author, coauthor, editor and coeditor of more than 100 reports and articles and three books. He is a regular columnist on financial subjects for *The Bottom Line.* In 2001 the Public Library Association awarded him the Charlie Robinson Award for his creative contributions to the field. He is one of twenty librarians from throughout the world who serves as an International Networker in the Bertelsmann Foundation's program to devise best practices and innovative models for public libraries.

Roberta S. Johnson was born and raised in Ohio. She received her undergraduate degree in theater from Kent State University while working in a bookstore and for Encyclopedia Britannica. She has worked at the Skokie Public Library in circulation and at the Morton Grove Public Library as a readers' service assistant. She earned her MLIS at Dominican University (the Rosary College). While at Morton Grove, Johnson created and maintained the readers' services section of the library's Web site (the Webrary at http://www.webrary.org), as well as presented programs on using the Internet for readers' advisory at ALA, PLA, and other conferences. In 1998 Johnson joined the Des Plaines Public Library staff as a Reference Librarian. In April 2000 she was made Readers' Services Librarian and created a new department to serve the library's popular materials floor: fiction, audiovisual, large type, foreign language, and high school collections. She currently reviews science fiction and fantasy for *Booklist* magazine and continues to present readers' advisory workshops around the country.

Anne K. May is a librarian in the Business, Science, and Technology Division of Queens Central Library (Jamaica, New York), the research library of the Queens Borough Public Library System. She holds a BA in history from SUNY-Binghamton and a JD from New York University School of Law. She is a recent graduate of the Graduate School of Library and Information Studies of Queens College. May was a presenter at PLA 2000 Readers' Advisory Preconference: "The State of Readers' Advisory Service." She was lead author of "A Look at Reader's Advisory Services" (*Library Journal*).

Randy Pitman is the editor of "Video Librarian," the video review guide for libraries. He is the author of *The Video Librarian's Guide to Collection Development and Management* (G. K. Hall), *Video Movies: A Core Collection for Libraries* (ABC-CLIO), *The Librarian's Video Primer* (video, ALA), and numerous articles for various library publications. An outspoken advocate for the use of video in libraries, he is also the past chair of the Video Round Table of ALA.

Catherine Sheldrick Ross is Professor and Acting Dean of the Faculty of Information and Media Studies at The University of Western Ontario. With a Ph.D. in English and an MLIS degree, she has long been interested in the transactions between readers and texts. Her publications include *Communicating Professionally,* written with Patricia Dewdney (1998), *A Double Life: A Biography of Alice Munro* (1992), four nonfiction books for children published by Kids Can Press, as well as numerous scholarly articles on the following topics: the reference transaction from the users' perspective; the reference interview; and readers' advisory. Her longstanding research interest is reading for pleasure; drawing from this work, she has given many workshops for library professionals on readers' advisory.

Joyce G. Saricks has worked as Coordinator of the Literature and Audio Services department at the Downers Grove (Illinois) Public Library since 1983. She joined the library staff as a reference librarian after receiving her MA/MAT in library science from the University of Chicago, and she has also worked as head of Technical Services at Downers Grove. She has written two books on readers' advisory—*Readers' Advisory Guide to Genre Fiction* (2001) and, with Nancy Brown, *Readers' Advisory Service* *in the Public Library* (1989, rev. 1997). She has written several articles on readers' advisory, presented workshops on that topic for public libraries and library systems, and spoken at state, regional, and national library conferences. In 1989 she won the Public Library Association's Allie Beth Martin Award, and in 2000 she was named Librarian of the Year by the Romance Writers of America.

Kenneth Shearer is a Professor at the School of Library and Information Sciences at North Carolina Central University. An honors graduate of Amherst College, he earned an MLS and a Ph.D. at Rutgers University. He has worked in public libraries in New York and Michigan. His teaching areas are public librarianship, readers' advisory, libraries in the political process, and research methods. He was the editor of *Public Libraries* from 1978 to 1988; he has written approximately forty articles for the professional literature and has edited or coedited several books, including *Guiding the Reader to the Next Book* (1996) and *Politics and the Support of Libraries* (with E. J. Josey 1990). Long professionally active, he is currently the chair of the Committee on Research and Statistics for the American Library Association. One of his three sons, Timothy, is an academic librarian who is concurrently working on a Ph.D. in LIS and has therefore become his most successful recruitment effort.

Duncan Smith is the Creator and Product Manager of EBSCO Publishing's electronic readers' advisory resource NoveList. He is a nationally recognized trainer in the area of readers' advisory services. Smith is also the author of several articles on readers' advisory services, including two chapters in *Guiding the Reader to the Next Book* (1996)—the first book to focus on research in the area of readers' advisory services. His most recent publication is "Talking with Readers: A Competency Based Approach to Readers' Advisory Service," *Reference and User Services Quarterly*. Prior to joining EBSCO Publishing, Smith was the Coordinator of the North Carolina Library Staff Development Program, a statewide continuing education program for library staff in North Carolina. He has worked in public libraries in North Carolina and Georgia. He holds an MSLS and a BA in English from the University of North Carolina at Chapel Hill. Smith is also a past-president of the American Library Association's Continuing Library Education Network/Exchange (CLENE) Round Table. In 1997 he received the Margaret E. Monroe Award for Library Adult Services from the American Library Association's Reference and User Services Division.

Brian Sturm is Assistant Professor for the School of Information and Library Science at the University of North Carolina at Chapel Hill. He obtained an MLS (1991) and a Ph.D. in Library and Information Science

(1998) from Indiana University. His research interests focus on the entrancing power of stories in both oral and written forms, and he has published articles in *The Journal of American Folklore, School Library Media Review,* and *Storytelling Magazine.* He is the coauthor (with Margaret Read MacDonald) of an index of children's folktale collections, *The Storyteller's Sourcebook, 1983–1999.* Sturm is also a freelance storyteller and has performed for conferences, libraries, and schools around the nation. He is active in several professional societies, including ALA, the Children's Literature Association, the Association for Library and Information Science Education, and the National Storytelling Association.

Connie Van Fleet is an Associate Professor in the School of Library and Information Studies, University of Oklahoma. She holds a BA in psychology (University of Oklahoma), an MLIS (Louisiana State University), and a Ph.D. in library and information science (Indiana University). She has been recognized for "distinguished teaching at the university level" (Louisiana State University), "excellence in grant writing" (Kent State University), and "significant contributions to library adult services" (ALA/ RUSA Margaret E. Monroe Library Adult Services Award). She has served on numerous local, state, and national committees and panels including the ALA Council, the Congress on Professional Education Steering Committee, and the National Endowment for the Humanities. She is coauthor (with Courtney Deines Jones) of *Preparing Staff to Serve Patrons with Disabilities* (1995) and a series of articles, with Erica Lilly, on accessibility of academic and public library home pages. Her most recent book (coauthored with Danny P. Wallace) is *Library Evaluation: A Casebook and Can-Do Guide* (2001). She is currently coeditor (with Danny P. Wallace) of *Reference and User Services Quarterly.*

Wayne A. Wiegand is a Professor of Library and Information Studies at the University of Wisconsin-Madison, and codirector of the Center for the History of Print Culture in Modern America (a joint program of the University and the State Historical Society of Wisconsin). He received his BA in history from the University of Wisconsin-Oshkosh (1968), his MA in history from the University of Wisconsin-Milwaukee (1970), and his MLS from Western Michigan University and Ph.D. in history from Southern Illinois University in 1974. He is the author of fifty scholarly articles and a number of books, including *Politics of an Emerging Profession: The American Library Association, 1876–1917* (1986), *An Active Instrument for Propaganda: American Public Libraries During World War I* (1989), and *Irrepressible Reformer: A Biography of Melvil Dewey* (1996), each of which received the G. K. Hall Award for Outstanding Contribution to Library Literature given by the American Library Association. In 1998 he coedited *Print Culture in a Diverse America* with Jim Danky, which received the 1999 Carey McWilliams Award for scholarly contribution to multicultural literature.

PART I

The Education of Advisors and
the Foundations for
Professional Practice

Introduction to Part I

Before librarians can practice readers' advisory well, they must be taught well. Before they can be properly taught, we must examine the context in which readers' advisory services take place. Consequently, the first part of this book looks at the related topics of educating librarians to be readers' advisors and establishing the foundations of readers' advisory services.

There is a clear need to prepare librarians to provide readers' advisory services well. The materials to build such a curriculum exist, but do the schools of library and information science actually provide the educational opportunities needed to prepare librarians to deliver these important services?

No, they clearly do not, argues Wayne Wiegand in Chapter 1. According to Wiegand, schools of library and information science almost totally ignore the literature on the social nature and act of reading, which would help explain who reads the stories that represent the largest part of libraries' business. In particular, Wiegand outlines how this neglect of the study of reading came to be, how the stories the majority of users desire became trivialized by the profession while information related to business and government achieved a privileged status. The chapter serves as a "wake up" call to the profession to give more attention to the subject of reading.

In Chapter 2 Kenneth Shearer and Robert Burgin examine the extent of the neglect of readers' advisory in the Master's programs at the ALA-accredited schools of library and information science. Their findings bolster Wiegand's argument that these schools almost completely neglect research on reading and readers. None of the eleven survey topics related to readers' advisory services was covered in the core curricula of even 40 percent of the responding schools, and although most respondents had some coverage of the topics in elective courses, these electives tended to rely on the interests of individual faculty members. Most of the programs do not even expose students to the idea of building adult popular collections and encouraging discretionary reading among the general public, activities that constitute the most common use of the public library.

Bill Crowley shows in Chapter 3 how readers' advisory is taught in a professional program of library and information science. Using his own experience in developing a course in readers' advisory services at Dominican University, Crowley also examines the academic context in which such curriculum development takes place and the reasons obstacles exist to the development of readers' advisory courses in schools of library and information science. The chapter is instructive to those in the profession who have not experienced the inner workings of academia and are unfamiliar with the curious world in which faculty operate. Crowley goes on to suggest a number of tactics for encouraging the development of readers' advisory instruction at the graduate level and even provides a syllabus from his own course to show what a readers' advisory course might encompass.

Professional education must, of course, be based on sound theory, and so the second half of Part A consists of three chapters that examine the foundations of readers' advisory services in the context of libraries and information services.

Chapter 4, by NoveList creator Duncan Smith, places readers' advisory services in the wider context of professional practice by examining both the similarities and differences between readers' advisory and more traditional reference services. Smith reminds us that readers' advisory questions are difficult because they ask us to explore unknown territory by requiring that we not only know something about our books and resources but also understand readers and the reading process. Smith maps several aspects of this unknown territory by examining the importance of staff interaction and personalized expert service, relating Kuhlthau's roles for information providers to readers' advisory service, outlining training protocols and models in this area, and affirming the importance of readers' advisory resources (both print and electronic).

Catherine Ross investigates the experience of reading in Chapter 5 by examining interviews that she and her students conducted with almost 200 heavy readers. She explores the ways readers themselves view the meaning of reading in their lives, the ways they choose books to read for pleasure, and elements that are required for a book to be "satisfying" for them. Consistent patterns emerge from the interviews:

- Heavy readers were read to as children

- Most were omnivorous readers as children

- They make time for reading

Importantly, Ross focuses on the relationship between the readers and their books and not on the texts themselves, as have most scholars in this area. This focus is consistent with Wiegand's emphasis on our gaining an understanding of the act of reading and Smith's emphasis on understanding reading in the context of the reader's life experiences.

In Chapter 6, Brian Sturm ends the first part of the book with a fascinating examination of the physiology and psychology of reading. Sturm asks what happens to us when we read. The answer is complex, and he examines the scientific literature on trance states, hemispheric dominance in the brain, and brainwave activity to suggest that reading—like listening to a story, being hypnotized, or meditating—may represent an altered state of consciousness. Sturm's suggested connections among the various research communities represents a promising research agenda for those who agree with Wiegand, Smith, and Ross that we need to understand more about the act of reading in order to provide better advisory services to readers.

This richer understanding of the act of reading and the complex relationship between readers and what they read is essential in helping librarians better serve their customers through readers' advisory services. The fact that few schools of library and information science choose to educate their students and future librarians in this area is regrettable, but the fact that the foundations for such education clearly exist is cause for hope.

—R.B.

CHAPTER 1

Missing the Real Story: Where Library and Information Science Fails the Library Profession

Wayne A. Wiegand

At the beginning of a course I teach titled "Information Agencies and Their Environments," which all first-semester University of Wisconsin-Madison School of Library and Information Studies students must take, I routinely run through a litany of statistics. The United States has more public libraries than McDonald's restaurants, I tell them; Americans make 3.5 billion visits to school, public, and college libraries every year—three times more than visits to movies. School children visit their library media centers 1.7 billion times during the school year—two times more than they visit state and national parks (American Library Association, Public Information Office 1998). As many children participate in summer reading programs as play Little League baseball. Generally, these statistics get their attention, but I don't quit there.

A revised version of this chapter was published in the October 27, 2000, Chronicle of Higher Education *as "Librarians Ignore the Value of Stories."*

College and university libraries lend 180 million items each year, the vast majority of which are books and periodicals. Two-thirds of Americans use a public library at least once per year, and of that number 80 percent (that's about 150 million people) go there to check out a book ("Poll finds..." 1996). For decades now, among the books they check out, fiction has consistently accounted for 65 to 75 percent of the circulation in these ubiquitous civil institutions. These statistics, I tell students, amply demonstrate that the millions of Americans of both genders, all ages, ethnicities, races, creeds, classes, and sexual orientations who frequent the thousands of libraries billions of times every year are coming primarily to fulfill needs and interests satisfied largely by the act of reading, and what they read is largely the stories (e.g., biographies, mysteries, Civil War battles, Newbery-Caldecott winners, romances, and African-American diaspora narratives) that contain cultural information they value.

Several weeks later I highlight the growing literature (now over a generation old) on the act and social nature of reading that helps explain who reads the stories all types of American libraries disseminate and why. I became interested in this literature twenty years ago as a library historian; its richness convinced me in 1992 to join with Jim Danky to establish the Center for the History of Print Culture in Modern America as a joint program at the University of Wisconsin-Madison and the State Historical Society of Wisconsin and to locate its university home in the School of Library and Information Studies.

The Act and Social Nature of Reading

The literature on the act and social nature of reading divides into four broad categories: (1) literacy studies, which demonstrate that understanding the social and historical context in which literacy is practiced is essential to understanding why it is being promoted; (2) reader-response theory, which shows that in the reading process the reader is an active agent who exercises a great deal of creativity in making sense of texts; (3) an ethnography of reading, which acknowledges that reading is often a communal activity based in a social infrastructure grounded on shared interpretive frameworks and practiced in shared institutions; and (4) a social history of books and reading (or, post-Gutenberg, "print culture history"), which proves that the act of reading is and for centuries has been a multilayered, highly complex process (see Wiegand 1997, endnotes 7 through 23). Print culture history is my personal favorite and the one most relevant to my own research. Through its literature I can easily see how all cultures—the dominant and marginalized—have always used stories to validate their existences, make sense of their worlds, and pass on to future generations what they regard as their culture's collective wisdom.

For students, however, I like to add cultural studies to this mix, in large part because it broadens questions about the act of reading to also address how people "read" nonprint cultural forms such as videos and compact discs, both of which libraries also circulate. The field of cultural studies argues that people make their own culture out of the resources and commodities provided to them and, in interacting with these resources and commodities, people freely "appropriate," "poach," and even "construct" new meaning from those resources and commodities in order to meet their own unique group or individual information needs. Thus, by combining contemporary scholarship on literacy studies, reader-response theory, the ethnography of reading, and print culture history with cultural studies, I hope that my students begin to see the broad outlines of the multiple answers to what is an essential question for anyone aspiring to positions in public, school, and academic libraries: Who reads the stories that thousands of libraries provide billions of times to millions of their patrons and why?

At the same time, however, I tell them that library and information science programs across the country almost totally ignore the literature on the social nature and act of reading that would help explain who reads these stories and why. I never have to work very hard to prove that statement. Four months ago, for example, I downloaded the catalogs of the top five library and information science programs listed in the *U.S. News and World Report* survey: Illinois, North Carolina, Syracuse, Michigan, and Pittsburgh. As I looked through the curricular offerings of these leading schools for references to the words "read" or "reading" or to the phrases "act of reading" or "social nature of reading," I found almost none. In several courses Michigan refers to "readers" or "readings" but only as required assignments for particular courses. Similarly, Syracuse talks about "key readings" in one course. North Carolina fails even to use words such as "read," "reading," or "act of reading" in any of its curricular offerings. Only in an "Advanced Problems in Librarianship" course does Illinois say it provides "directed and supervised investigation of selection problems in library resources, reference service, research libraries, reading, public libraries, or school libraries." And Pittsburgh has a History of Books, Printing, and Publishing course that covers "manuscript origins, the nature and development of the printing process, the reading public, the book trade, binding, and book illustration."

How the Oversight Evolved

As a library historian, I think I understand how this oversight evolved. Michel Foucault (1977) argues that centuries ago the "new order" we now call "modernity" separated the way people experienced daily life into "work" and "leisure." Business and government (and the sciences that served their interests) assigned a very high value to the former and a very low value to the latter. Except for the stories that the state regarded as so essential to the social order that they had to be taught in institutions such as schools, the communication of stories—no matter what their cultural form—became categorized as "leisure" and thus trivialized by the dominant culture. On the other hand, information that served the interests of business and government became privileged. One of the earliest manifestations of this distinction in American library history occurred in 1732, when Benjamin Franklin sent out the Library Company of Philadelphia's first order. It included dictionaries, grammars, an atlas, and books on science and agriculture "suited to the tastes and purses of young tradesmen"—almost entirely "useful knowledge" here, very few stories—and none of the religious kind that dominated the world around them (Harris 1978).

Three events in twentieth-century American library history reinforced or deeply influenced these value distinctions between useful knowledge and stories. First, with the help of a substantial grant from the Carnegie Corporation, the University of Chicago opened a graduate library school in 1928 to offer the profession's first doctoral program, which promised to concentrate on research. At the time Chicago led the nation in efforts to make the social sciences more "scientific." The nomothetic positivism practiced at Chicago effectively established the parameters of a professional discourse and quickly became the model that library and information science research has emulated ever since. And although in the first decade of its existence, the Chicago faculty (and especially Douglas Waples) focused much of their research on the "scientific" investigation of reading, their scope betrayed a cultural bias. They ignored fiction (the stories most library patrons wanted) and instead concentrated on (and thus favored) the kinds of nonfiction information (i.e., useful knowledge) patrons were more likely to look up at the library's reference desk.

Second, in 1939 the American Library Association (ALA) adopted its first version of the Library Bill of Rights, which not only made ALA (at least rhetorically) a champion of intellectual freedom but also made questions of what patrons read, and why, irrelevant to the profession's interests beyond supply and demand. Henceforth patrons were looked upon more as consumers whose transactions with the library ought to be kept confidential. Curiosity about—and investigation into—who reads the stories libraries circulate and why came to seem like an invasion of privacy or a breech of professional ethics.

Third, at midcentury the Carnegie Corporation funded a "Public Library Inquiry" to examine the public library's purpose. Led by Robert D. Leigh of Chicago's political science department, project investigators (including Bernard Berelson, Oliver Garceau, and Alice Bryan) concluded that American public libraries ought to minimize their practice of supplying the popular reading desired by nearly three-quarters of their users and instead concentrate on a small but more influential combination of "serious" readers, community leaders, and students of adult education who use public libraries to obtain useful knowledge. Like the research agenda at Chicago's Graduate Library School, however, the Public Library Inquiry's research scope was culturally biased. Because it favored useful knowledge over stories, the Inquiry overlooked entire patron groups (including children, who accounted for nearly half the American public libraries' user population) whose needs and interests at the time were satisfied by the act of reading.

As a result of these developments, by 1975 library and information science education had become convinced (along with most of the rest of the library profession) that access to "useful" information—and especially the kind that librarians thought people needed to become informed citizens and intelligent consumers—constituted librarianship's most important professional responsibility. At conferences and in the research literature, discussions about the stories most patrons wanted were either marginalized or ignored. Little wonder, then, that in the 1980s, when middle-class patrons began using computers to obtain the kinds of information that Franklin, Waples, and Leigh considered most valuable and that librarians thought they were trained to supply, a substantial fraction of library and information science education leaders (and especially those with business, computer science, engineering, and science backgrounds, whose training taught them to privilege information that business and government appreciated most) began moving their curricula toward a definition of information that emerging technologies were largely driving. By the year 2000 library and information science education had evolved a distinct professional discourse. If a computer couldn't handle it, many library and information science educators seemed to argue, then it wasn't information. And any library and information science education program that wanted to be considered "on the cutting edge" didn't even have to add the words "of technology." It went without saying.

This discourse proved so powerful that library and information science educators took no notice of another cutting-edge body of emerging research, this one taking place mostly in the humanities. While library and information science education was shifting its definition of "information" to one driven almost entirely by technology, increasing numbers of humanities scholars began shifting their focus from "culture as text" to "culture as agency" and "culture as practice." This new focus concentrated on how people use the multiple cultural forms available to them to validate their existences and make sense of their worlds. It also studied the cultural information that author/creator passed to reader/listener/viewer. From this shift the literature on the act of and social nature of reading itself emerged. And like its parent body of research, it concentrated not on "culture as text" but on "culture as agency" and "culture as practice."

By analyzing what library and information science education does with the literature on the act of reading, the controlling nature of its current discursive formations becomes readily apparent. Foundation texts that library and information science students must read in core courses include little or no coverage of literature on reading. With faculty advice and financial aid, library and information science doctoral programs mostly recruit and encourage students to investigate information topics connected to newer technologies with traditional social science methodologies. Vacancy notices for new library and information science faculty positions almost always emphasize teaching skills and research expertise in information technologies and never mention a need to develop an understanding of the information that millions in America's multicultural society find in the stories libraries collect and circulate. And in some "schools of information," story-centered courses and teaching positions—such as children's librarianship—have been eliminated entirely. Even attempts at oppositional thinking can't seem to venture "outside the box." For example, in its May 12, 2000, issue, the *Chronicle of Higher Education* published nine letters to the editor that sought to debunk and/or clarify an April 7 article titled "In Revamped Library Schools, Information Trumps Books." Not one of those letters cited the library's primary role as a reading institution. Instead, what united all correspondents was agreement that "libraries are more than just books."

The blindered thinking effected by professional discourse in which technology drives the definition of information was made even more obvious when some library and information science educators who received a Kellogg Foundation grant to redefine the library and information science curriculum met in Washington, D.C., in 1996. Before them they had a Benton Foundation report of a focus group of suburban public library users who, in response to a number of questions, nonetheless collectively identified the following as their top two public library services: (1) "providing reading hours and other programs for children" and (2) "purchasing new books and other printed materials" ("Benton Study..." 1996, 112). Although any well-informed students of the scholarship on reading would immediately sense that focus group members are here bearing witness to the value they place on the culturally informing potential of stories that reading releases, the Benton Foundation seemed unable to tease out this possibility. As a result, the Kellogg grantees seemed unable to fathom a potentially broader significance of these priorities as they contemplated a curriculum to fill the future needs of the profession.

Another example drawn from the same focus group activity speaks to another failing. In oral remarks, one focus group participant criticized libraries for not stocking enough popular titles. "If you want to get the book that everybody is reading right now, it is just not in," the participant complained. Although scholars of the act of reading—and especially its social nature—would immediately recognize this as a plea for increased access to a community-based information-sharing activity, such a possibility seems never to have occurred to focus group organizers or Kellogg grantees, who otherwise liked what the Benton Report said about the library's need to upgrade technology.

But this kind of blindered thinking about reading is not unique to library and information science discourse. With rare exceptions, English, history, and education departments have also failed to look at libraries as significant cultural, literary, intellectual, social, or even educational institutions. Scholars in American, cultural, and area studies have been equally remiss. For example, in "Reading Groups Are Bridging Academic and Popular Culture," an article that the *Chronicle of Higher Education* published in its December 19, 1997, issue, author Mary Cregan notes that Americans spend more time reading than surfing the Internet or watching movies. She quotes a Census Bureau study of mass-media use recently published in the *New York Times:* "While people have been devoting less time to reading newspapers and magazines over the last decade, they have actually increased the time they spend on books" to average over 100 hours per year (Cregan 1997, B4–B5). She then summarizes the proliferation of reading groups across the country as a manifestation of this increased activity and argues that the groups have potential to serve as a bridge between academic and popular culture. "People are turning back to books," she concludes, "refusing to give up the opportunity for meditative insight, for meaning, for the connection and community that reading—and discussing what one reads with friends—can bring" (Cregan 1997, B5). In the article Cregan never mentions the role that professionals in American public, school, and academic libraries (who in my opinion are better placed institutionally to function as the bridge) already play in this phenomenon.

Please let no one conclude from reading this chapter that I am antitechnology. Not at all. Librarians—and the programs that educate them—absolutely have to tap the potential of information technologies to serve their patrons. But the contrast between the statistics cited in the first two paragraphs and the near total absence of attention to reading in library and information science programs at universities across the country provides ample evidence of the kind of cultural and intellectual blinders that powerful academic discourses can unknowingly effect. I would argue that rather than restricting the definition of information for library and information science programs to what the technology provides, we should greatly expand our focus to be more inclusive and less culturally biased by looking at the act of reading that the library facilitates, whether it comes from the printed page, the video monitor, or the computer screen. Only then can we begin to explore entire information cultures and not just those fractions affected by technologies. Expanding our focus in this way would allow us to correct the major oversights committed by the Graduate Library School and the Public Library Inquiry, which I see repeated in contemporary library and information science education by encouraging us to take as seriously as the millions of its readers do the stories that thousands of libraries circulate to them as patrons billions of times every year.

In the next year, schools of "information" and "information and library science" will be graduating nearly five thousand students from ALA-accredited programs into positions in public, school, and academic libraries, where reading stories that contain multicultural information continues to constitute the library's major source of activity. Although a literature now exists to enable these students to acquire some knowledge of who reads these stories and why, the vast majority won't have a clue. Worse yet, they will have been schooled to think that an intellectual curiosity about what millions of their patrons read, and why, is not only beyond the scope of their practice as an information professional but actually none of their professional business. What a shame.

References

American Library Association, Public Information Office. 1998. *Quotable Facts About America's Libraries*. Brochure.

Benton Study: Librarians Need to Work on Message to Public. 1996. *Library Journal* 121 (September 1): 112.

Cregan, Mary. 1997. Reading Groups Are Bridging Academic and Popular Culture. *Chronicle of Higher Education* 44 (December 19): B4–B5.

Foucault, Michel. 1977. *Discipline and Punish: The Birth of the Prison*. New York: Pantheon Books.

Harris, Michael H. 1978. Franklin, Benjamin (1706–1790). In *Dictionary of American Biography*, ed. Bohdan Wynar, 186–87. Littleton, CO: Libraries Unlimited.

Poll Finds Library Use on Rise. 1996. *American Libraries* 27 (February): 15.

Wiegand, Wayne A. 1997. Out of Sight and Out of Mind: Why Don't We Have Any Schools of Library and Reading Studies? *Journal of Library and Information Science Education* 38: 316–26.

CHAPTER 2

Partly Out of Sight; Not Much in Mind: Master's Level Education for Adult Readers' Advisory Services

Kenneth D. Shearer and Robert Burgin

Background

"Many library school administrators have decided that all public library patrons care about is computer technology, and the majority of schools are supporting their belief with no course offerings in readers' advisory services. Library school graduates who choose a career in public libraries are not prepared to make recommendations to adult readers," writes Cathleen Towey in a recent issue of *American Libraries*, contrasting the education of adult services librarians to that of children's librarians (Towey 1997, 31). She regrets that "[t]he readers' advisory services that are so enthusiastically provided in the children's room no longer exist when patrons step up to the adult collection."

Towey views the educational preparation of public librarians for work with adult readers of popular materials as deficient. Many others in the field of library and information science share her view. Likewise, on the Fiction_L list, contributors reflect their concerns about the dearth of education for adult readers' advisory services. Georgine Olson reports that one contributor wrote that "[p]eople coming out of library schools don't have the background in books that readers' advisory calls for." Another wanted to "[m]ake it known to library schools that their graduates are unacceptable." A third contributor asked, "Has anyone ever written to ALA's Committee on Accreditation about this?" (Olson 1998)

A survey of over 100 professional and paraprofessional librarians who attended a 1993 conference on readers' advisory shows that paraprofessional staff members handled more adult readers' advisory questions than did professionals (Burgin 1996). This is evidence of a lack of preparation in advisory services among professionally trained librarians. It is not clear why this was the case, but perhaps there was little difference in the performance of the professionals and paraprofessionals, and so patrons opted for the most conveniently located staff; perhaps the graduates of the Master's programs were merely reflecting in their behavior the neglect of the topic in the curricula of those programs. In any case, there is no evidence to suggest that most library and information science programs are adequately preparing their graduates for work in this area.

At a 2000 Public Library Association preconference on adult fiction readers' advisory, an attendee approached one of the authors after a session and expressed concern about the quality of education for people planning to serve adults in public libraries. She asked whether the program that she had graduated from and a couple of others that she knew about were typical in their lack of attention to public library services to adults. She said that people who were planning to enter the field and work in public libraries often ask her what school they should attend. In order to answer their questions, she wanted to know which schools prepare students to serve adult readers with advisory services. She did not know where to steer new candidates and whether the deficiencies she had noted were common. The author she had approached named some programs that offer strong electives in adult readers' advisory but did not have the information for all ALA-accredited schools, the information the attendee desired. This chapter reports on a survey that begins to remedy that gap in our knowledge.

In the preceding chapter of this book and in other articles, Wayne Wiegand makes the case that research on reading and readers, which he views as an essential part of professional education, is almost completely neglected in schools of library and information science, to the great detriment of the profession (Wiegand 1997a, 1997b, 2000). In fact, Wiegand's presentation at the 1997 Association for Library and Information Science

Education conference, although very enthusiastically received by perhaps half the audience, was seen as retrograde by a sizeable group of those in attendance. Some attendees remarked, "Here we go again! Back to the book!" and others felt that Wiegand's points were anticomputer and anti-information science.

What Wiegand urges, however, is not that the field halt its development of services based on newer technologies. Instead, he argues that the field should build carefully on its hard-won, preeminent position in reader services. Indeed, the either/or approach to print sources and computer sources is simplistic and, if used to guide curricula, does not allow the field to mature appropriately or to best advantage. Whether a book is published in a hardcover or paperback or an e-book format is not the issue. The issue is readers and reading and the librarian's ability to match them up skillfully. Wiegand points out that there is much recent scholarship on reading that lays the foundation for a renewed commitment to readers' services, including "(1) literacy studies; (2) a social history of books and reading...; (3) reader-response theory; and (4) ethnography of reading," along with genre fiction research from cultural studies (Wiegand 1997b, 316).

However, for guidelines, scholarship, and research on advisory services we may look not only to disciplines outside the field. Librarians and educators within the field have been hard at work in recent years in the area of advisory services. Joyce Saricks and Nancy Brown have written a text on the subject (Saricks and Brown 1997). Kenneth Shearer's *Guiding the Reader to the Next Book* assembles research on the subject (Shearer 1996). Anne May and colleagues, whose research is the focus of Chapter 7 in this book, build on an earlier study of readers' advisory transactions (Lackner, May, Miltenberg, and Olesh 1998). Catherine Ross won a coveted Jesse H. Shera Research Award for work that shows that reading series books, such as Nancy Drew or the Hardy Boys, enhances reading skills and is seen as an important step in reading development among many heavy readers (Ross 1995). She has expanded upon her research into readers and reading in Chapter 5 of this book and in other recently published work (Ross 2001). Along with her many contributions to readers' advisory and popular collection development, Sharon Baker has speculated on personality types (as revealed in the Myers-Briggs Type Indicator) and their use in advising adult readers (Baker 1994). The Adult Reading Round Table of Illinois (1999) has produced a self-evaluative bibliography for fiction librarians. NoveList has collaborated with the Library Development and Services department of the Minnesota Department of Children, Families, and Learning and Minnesota library staff to prepare a workbook for readers' advisory (Talking with Readers 2000). Liang Yu and Ann O'Brien have recently provided a clear and comprehensive overview of the professional literature on fiction provision in libraries (Yu and O'Brien 1996).

Although impressive, this list *by no means* exhausts recent contributions, and it *does not begin* to address the renaissance in print advisory tools, such as *Genreflecting*, that have added to old standbys such as *Fiction Catalog*, lists such as Fiction_L,[1] or Web sites with extensive readers' advisory assistance such as Webrary (URL: http://www.webrary.org/ [accessed December 26, 2000]). By examining the references in this book, the reader will reap rewards. The literature, once negligible, is growing rapidly.

The Study

Keeping this background in mind, the authors surveyed the Master's programs at the ALA-accredited schools of library and information science to learn whether the anecdotal evidence and the opinions of prominent professionals—that readers' advisory for adult users is neglected in library and information science education—was mostly true or mostly false. The need for preparation in advisory services for adult users is clear, and the materials to build such a curriculum exist, but do the schools provide the educational opportunities needed to prepare professionals?

A copy of a questionnaire titled "Adult Readers' Advisory in the Curriculum" was sent to deans and directors of ALA-accredited programs in 1999; the cover letter asked the dean or director to complete the questionnaire or forward it to the faculty member best able to answer it. The instrument asked whether eleven topics related to adult readers' advisory were offered in their programs during the 1998/1999 academic year and whether the eleven topics were included in *required* and/or *elective* courses. The topics ranged from the broad topic "Readers' advisory in general" to the narrower "Classification and arrangement of popular materials" to a topic as specific as "Readers' advisory tools: Electronic (NoveList, e.g.)."

The rate of response—only twenty replies—to the original mailing was discouraging. We chose to follow up with a second mailing to the twenty-nine schools that had not responded to the first one. This time the instrument was directed to the person on the faculty most likely to know and care about the subject. We based our choice, when possible, on our personal knowledge and, when not possible, on the subject interests of faculty as provided in the 1998/1999 ALISE *Membership Directory*.

This strategy improved our coverage, and of the forty-nine ALA-accredited programs, we eventually received thirty-four responses, or 69 percent. Although we would prefer to be able to provide a census—because we suspect that the findings are somewhat biased and more likely to include data from the schools that pay some attention to readers' advisory—more than two thirds of the schools responded, and the information should have considerable validity.

The Findings

Tables 2.1 and 2.2 report the results of the survey. Table 2.1 shows the number of respondents who report that a topic is covered in either required courses or electives. Table 2.2 breaks down the results further by showing which schools report that a topic is covered in both required courses and electives, in required courses only, and in electives only.

Table 2.1. Survey Responses from 33 ALA-Accredited Schools of Library and Information Science in the United States

	Yes, in Required Courses	Yes, in Electives	No	N
Readers' advisory in general	12 (36%)	26 (79%)	2 (6%)	33
Theoretical foundations (such as reading behavior, reader-response theory, and print collection history)	8 (26%)	20 (65%)	5 (16%)	31
Classification and arrangement of popular materials	10 (33%)	17 (57%)	5 (17%)	30
Popular materials (bestsellers, genre fiction, etc.)	3 (9%)	26 (81%)	4 (13%)	32
Promotion (e.g., booktalks)	4 (13%)	25 (78%)	5 (16%)	32
Readers' advisory interviews	3 (9%)	24 (75%)	6 (19%)	32
Readers' advisory programming	1 (3%)	26 (84%)	4 (13%)	31
Readers' advisory tools:				
a. Electronic (e.g., NoveList)	2 (6%)	26 (79%)	5 (15%)	33
b. Internet (e.g., FICTION-L)	1 (3%)	25 (78%)	6 (19%)	32
c. Print (e.g., *Genreflecting*)	2 (6%)	27 (82%)	4 (12%)	33
Review media for the selection of adult popular materials	11 (36%)	22 (71%)	3 (9%)	31
Other	1	4	4	8

**Table 2.2. Survey Responses from 33 ALA-Accredited Schools
of Library and Information Science in the United States**

	Yes, in Both Required Courses and Electives	Yes, in Required Courses Only	Yes, in Electives Only	No	N
Readers' advisory in general	7 (21%)	5 (15%)	19 (58%)	2 (6%)	33
Theoretical foundations (such as reading behavior, reader-response theory, and print collection history)	2 (6%)	6 (19%)	18 (58%)	5 (16%)	31
Classification and arrangement of popular materials	2 (7%)	8 (27%)	15 (50%)	5 (17%)	30
Popular materials (bestsellers, genre fiction, etc.)	1 (3%)	2 (6%)	25 (78%)	4 (13%)	32
Promotion (e.g., booktalks)	2 (6%)	2 (6%)	23 (72%)	5 (16%)	32
Readers' advisory interviews	1 (3%)	2 (6%)	23 (72%)	6 (19%)	32
Readers' advisory programming	0 (0%)	1 (3%)	26 (84%)	4 (13%)	31
Readers' advisory tools:					
a. Electronic (e.g., NoveList)	0 (0%)	2 (6%)	26 (79%)	5 (15%)	33
b. Internet (e.g., FICTION-L)	0 (0%)	1 (3%)	25 (78%)	6 (19%)	32
80c. Print (e.g., *Genreflecting*)	0 (0%)	2 (6%)	27 (82%)	4 (12%)	33
Review media for the selection of adult popular materials	5 (16%)	6 (19%)	17 (55%)	3 (10%)	31
Other	1	0	3	4	8

Table 2.1 reflects the attention paid to readers' advisory in ALA-accredited programs in *required courses* (hereafter referred to as the core). The two most prevalent topics—"Readers' advisory in general" and "Review media for the selection of adult popular materials"—are included in the 1998/1999 core curricula of 36 percent of the respondents' programs. These represent the topics that are most often common knowledge among students graduating from ALA-accredited Master's degree programs with respect to readers' advisory. In contrast, only one program (3 percent of those responding) included the topic "Internet readers' advisory tools (Fiction_L, e.g.)" in its core, and only one program included the topic "Readers' advisory programming" in its core.

Given the fact that no topic was covered in the core curricula of even 40 percent of the responding schools, it seems safe to conclude that *most* ALA-accredited programs did not pay any attention whatever to readers' advisory in the *core* curriculum in the 1998/1999 academic year. Students who are not exposed to the idea of readers' advisory may not realize that this is a potential area of professional interest.

Although this regrettable deficiency appears to be easily remedied through Wiegand's suggestion of incorporating research on readers and reading in the curriculum, the topic that best represents that suggestion on the questionnaire—"Theoretical foundations (such as reading behavior, reader-response theory, and print collection history)"—is offered in the core of unfortunately only one-fourth (26 percent) of the programs that responded to the survey.

Because many programs offer as few as six semester hours in the core, one may well ask whether it is even fair to measure a school's attention to readers' advisory by the inclusion of constituent topics in core courses. After all, if potential special librarians, for example, are expected to find the core relevant to their needs, perhaps it is unnecessary to include readers' advisory in the core. Just as the school media or public library specialists in core courses may not desire to learn about maintenance of archives or strategies to contribute to corporate profitability, curriculum designers may view readers' advisory as elective material. (This approach presumes, of course, that students have sufficient knowledge of major aspects of the profession to enable them to chose the best specialization for themselves without an orientation to major aspects of professional practice.)

The next question, then, is whether the students who know they want to practice in adult services have the opportunity to explore readers' advisory topics in all programs. To explore that question, one may look at the column of Table 2.1 labeled "No." This column provides information on the number of responding programs that do not include readers' advisory topics for adults in either required *or* elective courses. Apparently two of the responding programs (6 percent) do not deal anywhere in their curricula with the topic "Readers' advisory in general." (We cannot help but wonder whether those fifteen programs that failed to respond might disproportionately include other library and information science curricula completely inattentive to readers' advisory.) Three responses (9 percent) include nothing in either their required *or* elective courses on "Review media for the selection of adult popular materials." Their graduates will apparently be as inept at building the adult collection of a public library as any college graduate off the street, a deficiency that the ALA Committee on Accreditation should certainly look into. Table 2.1 further shows that about one-fifth of the responding programs had no inclusion of readers' advisory interviews, which differ so markedly from reference interviews, or any coverage of advisory tools on the Internet, which increasingly offers an arena for advisors to share their expertise and a "gold mine" of advice on reading.

On a more optimistic note, the findings do indicate that all eleven topics from the questionnaire were included *somewhere* in the curricula of four-fifths of the responding programs.

Table 2.2 explores the degree to which schools represent readers' advisory topics in *both required* and *elective* courses. Perhaps not surprisingly, "Readers' advisory in general" and "Review media for the selection of adult popular materials" are most likely to appear in both required and elective coursework. Inclusion of the first would ensure student familiarity with the *idea* that librarians work creatively with adults to enjoy leisure reading, and the latter would come up in general collection building coursework and in more specialized discussions.

The column of Table 2.2 labeled "Yes, in Required Courses Only" presents a somewhat startling bit of information: Programs that include adult readers' advisory topics only in required courses may have difficulty preparing adult services librarians who have sufficient preparation for successful practice. Some cores are eighteen semester hours long and include both a course in collection building and a course in technical services. If curriculum designers have decided that *all* the students who enter their programs should be able to build and arrange popular collections well and offer adequate preparation for advisory service designed for adult leisure readers, then they may be exceptions, at least with respect to these two skills. However, if sufficient preparation is included in their *cores* to prepare for *adult* readers' advisory service in public libraries, the question becomes whether these programs are shortchanging their school, academic, and special library candidates, who presumably would be better served by an emphasis on other topics and skills.

The questionnaire had an open-ended question that allowed respondents to indicate topics that they cover other than the eleven specifically named. Several respondents provided this information, and the topics they mentioned ranged over a wide territory, including "Competition to library readers' advisory in the for-profit sector" and background topics such as the history of readers' advisory, community analysis, and use and user studies, along with a unit on reading and culture. Genre sources on the Internet and large-print books were mentioned, and two respondents mentioned audiobooks. One respondent wrote that videos based on books, especially fiction and biography, were covered, and popular lifestyle magazines were mentioned as well.

Finally, we deduced that there is an individual faculty member interested in readers' advisory in certain schools. Where it is clear from the questionnaire or other sources that the school includes an emphasis on adult readers' advisory topics in the curriculum, we have listed these instructors. This list is a beginning, of course, and we do not claim that it is definitive.

SCHOOL	FACULTY MEMBER
Alabama	Anabel Stephens
Dominican	Bill Crowley
Illinois, Urbana-Champaign	Debra Johnson
North Carolina at Chapel Hill	David Carr, Barbara Moran, Brian Sturm
North Carolina at Greensboro	Julia Hersberger
North Carolina Central	Pauletta Bracy, Robert Burgin, Kenneth Shearer
Queens College	Mary K. Chelton
South Carolina	Linda Lucas Walling
South Florida	Kathleen de la Peña McCook
SUNY Albany	Bill Katz
SUNY Buffalo	Lorna Peterson
Western Ontario	Catherine Sheldrick Ross
Wisconsin-Madison	Wayne Wiegand

Conclusions

Wayne Wiegand characterized the attitude toward recent scholarship on readers and reading in library and information science programs as "Out of Sight, and Out of Mind." We characterize the attitude toward adult readers' advisory services in library and information science programs as "Partly Out of Sight; Not Much in Mind." Most respondents had some inclusion of the readers' advisory topics listed on the questionnaire, and most of the coverage was in electives, although these electives seemed to rely on the interest of individual faculty members.

Perhaps our greatest concern on the basis of this survey is that most of the programs accredited by the American Library Association do not even expose students to the idea that they can develop a practice devoted to building adult popular collections and encouraging rewarding reading among the general public. In too many of these programs, even a basic preparation is not provided in the electives to the candidates who come to school knowing that this is the career they want. If it were not a fact that popular collections and reader guidance constitute the most common use of the public library, this might be excusable, but under the circumstances it is not.

Notes

1. To subscribe to Fiction_L, send an e-mail message to requests@maillist.webrary.org with *one* of the following commands in the subject or body of the message:

    subscribe fiction_l (to subscribe to the regular list)

    subscribe digest fiction_l (to subscribe to the digest)

    Within an hour, you should receive the Fiction_L welcome message. If you do not receive it or if you have any questions about the list, please contact Natalya Fishman, Fiction_L Manager, at fladmin@ webrary.org.

References

Adult Reading Round Table of Illinois. 1999. *The ARRT Genre Fiction List: A Self-Evaluation Bibliography for Fiction Librarians.* Illinois: Adult Reading Round Table of Illinois.

Baker, Sharon L. 1994. What Patrons Read and Why: The Link Between Personality and Reading. In *Research Issues in Public Libraries: Trends for the Future,* ed. Joy M. Greiner, 131–17. Westport, CT: Greenwood.

Burgin, Robert. 1996. Readers' Advisory in Public Libraries: An Overview of Current Practices. In *Guiding the Reader to the Next Book,* ed. Kenneth Shearer, 71–88. New York: Neal-Schuman.

Lackner, Catherine Patricia, Anne K. May, Anne Weidrich Miltenberg, and Elizabeth Olesh. 1998. An Investigation of Readers' Advisory Transactions in Nassau County (NY) Public Libraries. Master's thesis, Queen's College.

Olson, Georgine N. 1998. Fiction Acquisition/Fiction Management: Education and Training. *Acquisitions Librarian* 19: 1–9.

Ross, Catherine Sheldrick. 1995. If They Read Nancy Drew, So What? Series Readers Talk Back. *Library and Information Science Research* 17: 210–35.

———. 2001. Making Choices: What Readers Say About Choosing Books to Read for Pleasure. *Acquisitions Librarian* 25: 5–21.

Saricks, Joyce G., and Nancy Brown. 1997. *Readers' Advisory Service in the Public Library,* 2d ed. Chicago: American Library Association.

Shearer, Kenneth, ed. 1996. *Guiding the Reader to the Next Book.* New York: Neal-Schuman.

Talking with Readers. 2000. *Talking with Readers: A Workbook for Readers' Advisory.* A Cooperative Project of NoveList, Library Development and Services, Minnesota Department of Children, Families, and Learning and Minnesota Library Staff.

Towey, Cathleen A. 1997. We Need to Recommit to Readers' Advisory Services. *American Libraries* 28: 31.

Wiegand, Wayne A. 1997a. MisReading Library Education. *Library Journal* 122: 36–38.

———. 1997b. Out of Sight, and Out of Mind: Why Don't We Have Any Schools of Library and Reading Studies? *Journal of Library and Information Science Education* 38: 316–26.

———. 2000. Librarians Ignore the Value of Stories. *Chronicle of Higher Education* 47 (October 27): B20.

Yu, Liang, and Ann O'Brien. 1996. Domain of Fiction Librarianship. *Advances in Librarianship* 20: 151–89.

CHAPTER 3

"Taught at the University on a Higher Plane Than Elsewhere": The Graduate Education of Readers' Advisors

Bill Crowley

Overview

This chapter discusses the education of adult readers' advisors in the Chicago-area component of Dominican University's Graduate School of Library and Information Science (GSLIS). It does so in the context of a general examination of the prospects for advancing readers' advisory (RA) services in graduate programs accredited by the American Library Association. To this end, the chapter does the following:

- Describes the spectrum of RA students in the River Forest (Chicago area) component of the Dominican University GSLIS program

- Provides information on the author and describes how he came to RA

- Reviews the process through which Dominican University's GSLIS planned, tested, and added LIS 763 Readers' Advisory Services to its curriculum

- Explores the critical differences among the various cultures of higher education and the "off-campus worlds" of RA practitioners

- Considers the numerous obstacles to creating readers' advisory courses, including the difficulty of sustaining a research agenda in RA due, in part, to misperceptions about the field and a lack of rewards for faculty

- Offers practical suggestions for inducing ALA-accredited programs to offer courses in RA

- Provides a basic version of the author's current RA syllabus

What Kinds of Students Study RA?

What kinds of students register for LIS 763 Readers' Advisory Services in the Chicago-area component of Dominican University's GSLIS? In a class of fifteen students, for example, thirteen or fourteen will be female, and nine or ten will already be working in public libraries. However, if the course is offered at night or during the summer, it is likely that as many as four or five students intend to be school library media specialists or academic librarians. On occasion, because of a love of books and/or the happenstance of course scheduling, a current or would-be information specialist or knowledge manager will also enroll. To be more specific, the average RA class includes the following:

- *Public library* RA enthusiasts who delight in talking about books and exchanging ideas and suggestions with customers or patrons. They may be full-time students or already employed with the title of "librarian." If the lack of a Master's degree means that they must work as a clerk or library associate, perhaps at a circulation or information desk or even in the RA department, they take one or two courses a semester while balancing employer and family demands. Eventually, degree in hand, they apply for librarian positions in public service. If lucky, they are appointed as RA librarians or readers' services specialists (titles tend to vary). If and when they become heads of RA departments or public library directors, these same enthusiasts may plan to lead library book discussion groups and otherwise attempt to keep in touch though occasional work at the RA desk.

- *School library media specialists,* present or future, who also love books and encounter bright students with adult-level reading tastes and who are increasingly frustrated in classes where instructors "teach to the test." If currently employed as classroom teachers, these graduate students often find themselves talking about "the story" with, for example, high school students who seem to know everything about science fiction or fantasy and want to share their enthusiasm with an appreciative listener.

- *Academic library staff* who are working or plan to work in higher education institutions ranging from community colleges to research universities. Although knowing that they will be hired as reference or technical services librarians, they often plan to develop collections to support English department courses in science fiction, fantasy, western, or mystery genres or the many subgenres of inspirational or gay and lesbian literature. They may do the same for cross-disciplinary courses in popular culture taught by members of anthropology, sociology, or popular culture departments. These students know the value of both fiction and nonfiction stories and are likely to be the stalwarts of college or university book discussion groups, where they will deepen their knowledge of the reading interests of teaching and research faculty.

- *Writers* who intend to support themselves as librarians while pursuing their "other" calling.

- *Miscellaneous* students with corporate information and knowledge management interests.[1]

Therefore, awareness of the importance of adult-level RA is not limited to present and potential members of the public library community. It is a conviction that simply overflows the internal boundaries of the library and information world, demonstrating great appeal to certain members of the school library media, academic library, and other library communities. In addition, if we can agree that RA deals with works offering what Robert Coles (1989, 191) describes as a "compelling narrative"—however we choose to define both "compelling" and "narrative"—it makes no sense to overlook the stories that histories, biographies, self-help books, and other forms of nonfiction provide. The vast area of what Kenneth D. Shearer (1996, 182) rightly terms "discretionary reading" cannot be limited to fiction alone. To attempt to do so is to evidence a "theory" of RA that ignores the reality of RA "experience." Joyce G. Saricks, whose fundamentally important *Readers' Advisory Service in the Public Library* is a text in my course, mentioned to the fall 1999 class that she now sees nonfiction as included within RA.[2]

A Few Words About the Chapter Author

Unlike many faculty now being appointed to "new" American Library Association-accredited programs of *information science* (IS) or the more traditional programs of *library and information science* (LIS), I am a product of the "library" world. Prior to earning my doctorate, I spent twenty-three years in public libraries, library cooperatives, and state library agencies in New York, Alabama, Indiana, and Ohio. This experience includes employment as a reference librarian, public relations representative, consultant, multitype cooperative head, administrator of public services in a public library, and deputy state librarian. In 1993 I realized that I could either continue to complain about the direction of professional education or try to do something about it. Circumstances required that I remain in Ohio, a first-rate state that lacks a Ph.D. program in LIS. In consequence, I resigned the position as Ohio's Deputy State Library Librarian for Library Services, enrolled as a full-time student at Ohio University in Athens, earned a Ph.D. in higher education in two years with a dissertation on the academic library, and spent a third year as a researcher for the university's president emeritus.

In retrospect, earning a doctorate in higher education was a net positive. It left me with fewer illusions regarding how the academic world works. The setting aside of comforting misconceptions is important in any useful discussion of how to advance the cause of RA within ALA-accredited programs. We must understand the reasons for a "negative" RA climate in ALA-accredited programs before we can make further progress.

Although I started teaching Readers' Advisory Services in 1997, this is the first time I have written on RA. The reasons for this delay are important only because they can provide "real world" practitioners with a greater understanding of why the creation of RA courses is not more popular in academic environments. It is worth noting that Dominican University requires a teaching load for its library and information science faculty that is higher than that of most ALA-accredited programs. With little time for research while preparing for classes but knowing that Dominican University expects evidence of scholarly productivity for faculty to be retained, I followed the classic pattern of publication for first-year assistant professors. I did not do new research on RA. Instead, I mined my doctoral dissertation for publishable articles. My dissertation was on the academic library so I wrote about academic libraries (Crowley 1996, 1997). Had I earned my doctorate at a program where I was encouraged to do a dissertation on readers' advisory services, I would have written on RA. It's often just as simple as that—the articles and books that professors publish in their early years are likely to be related to the topic of their doctoral research.

While publishing articles culled from my dissertation, I also found myself on the unfashionable side of the library versus information dispute. It is ironic that supporters of RA are asking for new library courses at the same time the very concept of "library" is in retreat within ALA-accredited programs. Several years ago, acting in part on the theory that one has to preserve "library" in order to offer library-related RA courses, I put aside thoughts of writing about RA to join the ranks of those researching and publishing articles asserting that it was intellectually questionable and often misleading to argue that everything libraries do can be subsumed under the rubric of "information" (Crowley 1998, 1999b; Crowley and Brace 1999). Academics such as Sharon Baker, Mary K. Chelton, Kathleen de la Peña McCook, Catherine Sheldrick Ross, Kenneth Shearer, and Wayne A. Wiegand were already writing fundamentally important articles on RA. However, Mary K. Chelton and Wayne A. Wiegand seemed to be shouldering the larger burden of defending libraries within ALA-accredited professional education. With my background, I felt obligated to help.

Here we are talking about fundamentals. If the American Library Association ceases to enforce the provision of "library" education within library and information science or information science programs, most arguments regarding courses devoted to readers' advisory services—or even individual class sessions on RA—will become moot. There will be simply be no place in the curriculum for such instruction when separate offerings in public, academic, and school library administration/services are subsumed under generic classes dealing with the programs of "information organizations." Such an approach serves to free instructional time for the teaching of new information courses that happen to be more valued by faculty without a continuing library connection. Among the many reasons why this approach represents unproductive graduate education is the fact that it ignores what researchers have learned about the context-related or tacit knowledge of expert practitioners. Homogenized courses, classes that do not recognize the differences in context among the various library and information organizations, inevitably concentrate on "academic problems [that] are typically unrelated to an individual's ordinary experience" (Sternberg, Wagner, Williams, and Horvath 1995; Crowley 1999a). They are, in short, "unreal."

Adding Adult Readers' Advisory Services to the Curriculum

How did the teaching of RA come to Dominican University? Again, if this section presents an unusual number of details, it is only because I want to help practitioners gain a greater understanding of the worlds in which library and information faculty must fashion their careers. These worlds make certain demands on faculty, demands that we must understand—and address—if the library community is to expand the opportunities for RA education at the graduate level.

My "faculty" involvement with RA started on a spring day in 1997 when I was still a first-year assistant professor. I was walking by the GSLIS administrative offices when I saw then-Dean Peggy Sullivan in intense discussion with Ann Carlson, our expert on youth services and literature.

Peggy appeared to be troubled. Looking past Ann, she caught my eye and waved me into her office. Thirty minutes later, I was back at my desk. My ongoing concerns about student advising, retention, publication, and working on my next class were now overshadowed by the question of where I was going to find the time to design a new course in readers' advisory service.

Years later, I am quite pleased to have been "drafted" into RA. In any given semester LIS 763 Readers' Advisory Services can be the most enjoyable—and the most intellectually challenging—of the courses I am teaching. I also believe that it is a course in which I can make the greatest difference on the future direction of the library profession. In the spring of 1997, however, RA seemed to represent only more work in an already crowded schedule.

In retrospect, to mangle a traditional romance genre cliché, the stars seemed to be aligned in precisely the right order to add a course in RA to the curriculum of Dominican University's GSLIS. First, the university has a strong reputation for educating librarians to meet the reading needs of children and young adults. It was known that we were interested in people and reading. Second, Dean Peggy Sullivan, a renowned public librarian, academic leader, professional administrator, and storyteller, was completing her last year of a two-year term as head of the GSLIS program. Fortunately, Peggy's support for "library" programs has been maintained and extended by her successor, Dean Prudence Dalrymple. Third, the Dominican University GSLIS affiliate program at the College of St. Catherine in St. Paul, Minnesota, for the first time was actually offering a trial course on readers' advisory services, cotaught by Colleen Coghlan and Geraldine B. King in its spring 1997 session. Fourth, I had been hired the previous summer to fill a traditional "public library" faculty position. Despite the added work involved, I was already philosophically inclined to agree when Peggy—because Ann already handled children's and YA literature—asked me to offer a trial version of the adult readers' advisory services course in the fall 1997 semester.

However, beneath a fairly placid surface a number of issues were in play. Although the program offered by Dominican University GSLIS in the Chicago-metropolitan area and the affiliated College of St. Catherine in St. Paul, Minnesota—known locally as St. Kate's—are technically the same, it is one thing to start a class at an affiliate and quite another to address curriculum issues at a program's main campus. To put it bluntly, several Chicago-area faculty had significant concerns about a course in RA. They had read the literature, observed its apparent concentration on technique, and wondered whether RA could support a respectable research agenda in an information age. Although these arguments were delivered in one-to-one and small-group discussions on the River Forest campus, I believe that they reflect sentiments that will need to be addressed whenever RA practitioners pressure any ALA-accredited program to offer a similar course.

Planning the RA Course

As with many LIS programs, Dominican University's GSLIS does *not* reduce faculty workloads when a professor is asked to create a new course. Instead, our tradition is for professors to do the necessary work on top of their regular duties. An undiminished course load and the necessity of teaching in at least one of our two summer sessions because of the Chicago area's cost of living meant I had only a limited amount of time to design the RA class. That effort also included putting in place the necessary infrastructure, including print library resources and access to databases such as NoveList and What Do I Read Next? In order to (a) alleviate the doubts of senior faculty regarding the suitability of a course in RA and (b) address concerns about a trial course developed in St. Paul, which the majority of the GSLIS Council (the body ultimately responsible for adding courses to the GSLIS syllabus) could not observe, I decided not to follow the St. Kate's syllabus. Instead, while borrowing useful ideas from St. Kate's, I drew on a larger spectrum and adapted, with permission, from the syllabi of the few related courses that I could identify in other ALA-accredited programs.[3] I also decided to seek the advice of a planning group of RA professionals who were working in public libraries in Illinois, Indiana, and Wisconsin.

Unfortunately, bringing practitioners into the development of the RA course led to unexpected criticism from several colleagues whom I greatly respect. As my fellow faculty reminded me, the right to develop our own courses is cherished by all university faculty worthy of the name. Summed up by the German word *Lehrfreiheit,* this freedom to teach and research allows faculty to (1) pursue "investigations wherever they might lead," (2) draw from research "whatever conclusions were warranted," and (3) disseminate the results "through teaching or publication without hindrance or interference from external authorities" (Lucas 1994, 172). Such freedom in dissemination clearly includes crafting the syllabus for a new course (Crowley in press). Some of my colleagues stressed that, in bringing practitioners so strongly into the course development process, I was raising issues of academic freedom that potentially affected all GSLIS faculty members.

The meeting with practitioners, recruited through requests for volunteers placed on mailing lists such as Fiction_L and Libref_L and formalized as the Readers' Advisory Course Planning Committee, took place on Thursday, June 12, 1997. Members of the committee who participated at the meeting or who provided postmeeting follow-up included Tina Hubert, Merle Jacob, Roberta S. Johnson, Leslie Kuizema, Gary Warren Niebuhr, Ricki Nordmeyer, Lela Jones Olszewski, Anne Paradise, Joyce Saricks, and Debra Walker. [Saricks and Johnson contributed Chapters 9 and 11, respectively, to this book.] As readers will note, the membership of the committee included national leaders in RA. Also present, lending both her expertise and the support of her office, was Dean Peggy Sullivan.

As it developed, the meeting proved to be both a source of needed information and an opportunity for practitioners to reflect on the present status of RA within their institutions, in nearly all cases public libraries. There was general agreement that RA was still fighting for equal treatment with reference services, and not always successfully. After the meeting one participant communicated to me that she felt those present were clearly "very demanding about what they thought were musts in the course." Although expressed with good humor, the "very demanding" observation is almost an understatement. At several points it became necessary to gently point out to the committee members that, despite their quite valuable input, course development is a faculty-driven process. The final responsibility for designing the course rested with the instructor. In this context, for example, I insisted that the class would deal extensively with reading theory, as well as the history of reading in American culture, and would include nonfiction, specifically history, biography, self-help, and inspirational books within the definition of RA.

Although Dominican University's Crown Library changed its policy in the year 2000, the RA course came into existence in 1997, a time when the library could not allocate the resources necessary to support a new course with potentially unlimited demands for resources. The library, however, would purchase or subscribe to the tools necessary to access genre and other fiction. Tools for using nonfiction, such as the Illinois Online catalog, were on hand. In general, since genre fiction and nonfiction are readily available, students had easy access to materials required for the course. However, it was also necessary for me to spend July and August of 1997 writing, telephoning, faxing, and e-mailing publishers to request the donation of a spectrum of fiction and nonfiction genres, as well as hard copy and online reference material, even as I developed and refined the course syllabus. (*Note:* A generic version of the LIS 763 Readers' Advisory Services syllabus, supplied for the assistance of those who might be planning or agitating for RA courses, is appended to this chapter.) These donated materials, accessed through the library Web page, added to the library collection, or kept in cardboard boxes in my office, are heavily used by students in the class. They also serve as useful examples for class discussions. However, developing the support collections and refining the class syllabus required months that I had originally planned to use writing articles for publication. This sort of time allocation is often possible at a teaching university such as Dominican. On the other hand, it may be impossible for an untenured faculty member trying to make a career in programs where research is the priority emphasis for decisions on retention and promotion.

Since 1997 I have asked my graduate assistants to write letters to publishers asking for donated copies of works in RA areas that I want to emphasize in succeeding years. In the past, on the recommendation of the planning committee, securing materials for gay and lesbian literature was a priority. Currently, inspirational literature, both fiction and nonfiction, has become an area for development. Future plans include trying to build up resources for the African-American and Latino genres. As noted earlier, in the year 2000 Dominican University's Crown Library changed its policies and plans to establish a "Popular Materials Collection." This change was facilitated through a multipurpose grant to the GSLIS from the Illinois State Library. The creation of this multigenre collection, combing both classics and more recent materials, is expected to limit my own need to solicit donated works from publishers.

Over the next year, both the Dominican University programs at St. Kate's and at River Forest offered Readers' Advisory Services on an experimental basis. In 1998, on behalf of Colleen Coghlan, Geraldine B. King, and myself, I carried the course to the Dominican University GSLIS Curriculum Committee. After receiving a favorable recommendation at the committee level, the course was approved by the full GSLIS Council and added to the curriculum. It has been offered in St. Paul and in the Chicago area ever since.

Conflicting Cultures

In an April 1997 Fiction_L posting, Ricki Nordmeyer of the Skokie Public Library recalled that the Chicago-area Adult Reading Roundtable (ARRT) "sent a letter to all of the library schools in the country emphasizing the need for Reader's Advisory coursework in their MLS programs and offering to suggest names of those who could help them develop such a curriculum." According to Nordmeyer, ARRT "heard from only 3 or 4 of them, most of which felt that they were already addressing that need" (Nordmeyer 1997). There are a number of possible reasons for this lack of response, and most will be discussed later in this chapter.

For now it is sufficient to stress that there are no longer "library schools" in the United States and Canada. From the library perspective, American Library Association-accredited programs are, at best, schools of library and information science where "library," "information," and even "archives" exist more or less as partners. At their worst, again from a library perspective, the more extreme versions of information programs seem to tolerate library education only because library students represent a reliable source of tuition revenue. In state-assisted institutions, tuition dollars from future librarians and other students are often matched by a state subsidy. But tuition dollars and state subsidy funds based on library enrollment do not have to be spent on library-related courses and increasingly are not. The point cannot be stressed strongly enough. We now live in an "information" world, and readers' advisory services supporters seeking courses in ALA-accredited institutions had better learn the insider rules if they want to have any chance at all of securing RA-relevant education. (Recent evidence of the dominance of "information" over "library" can be found in Association for Library and Information Science Education [2000].)

Understanding the Research and Publication Imperative

In a recent advertisement for a faculty search, the University of Washington stressed that it "continues to engage in a major transformation and expansion of its Information School (formerly known as the School of Library and Information Science)" and asserted that it was "committed to creating one of the top information schools in the world." To advance this effort, the "Information School" was looking for candidates evidencing "cutting-edge research and teaching excellence in one or more of the following areas":

> Computer networking, computer-supported cooperative work, database management systems, data mining, distributed systems, embedded systems, human-computer interaction, information retrieval, information visualization, markup languages, metadata, multimedia, network information discovery and retrieval, participatory design, tangible user interfaces, telecommunications, ubiquitous computing, user interface design, and system design.

The University of Washington is not alone in its emphasis on concerns that seem to be directed at a world entirely distinct from the working lives of readers' advisors. We could cite many other instances. For example, at the same time the University of Washington posting appeared, the University of Wisconsin-Madison (UWM) School of Library and Information Studies announced that it was also seeking new faculty. In its advertisement, UWM revealed that it sought faculty interested in "information policy; transborder data flow; information economy; science communication; intellectual property; electronic publishing; 'underground' use of technologies; effects of technology on ethnic cultures; the interaction between technology and both individuals and groups."

In discussing the effect of the movement of ALA-accredited programs away from "library," it is important to review the impact that this transformation may have on the lives of individual faculty. First, new faculty are more likely to be recruited from other disciplines. Even if appointed from the new ALA-accredited information programs, such faculty are increasingly unlikely to have been educated in areas relevant to RA. Second, the scholarship and publications of such faculty, as revealed in their dissertations and early publications, are not likely to address RA issues. Third, when hired to teach and research course areas similar to those sought by Washington and Wisconsin-Madison, new faculty members, even if interested, are unlikely to be able to fit RA into their teaching. This is because many graduate faculty teach as few as two courses a semester. With such a limited teaching load, these faculty simply cannot shoehorn RA into schedules dominated by courses in information visualization and transborder data flow.

At institutions with less of a research emphasis, such as Dominican University, faculty teach three courses a semester. This provides a little more flexibility for the teaching of RA. However, in order to remain competitive and responsive to their markets, Dominican University and its counterparts must also provide courses to meet the emerging needs of the information and knowledge management communities.

Further Obstacles to Creating RA Courses

In addition to a diminished interest in traditional library issues by the information culture, which is increasingly prioritized in ALA-accredited programs, supporters of RA face two obstacles that serve to distance the area even from faculty who might otherwise prize a library connection. First, RA is perceived, albeit incorrectly, as an effective technique lacking both educational and theoretical justification. Second, and more accurately, RA lacks an adequate faculty rewards system.

Technique and Theory in the University and RA

For more than 130 years, American higher education has taught an increasingly wider spectrum of courses and offered an expanding range of degrees largely on the basis of a fundamentally important assertion of Charles W. Eliot, later to become a well-known president of Harvard University. According to Eliot,

It cannot be said too loudly or too often, that no subject of human inquiry can be out of place in the programme of a real university. It is only necessary that every subject should be taught at the university on a higher plane than elsewhere. (1869, 215–16)

Although Eliot's dictum lays a firm foundation for teaching RA courses in ALA-accredited programs, its implementation encounters a number of very practical limitations. Even if adequate faculty time is available, practitioners need to understand that contemporary professors considering teaching and researching RA are likely to translate Eliot's nineteenth-century "taught at the university on a higher plane than elsewhere" into a number of twenty-first-century questions. These questions are likely to include "Is RA capable of sustaining a research program with adequate funding and appropriate recognition?" and "Will teaching RA help me achieve promotion and tenure?"

Both time constraints and previous research commitments prevented me from contacting ALA-accredited programs to ask why RA is or is not taught. [See Chapter 2 for a survey of RA education in ALA-accredited programs.] However, as indicated by Ricki Nordmeyer's discussion of the unfruitful ARRT survey of library schools (earlier in this chapter), it seems unlikely that the effort would have produced many useful data (Nordmeyer 1997). Few ALA-accredited programs will openly admit that they slight library issues in their information environments. Additionally, no one below the rank of dean or director can force a faculty member to complete a survey questionnaire. If the faculty member is a full professor with tenure, such pressure may even be counterproductive. In lieu of the data such a survey may or may not supply, I first analyze an in-print assertion from a practitioner-turned-vendor-representative and trainer who maintains a leadership position within RA. The quotation addresses the historic dilemma of whether to judge the quality of works customers or patrons read. Then I apply "internal" understandings of how higher education works to demonstrate why the view he asserts is (a) problematic in light of the known practice of RA and (b) off-putting to potential RA educators.

Writing in *North Carolina Libraries*, Duncan Smith observed:

> It is both difficult and dangerous to speculate about which texts meet the highest need or which serve the highest purpose. To do so would involve judging not only the value of the texts, but also the worth of the individuals who read them. Both types of judgment are inappropriate for a democratic society and for a profession with democratic ideals. (1992, 205)

From my experience in discussing RA with numerous current and future practitioners, I can feel fairly safe in asserting that Smith's comments are representative of the views of many in the field. However, they do not capture crucial aspects of a reality where RA practitioners make and often follow judgments regarding book quality on a daily basis. For example, Diana

Tixier Herald's *Genreflecting,* another class text, discusses "awards" throughout its chapters (Herald 2000). Awards, by definition, represent some judgment of quality, however defined. Additionally, mailing lists such as Fiction_L bring RA recommendations, often involving assertions of quality, on a near-daily basis. Finally, to address the most fundamental issue Smith mentioned, informed judgments regarding the value of texts and the worth of people are fully compatible with both democratic ideals and experience. The pragmatic philosopher and educational theorist John Dewey, whose commitment to popular sovereignty was second to none, stressed that the future of democracy itself is dependent "upon freeing and perfecting the processes of inquiry and of dissemination of their conclusions" (Dewey 1984, 365). For Dewey and other pragmatists, effective public decisions are informed decisions. To declare areas of RA inappropriate for faculty and practitioner investigations is to impoverish the quality of the very discussions necessary to advance readers' advisory programs in a representative democracy.

The seeming reality that RA practitioners can both scorn and embrace determinations of quality is not evidence of professional duplicity. Rather, it may simply be yet another example of seemingly predictable divergence in what Chris Argyris has termed "theories of action." According to Argyris, human beings hold two such theories: "There is the one that they espouse, which is usually expressed in the form of stated beliefs and values. Then there is the theory they actually use; this can only be inferred from observing their actions, that is, their actual behavior" (Argyris 1999, 126). At a minimum, the real possibility that RA "as professed" is often different from RA "as delivered" represents an interesting research topic in itself. So does determining whether, when, and how books of certain types affect the lives of their readers.

It is possible to make the case for teaching and researching RA and for demonstrating why practitioners should be offered instruction in how to develop, manage, and further a vital library program. However, the fundamental condition for offering RA courses in a university environment is likely to be controversial for some within the practitioner communities. It requires accepting the real possibility that readers' advisory service is, in part, an educational program and that, for example, an adult book discussion can represent a particularly intense form of self- and group education disguised as a recreational activity. Once practitioners accept the prospect that RA can be an essential component of the educational mission of the public library, school library media center, and academic library, the necessary conditions for a graduate course start falling into place.[4] Ignore the educational component of RA and it becomes a matter of technique that is best taught in a workshop environment.

The equation is quite simple. To the same degree that RA substitutes ideology for inquiry and to the extent that it denies the right of scholars and practitioners to analyze and judge both the quality of reading materials and the effects of reading on readers, it is distanced from the sphere of the university.

Readers' Advisory and the Faculty Rewards System

Writing in the October 27, 2000, issue of the *Chronicle of Higher Education*, Wayne A. Wiegand discusses the "shame" of five thousand or so new graduates of American Library Association-accredited programs who are unable to understand the needs of readers when they take jobs in "public, school, and academic libraries whose patrons use them chiefly to get reading material." [See Chapter 1 for Wiegand's discussion of this issue.] For Wiegand, these professional limitations seem to be directly related to a commitment by such programs to hiring professors with interests in "teaching skills and research expertise in information technologies" (Wiegand 2000, B20). Although I agree with Wiegand, I am also aware that the move away from both libraries and reading is the result of a spectrum of causes, including the lure of an "information economy," the striving of nonlibrary professors in ALA-accredited programs to remake their schools in the image of their home disciplines, and the historic efforts of faculty to escape the control of practitioners (Crowley 1999b). The world of ALA education has changed, and it is not going back. The problem now becomes how to maximize library concerns—including RA—in ALA-accredited programs that privilege "information." In this effort we can follow, with profit, the reminder of the Ohio Board of Regents, published in its *Report of the Regents' Advisory Committee on Faculty Workload Standards and Guidelines: February 18, 1994*, that faculty gravitate "toward those activities that...[are] more highly valued and rewarded" (Ohio Board of Regents 1994). Restated, supporters of RA must ensure that faculty in ALA-accredited programs find it to their advantage—in terms of their academic careers—to teach and research in the area of readers' advisory services. This is not going to be an easy task. And there are no guarantees regarding the likelihood of success.

Tactics for Securing RA-Relevant Education

I must stress that pleas for creating RA courses based on shared values and common histories are unlikely to elicit much response from today's ALA-accredited programs. For such programs, the "library" world has diminished to a subset of the information universe. Increasingly, faculty who are educating future librarians have little or no library experience, and many even lack library-related degrees. More university funding and outside grants than ever before are becoming available to ALA-programs because of their new information emphasis. University administrators interested in their share of a trillion-dollar information economy are approving new faculty positions. In this somewhat negative library context, I suggest the following tactics, listed in a roughly increasing order of difficulty.

1. State associations can provide seed money for an in-state ALA-accredited program to develop a course in RA. Such support could enable a full-time faculty member—who might otherwise have to teach in a summer session for financial reasons—to create the new course. Even if an adjunct or part-time instructor then does the actual teaching of RA, a full-time professor will have had the responsibility for developing it. In the academic context, a course is usually deemed more valuable if taught, or at least developed, by a full-time professor.

2. State associations might negotiate with their in-state ALA-accredited program to arrange for an out-of-state program with one or more RA-related courses to educate local students through telecommunicated or Web-based technology.

3. Relevant divisions within ALA and state library associations might allocate their own funds or secure outside support for grants to Ph.D. students willing to do a dissertation in the area of readers' advisory services. At least in their early years as professors, such students are likely to draw on their dissertations for scholarly and other RA articles. In addition, they might volunteer to teach RA—or support the teaching of a course by a part-time instructor—when appointed to positions in ALA-accredited programs.

4. Practitioners could work with ALA-accredited programs to secure funding to create endowed chairs that are dedicated to studying the complex interactions among, for example, publishers, libraries, librarians, books, booksellers, and the many reading publics.

5. RA practitioners might join forces with other librarians to force changes in the standards for accrediting ALA programs to require the teaching of certain library courses, including RA. Because ALA-accreditation has value for numerous students through either state laws or library traditions, this might actually work. However, there is likely to be a price. Some universities might give up accreditation if it requires the diversion of faculty time and other resources from more profitable "information" to less lucrative "library" concerns.

6.   Readers' advisors and other library practitioners could work with local universities to create new ALA-accredited programs with a greater library emphasis. However, unless ALA accreditation requirements are also changed in a more "library" direction, such new programs will also face the temptation of minimizing library while educating for the wealth-producing information environment.

A "Basic" Readers' Advisory Syllabus

A basic version of my LIS 763 Readers' Advisory Services syllabus is provided as an attachment to this chapter. Although RA, as it is practiced in public, school, and academic libraries is highly context-specific, certain principles regarding reading, culture, the fluid nature of genres, and the unifying role of story across fiction and nonfiction boundaries seem to have a remarkable resilience.

Conclusions

This chapter, written by a librarian turned academic, recounts a process that happened through a combination of luck, professional experience, personal interest, and the enthusiasm and cooperation of many RA practitioners. The result was LIS 763 Readers' Advisory Services, a course taken by students in both the Chicago-area and St. Paul components of Dominican University's GSLIS since 1997. Throughout, I have stressed the point that awareness of differences, in effect a realistic knowledge of the bridgeable gulf that separates the demands of the academic world and the requirements of off-campus contexts, is absolutely essential for those seeking to establish RA-appropriate education at ALA-accredited institutions. This consciousness needs to be combined with an understanding that the diminishing power of the historic library ties between professors and practitioners cannot compete with either changing academic demands or the pull of an information world. When we combine such realism with the Ohio Board of Regents' reminder that faculty respond best when activities are "highly valued and rewarded," we can make real progress in achieving RA education.

Notes

1.   These categories were from index cards filled out by students and information obtained from in-class and other discussions held since 1997.

2. Saricks's now repudiated remarks limiting adult RA in the public library to fiction are found in Saricks and Brown (1997, 1). During her last appearance as a guest lecturer in my class, Saricks gave me permission to share with others her change of mind on RA and nonfiction. [See Chapter 12, in which Burgin explores nonfiction RA.]

3. Syllabi and other assistance were received from Lorna Peterson (SUNY Buffalo) and, through her, Helen Huguenor Lyman and Linda Lucas Walling (University of South Carolina) and Bill Summers (Florida State University). In addition, because she was in the Chicago area meeting with a coauthor, I was able to spend a Sunday brunch picking the mind of Sharon (Shay) Baker of the University of Iowa.

4. The laws of the State of Illinois, for example, allow for the creation of public libraries as "local public institutions of general education for citizens" (Illinois Library Association, *Illinois Library Laws in Effect, January 1997* (1997), 75 ILCS: 16/1–10).

References

Argyris, Chris. 1999. Tacit Knowledge and Management. In *Tacit Knowledge in Professional Practice,* ed. Robert J. Sternberg and Joseph A. Horvath, 123–40. Mahwah, NJ: Lawrence Erlbaum Associates.

Association for Library and Information Science Education (ALISE). 2000. *Educating Library and Information Science Professionals for a New Century: The KALIPER Report- Executive Summary.* Reston, VA: ALISE. (KALIPER stands for the Kellogg-ALISE Information Professions and Education Renewal project.)

Coles, Robert. 1989. *The Call of Stories.* Boston: Houghton Mifflin.

Crowley, Bill. 1996. Redefining the Status of the Librarian in Higher Education. *College and Research Libraries* 57: 113–21.

———. 1997. The Dilemma of the Librarian in Canadian Higher Education. *Canadian Journal of Information and Library Science* 22: 1–18.

———. 1998. Dumping the "Library." *Library Journal* 120 (July): 48–49.

———. 1999a. Building Useful Theory: Tacit Knowledge, Practitioner Reports, and Culture of LIS Inquiry. *Journal of Education for Library and Information Science* 40: 282–95.

———. 1999b. The Control and Direction of Professional Education. *Journal of the American Society for Information Science* 50: 1127–35.

———. In press. *Building Useful Theory: Enhancing the Research Effectiveness of Faculty, Consultants, and Practitioners.* Metuchen, NJ: Scarecrow Press.

Crowley, Bill, and Bill Brace. 1999. A Choice of Futures: Is It Libraries Versus Information? *American Libraries* 30 (April): 76–77, 79.

Dewey, John. 1984. *The Public and Its Problems.* In *John Dewey: The Later Works, 1925–1953, Volume 2: 1925–1927,* ed. Jo Ann Boydston, 235–372. Carbondale and Edwardsville, IL: Southern Illinois University Press.

Eliot, Charles W. 1869. The New Education: Its Organization (Part 1). *Atlantic Monthly* 23 (February): 215–16.

Herald, Diana Tixier. 2000. *Genreflecting,* 5th ed. Englewood, CO: Libraries Unlimited.

Lucas, Christopher J. 1994. *American Higher Education: A History.* New York: St. Martin's Press.

Nordmeyer, Ricki. 1997. RE: Fiction in Libraries. Posting to Fiction_L. Monday, April 7, 1997, 09:16:58–0500 (CDT).

Ohio Board of Regents. 1994. *Report of the Regents' Advisory Committee on Faculty Workload Standards and Guidelines: February 18, 1994.* (URL: http://summit.bor.ohio.gov.plandocs.workload.html [accessed March 24, 1999])

Saricks, Joyce G., and Nancy Brown. 1997. *Readers' Advisory Service in the Public Library,* 2d ed. Chicago: American Library Association.

Shearer, Kenneth. 1996. Reflections on the Findings and Implications for Practice. In *Guiding the Reader to the Next Book,* ed. Kenneth Shearer, 169–83. New York: Neal-Schuman.

Smith, Duncan. 1992. All Readers Their Books: Providing Access to Popular Fiction. *North Carolina Libraries* 50 (Winter): 204–7.

Sternberg, Robert J., Richard K. Wagner, Wendy M. Williams, and Joseph A. Horvath. 1995. Teaching Common Sense. *American Psychologist* 50: 914.

Wiegand, Wayne A. 2000. Librarians Ignore the Value of Stories. *Chronicle of Higher Education* 47 (October 27): B20.

Attachment: "Core" RA Syllabus

LIS 763-04-01 Readers Advisory Services
Dominican University Graduate School of Library
and Information Science (GSLIS)
River Forest, Illinois
Sample Syllabus [circa 2001]
Instructor: Bill Crowley, Associate Professor, GSLIS

Overview: Dominican University offers a basic readers advisory course titled LIS 763-04-01 Readers Advisory Services. Due to a sense that the term is evolving, a decision was made in 1997 by the then dean and present instructor to eliminate the apostrophe in "Readers" and ignore any complaints from those who believe it is too soon to make such a change.

TEXTS

Abbott, Lee K. 1995. "Twenty Things Good Stories Have in Common." *Impromptu: A Newsletter* 12, no. 2 (Autumn): 1–5 (Syllabus—Appendix E).

Adult Reading Round Table Steering Committee (Illinois). *ARRT Genre Fiction List: A Self-Evaluation Bibliography for Fiction Librarians*.

Balcom, Ted. 1992. *Book Discussions for Adults: A Leader's Guide*. Chicago: American Library Association.

Crowley, Bill. 1999. "Building Useful Theory: Tacit Knowledge, Practitioner Reports, and the Culture of LIS Inquiry." *Journal of Education for Library and Information Science* 40 (Fall): 282–95.

Discussion book (selected by the book discussion leader each semester)

Herald, Diana Tixier. *Genreflecting: A Guide to Reading Interests in Genre Fiction* (Latest edition).

[Payn, James]. 1864. "The Blessedness of Books." *Chambers's Journal of Popular Literature, Science, and Art*, September 10: 577–79.

Saricks, Joyce G., and Brown, Nancy. *Readers' Advisory Service in the Public Library* (Latest edition).

Sources of Reading Theory

In addressing reading theory, the course draws on a number of sources, including A. J. Appleyard, SJ, *Becoming a Reader: The Experience of Fiction from Childhood to Adulthood* (New York: Cambridge University Press, 1990); R. Patton Howell, ed., *Beyond Literary: The Second*

Gutenberg Revolution (San Francisco: Saybrook, 1989); and Victor Nell, *Lost in a Book: The Psychology of Reading for Pleasure* (New Haven, CT: Yale University Press, 1988). Numerous other works on reading in general and reading in the genres also provide sources of insight for various class discussions.

Writing Guide

Kate L. Turabian's *Manual for Writers of Term Papers, Theses, and Dissertations* (Latest edition). Useful for both citations and English grammar. A brief, electronic interpretation of Turabian's *Manual* is available at the University Libraries of the University of Southern Mississippi. However, this electronic resource cannot help with issues involving English grammar. http://www.lib.usm.edu/~instruct/guides/turabian.html

Overview

LIS 763 Readers Advisory Services is a graduate course offered by a professional school. By design, the content is set at a higher level than normally found in library, information, and media workshops or community college offerings. In combining practical instruction in techniques and tools with equally relevant research and theory, Readers Advisory Services tries to live up to the spirit of the following:

The Intrinsic Value of Reading

I had hundreds of books under my skin already. Not selected reading, all of it. Some of it could be called trashy. I had been through Nick Carter, Horatio Alger, Bertha M. Clay, and the whole slew of dime novelists in addition to some really constructive reading. It was help, because acquiring the reading habit early is the important thing. Taste and natural development will take care of the rest later on. (Zora Neale Hurston, *Dust Tracks on a Road,* Lippincott 1942; reprint, New York: Harper, 1996, 125. Citation refers to the reprint edition.)

Zora Neale Hurston (1891–1960) was a famed African-American novelist, folklorist, and anthropologist. Her fictional and factual work includes *Their Eyes Were Watching God, Jonah's Gourd Vine, Tell My Horse,* and *Mules and Men.*

On the Relevance of Theory to the Real World

Efficient practice precedes the theory of it; methodologies presuppose the application of the methods, of the critical investigation of which they are the products. It was because Aristotle found himself and others reasoning now intelligently and now stupidly and it was because Izaak Walton [*The Compleat Angler*] found himself and others angling sometimes effectively and sometimes ineffectively that both were able to give to their pupils the maxims and prescriptions of their arts. (Gilbert Ryle, *The Concept of Mind,* London: Hutchinson, 1949/1958, 30)

Gilbert Ryle (1900–1976) of the University of Oxford was a leader in "ordinary language philosophy," which holds that many profound philosophical problems can be solved by returning to the meaning of language as it is spoken in everyday life.

Computer Accounts

Information is provided on securing a Dominican University e-mail account.

Basic Electronic Resources

Fiction_L (instructions on subscribing and unsubscribing)

Home page of *Genreflecting* author Diana Tixier Herald: http://www.Genreflecting.com/

NoveList (instructions on the use of the university's subscription)

What Do I Read Next? is on the Web at (information supplied)

The Reader's Advisor

Fiction Catalog (latest hard copy and electronic edition)

Needle in a Cyberstack, in particular the following pages

"Popular Fiction" http://members.home.net/albeej/pages/ PopularFiction.html

"Books and Book Reviews" http://members.home.net/ albeej/pages/Books.html

What's Next? from the Kent District Library (Michigan) helps you search adult fiction in a series. http://www.kentlibrary.lib.mi.us/whats_next.htm

Course Description

A course on adult fiction and nonfiction reading. Includes the relationships of readers advisory (RA) with reference and other library services, research on adult reading and learning, and the roles of popular reading in an information society. Students will also gain experience in adult book discussion. Sessions on fiction genres (mystery, science fiction, romance, Western, etc.), nonfiction (self-help, biography, and history), and links among the fiction and nonfiction categories.

Goal of the Course

LIS 763 is designed to blend theory and practice to enhance student expertise in meeting the fiction and nonfiction reading needs of adult library users. To this end, it aims to strengthen students' written and verbal communication effectiveness. Course activities have been devised to encourage the student to develop a philosophy of RA service grounded in an understanding of the roles of reading in past and contemporary cultures, as well as a commitment to effective, customer-centered service.

Course Objectives

LIS 763 Readers Advisory Services has several overlapping objectives:

- To introduce students to the theory and practice of meeting adult reading needs through adult readers advisory services (RA)
- To explore adult RA as a critical aspect of the educational roles of public, high school, and academic libraries
- To introduce students to basic reference tools for adult RA
- To explore the historical development of adult American reading tastes
- To explore evaluating, selecting, and utilizing RA reference materials and other methods of facilitating access to fiction and nonfiction works sought by library customers
- To identify ongoing issues in delivering RA services
- To explore RA's place in a hierarchy privileging information and other educational programs

- To demonstrate the value of nonfiction in RA service

- To provide basic training in leading a book discussion group

- To explore such ethical issues as requiring staff to read on personal time

- To discern internal and external relationships among RA librarians and other library staff

- To understand factors that affect planning and budgeting for RA services

- To explore use of the Web for enhancing effective RA service

- To investigate marketing and other approaches for increasing the perceived value of RA services to potential customers within and without the library

Assignments and Grading

Writing and Analysis Assignment: Three Typed Pages (Minimum)

The first assignment will involve a close reading of "The Blessedness of Books" contained in the December 10, 1864 issue of *Chambers's Journal of Popular Literature, Science, and Art*. Drawing on Saricks and Brown, *Readers' Advisory Service in the Public Library*, 2d ed., students will describe how they will serve any, many, or all of the people described in "The Blessedness of Books." (Article to be distributed.)

Percentage of grade: 10%

Book Annotations and Class "Book Talks"

In addition to the class texts, students will read six (6) books. Five books will be read in the genres and four of these five will be "book talked." A sixth work, will be selected by the guest book discussion leader and will be read by the class for the book discussion. Because students tend to be less familiar with the inspirational and gay and lesbian genres, all students will read a work in both areas and present a book talk on one. For the most part, students can read and book talk works in areas they select, provided there is a rough proportionality in the number of class reports. (A) Students are urged to read in unfamiliar genres. (B) Book talks should take about ten (10) minutes.

Books Eligible for Book Talks

Eligible books for these assignments include (1) works listed in *Genreflecting,* (2) newer titles by authors discussed in *Genreflecting,* (3) works listed in NoveList or What Do I Read Next? (4) works listed in the *Fiction Catalog,* (5) works on best-seller or award lists, (6) works provided by the instructor, or (7) works otherwise approved by the instructor.

Annotations, which are to be single spaced but no more than one page in length, will follow a slightly amended version of the outline presented on page 88 of Saricks and Brown's *Readers' Advisory Service in the Public Library.* The addition consists of including "Relevant Nonfiction Works and Authors" or "Relevant Fiction Works and Authors" as the last category in the outline (Appendix A). Students may use their annotations as a prompt during their class presentations.

Percentage of grade: 25% (5% each)

Topic Papers: Ten Typed Pages Each (Minimum)

Students will complete two topic papers. One paper will serve as the class midterm; the other will serve as the class final. However, students will decide for themselves which of the topic areas to write in to meet the deadlines for the midterm and final. All students must do a paper in Topic Area 1 ("Visit") for either the midterm or the final. The other paper may be in Topic Area 2 or Topic Area 3.

Topic Area 1: RA Site Visit (Required)

Students will "visit"—in person, by telephone, via e-mail, and/or fax—one or more public, academic, high school, or other libraries offering RA service and will write a report on these visits. The report should address: planning for RA service, budgeting, staffing, in-service training, hours of service, collection development, electronic (including Web sites) or hard copy resources available, reading lists (electronic or hard copy), expectation for staff reading after official work hours, tacit knowledge of the RA staff (see Crowley article), nature of customer base, and so on. Students may visit as part of a group and report as a group or individually.

- Group visits must involve an actual trip to the library.

- Group reports will be marked on a group basis.

- All papers must be individual papers and will be marked on an individual basis.

- Students are expected to make their own contacts for the interview(s). However, a listing of RA librarians who have volunteered to be interviewed is provided in Appendix B.

- Simply visiting the Web pages of one or more libraries is not sufficient to meet the visit requirement. Students must communicate electronically and/or in person with one or more real human beings!

Topic Area 2: The Social History of a Book (Borrowed with Permission from Dr. Linda Walling of the University of South Carolina)

In this option a student will seek the approval of the instructor for a "book that had an impact." Afterward the student will do the following:

- Read the book and evaluate it. (For example, was it as you expected from just hearing about it or seeing the movie? If not, how was it different from what you expected? Who is the book's audience? What is its appeal?)

- Locate and read reviews of the book at the time it was written. How was it received when it first appeared? How long did it take the book to have an impact?

- Research the era in which the book was written (historical events, social attitudes and values, economic situation, etc.)

- Determine what the book's history has been since it was written. Has it stayed in print? Is it included in literary histories and/or books on the history of the genre? How does it compare to other books by the author? How has it influenced other books on the subject or in the genre?

- Discuss the impact of the book with today's readers. What about its possible future impact?

Topic Area 3: Is the Author Using a Formula? Is He or She Using It Effectively?

In this option, the student will write a paper exploring how principles set forth by any author in any genre are (or are not) applied in the author's own work or the work of another writer in the same genre. For example, Raymond Chandler's "The Simple Art of Murder," published in *The Art of the Mystery Story* (on reserve), describes his standards for realistic mystery fiction. It is thus possible for a student to determine whether Chandler put his own theories to work in *The Big Sleep* and/or *The Long Goodbye*.

Alternatively, a student might examine whether Chandler's rules are of use in understanding, for example, Sue Grafton's *K Is for Killer*.

Regardless of the topic areas selected, the student will be expected to write full ten-page papers. Any attachments and bibliographies are not counted in the basic ten pages.

Percentage of grade: Per paper 20% (Total 40%)

Attendance and Class Participation

Quality class participation counts. Your grade may be affected if you miss more than two sessions. However, additional absences resulting from "acts of God"(e.g., prolonged illness, similar illness of spouse or spousal-equivalent, child, etc., can be addressed, for example, through an incomplete grade and makeup work).

Percentage of grade: 15%

Class Reports for Midterm or Final

Students will deliver a report, ten to fifteen minutes long, on either their midterm or final paper. "Appendix C: Effective Public Presentations" is the bible you should follow for the talks.

Percentage of grade: 10%

Grading Summary

Writing and analysis assignment	10%
Book annotations/class book talks	25%
Midterm topic paper	20%
Final topic paper	20%
Attendance/class participation	15%
Midterm or final presentation	10%
Total	100%

Additional Resources

Note: Appendix D provides a bibliography of works dealing with genre fiction, book publishing, history of the book, and so on.

Class Calendar

1. This calendar is flexible, but the instructor will provide reasons for changes. Class times, subject to negotiation over breaks, may vary.

2. At appropriate times throughout the semester the instructor will lecture and lead class discussions on the history of American popular reading since colonial times.

Class 1: Culture, Reading, Libraries, and RA Services

Introduction and Overview

- Distribution of inspirational, frontier/western, mystery works by instructor

- If feasible, please use Fiction Catalog (first choice for inspirational) or NoveList (second choice) or What Do I Read Next? (third choice) to find similar authors and related works. For locating relevant non-fiction works, students can use any public library catalog or What Do I Read Next?

Class 2: RA Tools and Reading Theory

Reading

Abbott, Lee K. "Twenty Things Good Stories Have in Common" (Syllabus—Appendix E)

Assignment

Secure an e-mail account.

Return "(1) Annotations, (2) Book Talks, (3) Midterm/Final" Form to Instructor.

Class 3: (A) "The Blessedness of Books"
(B) Saricks and Brown
(C) Tacit Knowledge as Useful Theory

Reading

James Payn, "The Blessedness of Books."

Saricks and Brown's *Readers' Advisory Service in the Public Library*.

Crowley, Bill. "Building Useful Theory: Tacit Knowledge, Practitioner Reports, and the Culture of LIS Inquiry," *Journal of Education for Library and Information Science* 40 (Fall 1999): 282–95.

Assignment

Three-page paper describing, per Saricks and Brown's *Readers' Advisory Service*, how you would serve any, many, or all of the people described in "The Blessedness of Books."

Class 4: Inspirational Literature

Reading

Inspirational book

Relevant pages in *Genreflecting* (Hint: not many)

Assignment

Appropriate students read book and complete a one-page annotation.

Class 5: Frontier/Western

Reading

All students read Chapter 2 (Western) in *Genreflecting*.

Relevant students read frontier/Western book

If it is your assignment, read frontier/Western book and complete an annotation.

Assignment

Appropriate students read book and complete a one-page annotation.

Class 6: Mystery/Suspense/Adventure

Reading

All students read Chapter 3 (Crime) and Chapter 4 (Adventure) in *Genreflecting.*

Assignment

Relevant students read book and complete a one-page annotation:

- Distribution of science fiction/fantasy/horror, romance, and nonfiction/history/biography books. If possible, use NoveList (first choice for nonfiction) or What Do I Read Next? (second choice), or Fiction Catalog (third choice) to find similar authors and related works. For locating relevant nonfiction works, students can use What Do I Read Next? or any public library catalog.

Class 7: Science Fiction/Fantasy/Horror Genres

Reading

All students read Chapters 6 (Science Fiction), 7 (Fantasy), and 8 (Horror) in *Genreflecting.*

Assignment

Appropriate students read book and complete a one-page annotation.

Class 8: Midterm Exam and Midterm Presentations

Class 9: Romance

Reading

All students read Chapter 5 (Romance) in *Genreflecting*

Assignment

Appropriate students read book and complete a one-page annotation.

Class 10: Managing the RA Program (Practitioner as Guest Instructor)

Class 11: Nonfiction/History/Biography

Reading

You can see how "history" is interwoven with the genres in *Genreflecting*.

Assignment

Appropriate students read book and complete a one-page annotation:

• Distribution of gay/lesbian books. Students may use any preferred electronic or hard copy tools.

Class 12: Gay/Lesbian

Reading

The limited material on gays and lesbians listed under the terms in *Genreflecting*.

Assignment

Appropriate students read book and complete a one-page annotation.

Class 13: Leading a Book Discussion and Book Discussion (Guest Instructor)

Class 14: Final Exam and Final Presentations

Observations by instructor.

Notes on the Selection of Genres

The course is predicated on the view that the boundaries among genres are permeable, unstable, and subject to redefinition. Throughout the semester, students are encouraged to develop genres appropriate to their "local" contexts. Depending on the instructor's understanding of current practitioner needs in the tristate Chicago metropolitan area, African-American, Hispanic, small press, or other traditional or instructor-generated genres may be substituted for either the inspirational or gay/lesbian genres. Due to time limitations, it is often necessary to discuss two or more genres in a given class.

Appendix A:
Required Format for Book Annotations

In the class syllabus the format for the annotations follows a slightly amended version of the outline presented on page 88 of Saricks and Brown's *Readers' Advisory Service in the Public Library.* The addition consists of including "Relevant Nonfiction Works and Authors" or "Relevant Fiction Works and Authors" as the last category in the outline. Following the custom in public libraries the annotations are single spaced but no more than one page in length.

Appendix B:
RA Personnel Who Volunteered to Be Interviewed

This appendix presents the names, addresses, e-mail listings, and voice and fax numbers of librarians willing to be interviewed by students on RA. The list, accumulated through periodic requests posted on Fiction_L, includes "local" Illinois, Indiana, and Minnesota librarians, as well as volunteers from such states as Kansas, North Carolina, New York, Oklahoma, South Carolina, and Virginia. Additionally, the list includes RA librarians from Australia and Canada. However, students are not limited to interviewing list members but may interview personnel with RA responsibilities in a public library, academic library, or school library media center.

Students are asked to address the following areas in their interviews, oral reports, and papers dealing with actual RA programs: planning for RA service, budgeting, staffing, in-service training, hours of service, collection development, available electronic (including Web sites) or hard copy resources, reading lists (electronic or hard copy), expectation for staff reading after official work hours, tacit knowledge of the RA staff (see Crowley article), nature of customer base, and so on. Students may visit and report as a group or individually.

Appendix C:
Effective Public Presentations

This appendix provides standard guidance on delivering public presentations.

Appendix D:
Selected Readers Advisory Reference Works

This appendix includes a substantial number of articles, books, and Web sites related to RA, adult reading, and related topics.

Appendix E:
"Twenty Things Good Stories Have in Common"

"Twenty Things Good Stories Have in Common" is reprinted as Appendix E with permission of its author. It appeared in the article "Lee K. Abbott," *Impromptu* 12, no. 2 (Autumn1995): 1–5 (published by the Department of English, College of Humanities, Ohio State University). Lee K. Abbott is professor of English and director of the Creative Writing Program at Ohio State University.

CHAPTER 4

Reinventing Readers' Advisory

Duncan Smith

Imagine witnessing the following scenario: A young man approaches the library reference desk and says, "I've just learned that my brother has diabetes. I'd like to learn more about it and find out what I can do to support him. What do you suggest?" To this the librarian responds, "Oh, that's too bad. I've never had diabetes, so I don't know anything about it."

Most of us would be appalled if we witnessed this transaction. If we were this librarian's manager, we would sit her down and discuss her performance. We would probably point out that it is inappropriate and against our profession's standards of practice to depend exclusively on our personal experiences to respond to requests for information. We might even threaten to "write her up" and put this incident in her file. After all, we know that the librarian should conduct an interview to learn more about the type of information the user needed and what would be most useful in responding to the situation. Then the librarian could employ the standard search strategies as appropriate.

As library professionals, we have models that tell us how to respond to reference questions. We even have tools in place that help us respond to requests for information. We have been trained in how to use reference sources, how to conduct reference interviews, and how to provide reference service. We have also learned that personal beliefs and biases have no place in professional practice. But repeated studies reveal that readers' advisory falls far short of the ideals and best practices we are taught in graduate school, just as the transaction in the earlier scenario falls short of the ideal.

When the question relates to helping someone find a good book to read, the resource we most frequently use is our personal reading (Burgin 1996). This strategy frequently results in service similar in quality to that provided in the opening scenario. For readers' advisory service, the profession lacks the structures that have professionalized librarianship's approach to reference work. How to answer a request for a good book to read is not often taught in the library science curriculum. [See Chapter 2 of this book for a survey of readers' advisory in library science curricula.] When we lack models, techniques, or resources or when we are unaware of their availability, we fall back on the only model we have—our personal conversations with family and friends about books. Personal recommendations work when we have established a relationship and sufficient rapport with the reader, but a different context exists for book-related conversations in the library. There we rarely have the luxury of serving someone we know. Most of our interactions are with strangers. We usually don't know where they grew up, their marital status, their line of work, their hopes, or their dreams. Our ignorance is not restricted to their life stories. We rarely know about the stories that support and nurture them. In these episodic, anonymous, and brief encounters, we are not likely to dispel our ignorance.

Typically, readers' advisory interactions take place in environments that are busy, crowded, and very public. It is difficult for patrons to share personal reading experiences at a reference or circulation desk. In this environment it is also difficult for staff, who are deeply engaged in the mental gymnastics of reference work, to shift their thinking to someone who is seeking help in finding a good book to read. Research has shown that within the typical library environment, readers' advisory services have failed to fully meet readers' needs.

Research Findings

Two unobtrusive studies support this assessment of the state of readers' advisory service in the library. Kenneth Shearer's groundbreaking study of readers' advisory service in selected North Carolina libraries involved students enrolled in a public library administration course at North Carolina Central University's School of Library and Information Sciences entering several North Carolina public libraries with a readers' advisory request (Shearer 1996). These students entered a library and made the following statement: "I enjoyed Harper Lee's *To Kill a Mockingbird* and would like something like it. Can you help me?" In at least 50 percent of the cases, the "patrons" received no assistance when they sought help in finding a good book to read. Another 30 percent of the students were told by the librarian to read book X, book Y, or book Z. One staff member recommended Knowles's *A Separate Peace* because she was currently reading this book and it reminded her of Lee's Pulitzer-Prize-winning novel. In only 20 percent of the cases did a staff member attempt to discover something about the reader's experience of *To Kill a Mockingbird*.

After they left the library, the surrogate patrons completed a questionnaire that assisted them in recording and analyzing their experience. They rated the overall quality of their experience and considered whether they would return with a similar request to the staff person who had served them. The 50 percent of the cases in which students received no service require no comment, but an interesting finding emerges from the remaining cases. The students tended to give high marks to those staff members who sought to find out something about their experience of *To Kill a Mockingbird*. In almost every case, these students stated that they would go back to these staff members with a similar request, even in cases where the staff member was unable to guide the reader to another author or title. An interesting corollary to this finding is that these students tended to give lower marks to staff who simply directed them to titles of no interest (*A Separate Peace*, for example), and they also tended to say that they would not return to these staff members. This was true even in cases where the students admitted that the staffs' suggestions were appropriate.

Discussions of readers' advisory service have tended to assume that, like reference, the product of the service is an answer. In the case of readers' advisory service, the answer is frequently a specific suggestion or a list of authors and titles. One of the interesting implications of Shearer's work is that it suggests that this view is too narrow. Readers apparently want an opportunity to share their personal reading experiences. This sharing seems as important as a reading suggestion, if not more so. Shearer's study seems to indicate that readers may value the conversations they have with staff as much as the reading suggestions themselves.

Another important study documents the value that patrons place on interaction with staff. In a cost-benefit analysis, a telephone survey sampled library cardholders of the St. Louis Public Library. Registered borrowers were asked to indicate which services they valued and to place dollar values on them. This study found the following:

Survey respondents placed the highest value on staff assistance, a category that accounted for nearly 40 percent of total direct user benefits, followed by adult books (29 percent), children's books (13 percent), and electronic materials (12 percent).

The staff help that is so highly prized by library users is not the perky, minimally trained, minimum-wage variety often found in shopping-mall bookstores. Instead, users favor reference and reader's advisory: the ability of well-trained staff to provide accurate answers and recommendations as to "the next best book." (Holt and Elliott 1998)

The personalized expert service that patrons value in Holt's study was not found in the majority of cases in Shearer's study of the readers' advisory service provided in North Carolina. Likewise, Anne May and colleagues studied readers' advisory service in public libraries in Nassau County on Long Island in New York (May et al. 2000). This study corroborates and expands on Shearer's earlier work. [See Chapter 7 of this book for more on May's work.] May and her fellow researchers summed up their experience with the following:

> Our study did not reveal any formal institutionalized RA protocol. Rather, our findings under-scored that a non-methodical, informal, and serendipitous response was the norm to a patron's request for a "good read." This is an approach that at times serves patrons brilliantly but more often offers unprofessional and unsatisfactory service. We can and must do better. (May et al. 2000, 43)

May points out that readers' advisory resources were infrequently consulted and that staff relied heavily on their personal reading. In cases where the reading interests of the staff member and the user were similar, the patron tended to receive good service. In cases where the staff member's personal reading did not correspond with the reader's interest, however, the result was frequently extremely poor service.

These studies show that a gap exists between the service readers value and the service that many librarians provide. The gap is not restricted to readers' advisory service. Reference exhibits a similar gap.

Both Shearer (1996) and May et al. (2000) use a methodology that was first employed to study reference services. Crowley (1968) and Childers (1970) found that reference librarians answered reference questions accurately only 55 percent of the time. In 1985 Gers and Seward published a study that identified six core behaviors that lead to providing accurate answers to reference questions. These behaviors include (a) using open-ended questions, (b) rephrasing or restating the patron's responses to ensure that the staff member understands the patron's request, and (c) asking a follow-up question such as "Does this completely answer your question?" It is interesting to note that the behaviors Gers and Seward (ibid.) identify are all interpersonal communication skills, skills that one would use to establish a relationship with a user.

In order to improve reference service in the state of Maryland, where Gers and Seward originally conducted their study, a series of workshops was used to train public library staff in the use of these six behaviors. A follow-up study found that as a result of these workshops, library staff in Maryland began using these behaviors and reference accuracy improved

(Stephan 1988). Additional studies in Maryland and elsewhere, however, have indicated that in order to apply these behaviors consistently, staff need continuous and ongoing reinforcement. A recent review of this topic concludes that professional performance in this area still needs improvement (Baker and Field 2000).

The Gers and Seward study was published in *Library Journal*, one of the profession's most widely circulated professional journals, but studies continue to appear that indicate we are still answering reference questions accurately only 55 percent of the time. Attempts to remedy this have continued to focus on (1) the need to recruit a different type of person to the profession, (2) staff training, and (3) incorporating the behaviors into staff performance evaluations. The effectiveness of these strategies is questionable because subsequent studies point to a continuing 55 percent accuracy rate.

May's study is filled with numerous insights into the current state of readers' advisory practice. She uses many quotes from the experiences of the students involved in this study to explain the study's findings. Two of the more interesting statements reflect librarians' dislike of readers' advisory transactions: "You know this is the query the reference desk dreads" and, muttered under a librarian's breath, "I hate this question." Why do readers' advisory questions generate more dread and hatred than other questions? The answer lies in the fact that these questions require us to move into unknown territory.

The Roles of the Readers' Advisor

Classification of reference queries is usually based on the level of effort they require and the definitiveness of the anticipated answer. Reference departments often keep track of questions by grouping them into ready reference or research. Ready reference questions are answered quickly and have a fairly specific answer. Librarians can answer these questions by consulting a standard reference source (an almanac, for example) or directing the patron to a particular section of the library's collection. Research questions require more staff time, and solutions are less defined. Examples include the following: "I need to write a paper on Hemingway's *Old Man and the Sea*. Can you help me get started?" or "I just learned that my wife has breast cancer. I would like to learn more about it and what I can do to support her. What do you suggest?" These questions require the staff member to probe for more information, and the resolution of these questions may require consulting several reference resources and referring the user to many different types of materials. The solution to these questions may also involve referring users to organizations or services outside of the library itself.

Readers' advisory service has the equivalents of ready reference and research questions. Examples of the ready readers' advisory would be "Who won the Nobel Prize for literature this year?" and "Do you have any mysteries that take place in Seattle?" One can resolve these questions by consulting standard resources. The research readers' advisory takes the form of "I just read X and I am looking for something like it. Can you help me?" (where X is a book the patron has read and enjoyed)—or in its most open-ended form, "I need a good book to read. What do you suggest?" To effectively respond to this question, a librarian must not only know something about books, collections, and resources but also has to understand the reader and something about the reading process itself. Although this level of knowledge about users and their experiences in seeking information might be desirable, it has not received much attention in reference work. It has not been part of the model for this service.

Regardless of whether a question is a reference question or a readers' advisory question and regardless of whether it is a ready reference or research question, librarians generally respond to it in the same way. They tend to view their role and responsibility as that of information provider. Not all questions are equal, however. They require different responses and different approaches. The role that staff plays in responding to ready reference questions and research questions is different. The role that staff plays in responding to reference questions and readers' advisory questions is also different. These varying types of questions may require a service stance and a service model that are different from the reference-based, information provider approach that dominates the profession.

In *Seeking Meaning: A Process Approach to Library and Information Services,* Carol Collier Kuhlthau has identified roles for information providers who support students who are writing research papers (Kuhlthau 1993). Kuhlthau identified five different roles in her work. In the *organizer* role, the staff organizes a collection for use but does not interact with the users of that collection. In the *locator* role, staff directs users to a specific source or provides the answer to a specific question (ready reference). The *identifier* role has staff involved in an interview process with the reader and consulting sources in no particular order. Kuhlthau's fourth role is *advisor*. For her, advisors have a sequence in mind as they respond to a question. There is no variance in response to the question. The focus is on having a patterned response to a frequently asked question and on guiding the reader through that sequence. For example, all readers who have placed John Grisham's most recent book on hold and want something like it to read while they are waiting would be given the results of a search on legal thrillers in standard readers' advisory resources. These readers might also be given a handout on how to search either the library's catalog or a variety of readers' advisory resources for themselves.

The *counselor* is Kuhlthau's final role. This is closest to the role required to respond to patrons' requests for a good book to read. This role involves interacting with readers about their personal experiences or needs. In this role, the staff member is working with the users to define the nature of their needs and then to develop strategies or solutions to meet those needs. Continuing with the example of the John Grisham reader, the staff member might ask the reader about the last John Grisham novel read. The staff member would then ask the reader about the aspects of their reading experience that were most important. These might include the fact that the story's pattern conforms to that of a legal thriller, that the hero is a male lawyer, or that the story moves at a rapid pace with a focus on plot. Staff members would then use this information to establish links to similar titles or to authors who write legal thrillers and specifically address the reader's needs. They would also explain to the reader the connections that exist between the books they are suggesting and the reader's interests. As part of this process, staff members might explore the reader's past reading experiences so that the reader becomes more aware of what interests him about the books that he is reading. Staff members would also explain how they identified suggested titles and the use of any resources they consulted.

In writing about the models of readers' advisory service that exist in the literature, May et al. (2000) are referring to models that support something like Kuhlthau's counselor role. This role is much more complex than the information provider role that reference work most often exercises. The counselor role is one that only the most dedicated, adept, and passionate readers' advisors employ. It is a role that few have been educated to assume and that many may not choose to accept. It is a role that may also be very difficult to consistently employ in today's library context.

Best Practices

Reference service provides us with a model to use to begin to educate ourselves to become readers' advisors. The studies already mentioned by Crowley, Childers, and Gers and Stephan identified not only the 55 percent accuracy rate but also the behaviors that lead to providing accurate answers. These studies also describe the development of a training protocol to instill these behaviors in library staff and a mechanism for supporting the ongoing use of these behaviors in the provision of reference service. A similar process is developing for readers' advisory service.

Smith and Mahmoodi (2000) describe the development of a competency-based readers' advisory manual in Minnesota. This manual was modeled after the self-assessment guides that the Minnesota Division of Library Development and Service has been using since the late 1970s. To develop this manual, a group of participants/observers, including practicing librarians, library managers, library educators, and members of the general public who were fiction readers analyzed videotapes of librarians providing readers' advisory service. After viewing each transaction, the group evaluated the overall quality of each transaction and suggested ways to improve it. They were asked to determine what the librarian would need to know in order to do a better job of meeting the reader's needs. The result of this process was the identification of more than 130 competencies in four broad knowledge areas. This process also illuminated some of the reasons why performing this function in today's library context is so challenging.

An examination of the four broad areas illustrates this point. The areas are as follows:

- An understanding of the reader

- An understanding of the appeal of books

- A background in fiction

- An understanding of the readers' advisory transaction

In order to meet the needs of fiction readers, library staff providing readers' advisory service need to understand readers. Children's librarians frequently learn about the developmental stages of children and how they learn to read. Library staff working with adults have rarely received a similar education in adult development and adult reading behavior. In fact, Wayne A. Wiegand has written that reading and the reader have virtually disappeared from library education programs (Wiegand 1997). [See Chapters 1, 2, and 3 in which Wiegand, Shearer, and Burgin and Crowley expand on this point.] The absence of this topic from library school curricula is not exclusively the fault of the faculty or the school's curriculum development committee. Research on adult reading behavior has been extremely limited. Very little information about the behavior of adult fiction readers is available.

A notable exception is the work of Catherine Sheldrick Ross (Ross 2001). Her analysis of 194 open-ended interviews provides much interesting information about how readers act and how they choose books. One significant finding is that experienced readers may use several factors when making a book choice. A hierarchy exists among the factors, and one factor usually receives precedence over another. Ross gives an example of a reader who is looking for a mystery story but also wants one with a female detective. In this case, the factor of genre (mystery story) is given precedence over the gender of the protagonist (female detective). The fact that several factors determine reading choice makes meeting the needs of a specific reader even more challenging in the library context where an interaction—if it occurs—is usually brief. The multivariate nature of reader choice is further complicated by the fact that many readers are browsers. [See

Chapter 5 for more of Ross's findings.] As Baker has also pointed out, the operant definition of "browsing" is looking for something without a clear idea of what one is looking for (Baker 1986). This means that many readers are open to suggestion and that they may find it difficult to articulate exactly what they are looking for. When library staff adopt the information-provider/ locator or identifier roles described by Kuhlthau, the typical role stance for reference service, they depend on the users to clearly articulate what they are seeking. In the case of readers' advisory service, this may be extremely difficult for many readers unless the staff member has a framework for understanding readers and asks the correct open-ended questions.

The Importance of Appeal

Understanding the appeal of books is another essential element to providing effective readers' advisory service. Joyce Saricks and Nancy Brown have extensively developed the concept of appeal (Saricks and Brown 1997). This concept embodies thinking about the language that readers use to describe what attracts them to books. It then applies this language to specific books to establish links that group books by the factors that draw readers to them. Many readers are drawn to books of a particular genre or subject. For example, a reader may be interested in reading novels about the experiences of women in distant countries (*Memoirs of a Geisha* would be an example of this kind of book). Saricks and Brown, however, have expanded the concept of appeal beyond categories that are traditionally covered by subject headings (genre, location, time period, character, and theme/topic) and include elements such as pacing (fast vs. slow), characterization (characters developed over time vs. stereotypes that we recognize immediately), and storyline (psychological vs. action oriented).

The framework that Saricks and Brown developed is beginning to appear in some published resources: Nancy Pearl's mainstream fiction resource *Now Read This!* uses character, language, story, and setting to group a set of mainstream fiction titles (Pearl 1999). Saricks has continued to expand her conceptualization of the concept of appeal. In a forthcoming book, she moves from the consideration of individual titles to the appeal elements that dominate a genre.

The appeal factors of books and the way they relate to the effective provision of readers' advisory service are knowledge that most staff must pick up on their own on the job. Library education programs have paid scant attention to the study of adult fiction and its appeal. Although several schools include a course in the study of genre fiction, these courses are electives, not a requirement. The number of library staff who have had an opportunity for the formal, structured study of popular adult fiction is very limited. [See Chapter 2 for a survey of readers' advisory service in library education.]

Without an understanding of readers and their motivations or an understanding of what draws readers to particular books, library staff lack a framework for supporting readers as they navigate through their many choices of books to read. And without these underpinnings, staff members tend to rely on knowledge acquired through their own experience. They do not often consider using resources as part of responding to requests for good books to read, partly because a question posed in a manner that solicits a personal response makes it awkward for the librarian to consult outside sources. Furthermore, the librarian may not be very familiar with the readers' advisory resources and tools at hand or may not know their capabilities, and the tools may not employ the vocabulary that matches the reader's request.

The readers' advisory questions posed in Shearer's and May's studies were the most complicated level of query entertained in most library practice. These studies involved readers who had enjoyed a book and wanted something like it. The vehicle for successfully responding to this query is a form of the reference interview known as the *readers' advisory transaction.* This terminology reinforces the conversational nature of the interaction rather than the one-way interrogation evoked by the term *interview.* The flow of this transaction and understanding its nuances are important parts of providing quality readers' advisory service. A successful reader's advisory transaction would be one that established an open and welcoming climate, the staff member verified what the reader said, the staff member exhibited enthusiasm for the reader's interests, and the staff member made reading suggestions in a nonjudgmental way.

Without formal education in the four areas mentioned earlier—understanding readers, understanding the appeal of books, a background in fiction, and understanding the readers' advisory transaction—staff are left to learn on their own. In a busy public service environment, where the focus is on the provision of service and not how to do the service differently or more effectively, staff respond to requests for readers' advisory service using the methods that they have used in the past. As Shearer (1996) and May et al. (2000) show, this approach often results in poor service.

Readers' advisory questions require engaging patrons in a more amorphous way—to understand more of a user's psyche than we normally do in reference. They require more knowledge about the suggested materials than customary in traditional reference. They require operating in an arena where, until recently, tools were limited and training in their use was even scarcer. They have required us to learn about dealing with questions largely on our own because the formal educational system has tended not to address this category of service adequately.

Reinventing Readers' Advisory

In recent years, readers' advisory service has undergone a renaissance. Public libraries have begun to acknowledge the importance of serving fiction readers (who account for at least 60 percent of total public library circulation). These institutions have begun to assess their current level of readers' advisory service and to design and implement readers' advisory service programs. The St. Louis Public Library is one major urban library that is engaged in this process through the creation of its Center for the Reader. [See Chapter 16 for an expansion of this topic.] In response to this resurgence of interest, publishers have begun to develop new print and electronic tools specifically geared to the readers' advisor's needs. Journals have also begun to address the needs of readers' advisors—with special columns devoted to genre fiction, for example, or with references to "read-alikes."

Many library professionals have begun to develop readers' advisory service as the focus of their practice and to develop their skills in this area. In Minnesota, the acknowledgment that readers' advisory service is a respected and worthwhile area of concentration for public librarians is reflected in the addition of readers' advisory service as an area of specialization in the state's Career Renewal Program for public library personnel. In addition to people who have chosen readers' advisory service as the focus of their practice, many people are also aware of the need to improve their ability to address these questions.

Earlier in this chapter I stated that library staff tend to treat unequal questions as equal. Some questions are more complex than others and require a different stance or service response. Another assumption that librarians tend to make is that all staff are equal. They are not. Different staff members have different levels of expertise in certain topic areas. They also have different interpersonal gifts and varying professional interests and goals. The profession has tended to promulgate a model that implies that all librarians should be able to respond to all questions equally well. The requirement placed on staff is that patrons will get the same level and quality of service regardless of which staff member is serving them. Although libraries should not deviate from this service goal, we need to acknowledge and deal with the fact that each staff member will need different resources and support structures if we are to achieve this goal. This is especially true in the area of readers' advisory service.

In the area of reference, we have been educated to use resources as our primary vehicle for addressing service requests from users. In the area of readers' advisory service, this has not been the case. Library staff members have worked in an environment where the central message is as follows: "In order to provide excellent readers' advisory service you must read, read,

read. In cases where you are not able to meet a patron's request for assistance in this area, you should read in that area so you can respond to patrons' requests in the future. If you are unable to help science fiction readers, you should read science fiction so that you will be able to respond to these questions in the future." This is a strategy used by many of those who are focusing on readers' advisory service. In *Readers' Advisory Service in the Public Library,* Saricks and Brown outline how to conduct a formal genre study (Saricks and Brown 1997). Even this dedicated group, however, admits that staff can never read enough and depend on resources to support them in their work.

The integration of resources into readers' advisory work is a strategy that all three of the groups mentioned earlier can use. Introducing resources into conversations with readers changes the nature of readers' advisory service in several ways. Resources help staff to cope with gaps in book knowledge by serving as added memory. When staff are able to depend on resources for potential suggestions or information about books, they are free to focus on the reader. This focus enables the staff member to use open-ended questions to gather information about the reader's previous reading experiences and learn what kind of book the reader is seeking. Through the use of resources, we can reduce the complexity of performing readers' advisory work. Resources can anchor the readers' advisory transaction itself.

The successful integration of resources into the flow of a readers' advisory transaction requires staff to talk about why they are consulting the resource and how they are going to use it to find books that will interest the reader. This linking of the consulted resource to the patron's need is the equivalent of linking suggested titles to the book the reader has read. Catherine Sheldrick Ross and Patricia Dewdney (1994) do an excellent job of discussing the necessity of this approach.

The Promise of Electronic Resources

Many new options are opening up for today's readers' advisor. We have access to more resources than ever—from books and electronic tools to educational and training opportunities. We may also find more financial and management support for readers' advisory services and activities. But in spite of all of these increased opportunities, I believe there are still opportunities for improvement.

One option that is beginning to be explored in the literature is the possibility of redesigning reference work itself. The profession's 55-percent accuracy rate may not be the "fault" of personnel. It may be the result of the way we have designed the service. If reengineering is a possibility for addressing the 55-percent accuracy rate, it should certainly be an issue that we examine given the low satisfaction rate indicated for readers' advisory service in studies such as Shearer's (1996). Let's examine some of the possible solutions to our dilemma that electronic resources offer.

As we learn more and more about readers and the types of conversations they require, we can use these models to introduce prompts into electronic resources that staff use when working with readers. The prompts could be run in a staff-only mode so that only staff would see them, or they could be designed for use in conjunction with a reader. Prompts could help guide inexperienced or overwhelmed staff through the readers' advisory transaction, who then use it as part of their conversation with the reader. One prompt in such a resource might say "Ask the reader to describe a book read and enjoyed." The next prompt might include sample elements to listen for: "Did the reader identify a genre, a location, a topic or theme?" "Did the patron use words such as 'fast-paced' or give detailed descriptions of characters?" In this case, the resource would be guiding the staff member through the process of the readers' advisory transaction. It is extending the concept of added memory from book knowledge to understanding the reader. The benefit to the staff member is the same. Rather than trying to remember what questions to ask or what to listen for, the resource would provide the structure and free the staff member to focus on the reader. As staff become more experienced or comfortable with the process of the readers' advisory transaction, they can turn this feature off in the same way those who use Microsoft products turn off the assistant "Clippy" when it is not needed or desired.

Another area in which electronic resources can support people who are serving fiction readers is in the identification of suggested titles. Ross indicates that the selection of a particular book by a reader involves several hierarchical variables (Ross 2001). The choice of a particular book is multivariate. It is difficult to understand the nuances of this hierarchy in a brief interaction with a reader. This requires interacting with a reader over time. "One Reader Reading" explores the presence of one reader's hierarchy (Smith 1996a). Future electronic resources will be able to allow readers to track their reading through time. These reader logs will indicate which books a specific reader has read and may even allow the reader to rate them according to a predetermined scale. With the reader's permission, library staff could access this information and deduce what interests the reader and which of these interests are most important.

The role of the advisor in this case would be to work with the reader to interpret and refine the hierarchy before searching for suggested titles. For example, an electronic resource might identify the fact that a reader enjoys both biographies about women and mainstream novels that have women characters who are making unusual life choices. The resource's filter would provide that information to the advisor, who would then use it as part of a conversation with the reader. For example, "I see from looking at your history that you like both biographies and novels about women. What are you in the mood for today?" The resource in this case would support the staff member in formulating a search strategy.

Electronic resources can also bring together a wide variety of information about a particular book. This information goes beyond subject headings and narrative descriptions of the titles. As more and more advisors identify appeal factors for specific titles, this information will begin to appear as another element in the description of a book. As more and more readers develop reading histories and become willing to share them, we will be able to use Bayesian and other models to establish links between books that we have not been able to see firsthand. In "The Science of the Sleeper," Malcolm Gladwell explores how resources based on Bayesian models mirror the expertise of a skilled independent bookstore owner (Gladwell 1999).

In reader response theory, the concept of interpretative communities is a popular one (Tompkins 1981). This concept indicates that different readers read books in different ways. Like questions and staff, readers are not unique. They are individuals, but they are not unique in their reading behavior. They tend to form interpretative communities, reading similar groups of books in similar ways. Electronic resources using Bayesian and other models will allow us to identify these communities and to use this information to provide another set of possible titles for a reader. One current use of this type of resource is Amazon.com's "Readers who bought this book also bought book X, book Y, and book Z." Resources that have access to reader logs or reader histories could make a similar feature available.

These last two features can form part of a framework that would allow librarians to consider and weigh a reader's hierarchy when they conduct searches of the resource's database. Ross informs us that readers have hierarchies (Ross 2001). We also know that some readers are content driven. They like a particular genre and even within that genre a particular type of main character (mystery stories with women detectives—the works of Nevada Barr, perhaps). What these new resources could also do is point us to authors and titles that other readers of Nevada Barr's titles have read and enjoyed. These suggestions may take us to genres and themes that other readers have discovered. Linkages that are known in this interpretative community have eluded us in the past because we did not have the data or a mechanism for locating them.

The creation of these resources could help move readers' advisory service out of the realm of Kuhlthau's counselor model (Kuhlthau 1993), a realm that is uncomfortable for many of us, into the more familiar standard reference intervention of the identifier role, the role that we have been educated to perform in providing reference service. The advent of these resources should result in a more standardized approach to providing readers' advisory service without sacrificing the depth of this service. These resources may enable us to engage all readers in productive conversations regardless of our personal knowledge of books or our knowledge of the reader we are serving and the books that reader enjoys.

Readers' Advisory in Cyberspace

The development of electronic resources will become even more critical as a trip to the library becomes something that readers do by logging onto the Internet instead of going to a physical facility. May and her colleagues also noted the absence of a readers' advisory presence on the Web pages of the libraries they visited (May et al. 2000, 42). This is not surprising because most library buildings lack signage or other visual clues that indicate the availability and location of services for fiction readers. A disadvantage for readers who are visiting the library's Web site, however, is that they do not have access to a knowledgeable staff member. They cannot engage in a conversation with a staff member because they are not physically in the library. Fiction readers visiting the library's Web page are also at a disadvantage because they cannot resort to their most common strategy—browsing the library's book collection. They are unable to do this because they are not physically in the library and because a lack of subject access to fiction prevents them from searching for unknown items. If I am looking for résumé books and I don't know an author or title, a subject search of the library's catalog via its Web site or dial-up connection will allow me to locate books on this topic. Because many libraries lack detailed subject access to fiction, readers accessing this same catalog or Web site cannot locate coming-of-age stories that deal with racism such as *To Kill a Mockingbird*. This two-tiered service model may send the message to fiction readers that they are not as important as users who are interested in nonfiction topics. It may lead fiction readers to take their business elsewhere.

In the Web world, holding onto customers is about understanding their needs and creating sites that engage them. As we learn more and more about readers and how they search for and experience books, we should develop resources and sites that engage them. This may mean reconfiguring the ways in which we describe and present information about books. For example, rather than presenting a traditional author/title list of bio-thrillers (an emerging subgenre in adventure/suspense), Michael Gannon created a quiz on Ebsco's online service NoveList that asks readers to "Guess That Biotoxin!" (Gannon 2000). In this quiz Gannon provides an author, a book title, and a partial spelling of the toxin the book deals with. The reader must then guess the toxin by supplying the missing letters from the partial spelling (e.g., A_TH_A_ = ANTHRAX). This activity and similar ones not only add a level of interactivity and engagement to a library's Web site; they also communicate what we know. By doing so, we show readers that we understand them and that they can trust us to provide suggestions that are likely to be appropriate and interesting. Ross has identified the importance of trust to readers who are seeking readers' advisory service (2001).

Conclusions

The effective provision of readers' advisory service requires that we move into a new and unmapped region. It is terrain that many library staff have chosen to explore and map for themselves. We have trusted that communicating this map to the profession through publication, education, and training programs would result in improved service to fiction readers. Reading the literature and participating in staff development programs have and will continue to lead to improved practice for some. The profession's history, however, indicates that unless these activities occur in a context that provides ongoing support, the changes that they engender will be neither significant nor sustained.

Many librarians are exemplary readers' advisors. Their knowledge has informed much of the literature on this topic, and many are gifted teachers. We do them and ourselves a great disservice, however, when we do not work to capture their expertise and incorporate it into resources that all staff members can use. Librarianship is a tool-focused profession. Rather than seeking to change that focus or to make us all expert readers' advisors, the profession should seek to create and use the resources that capture and generalize our combined expertise.

This does not mean that readers' advisory conversations will cease to occur in libraries. This does not mean that librarians should not continue to expand their book knowledge or to practice and develop their interpersonal skills. It does mean, however, that the combined knowledge and expertise of the profession can become a networked and shared resource. It promises an added strategy to ensure that all readers receive the best service possible.

References

Baker, Lynda M., and Judith J. Field. 2000. Reference Success: What Has Changed over the Past Ten Years? *Public Libraries* 39, no. 1: 23–30.

Baker, Sharon L. 1986. Overload, Browsers and Selections. *Library and Information Science Research* 8 (October): 315–29.

Burgin, Robert. 1996. Readers' Advisory in Public Libraries: An Overview of Current Practice. In *Guiding the Reader to the Next Book,* ed. Kenneth Shearer, 71–88. New York: Neal-Schuman.

Chelton, Mary K. 1993. Read Any Good Books Lately?: Helping Patrons Find What They Want. *Library Journal* 118, no. 8: 33–37.

Childers, Thomas A. 1970. Telephone Information Service in Public Libraries: Comparison of Performance and the Descriptive Statistics Collected by the State of New Jersey. Ph.D. diss., Rutgers University.

Crowley, Terrence. 1968. The Effectiveness of Information Service in Medium Sized Public Libraries. Ph.D. diss., Rutgers University.

Gannon, Michael. 2000. A Hypochondriac's Guide to Bio-Thrillers. URL: http://novelist.epnet.com (accessed December 25, 2000). *Note:* Available only through subscribing libraries.

Gers, Ralph, and Lillie J. Seward. 1985. Improving Reference Performance: Results of a Statewide Study. *Library Journal* 110, no. 18: 32–33.

Gladwell, Malcolm. 1999. The Science of the Sleeper. *New Yorker* 75, no. 29 (October 4): 48, 7p.

Holt, Glen E., and Donald Elliott. 1998. Proving Your Library's Worth: A Test Case. *Library Journal* 123, no. 18: 42–45.

Kuhlthau, Carol Collier. 1993. *Seeking Meaning: A Process Approach to Library and Information Services.* Norwood, NJ: Ablex Publishing.

May, Anne K., Elizabeth Olesh, Anne Weinlich Miltenberg, and Catherine Patricia Lackner. 2000. A Look at Reader's Advisory Services. *Library Journal* 125, no. 15: 40–43.

Pearl, Nancy. 1999. *Now Read This: A Guide to Mainstream Fiction, 1978–1998*. Englewood, CO: Libraries Unlimited.

Ross, Catherine Sheldrick. 1991. Readers' Advisory Service: New Directions. *Reference Quarterly* 30, no. 4 (Summer): 503–18.

———. 2001. Making Choices: What Readers Say About Choosing Books to Read for Pleasure. *The Acquisitions Librarian* 25: 5–22.

Ross, Catherine Sheldrick, and Patricia Dewdney. 1994. Best Practices: An Analysis of the Best (and Worst) in Fifty-Two Public Library Reference Transactions. *Public Libraries* 33 (September/October 1994): 261–66.

Saricks, Joyce G. 2001. *Readers' Advisory Guide to Genre Fiction*. Chicago: American Library Association. Forthcoming.

Saricks, Joyce G., and Nancy Brown. 1997. *Readers' Advisory Service in the Public Library*. Chicago: American Library Association.

Shearer, Kenneth. 1996. The Nature of the Readers' Advisory Transaction in Adult Reading. In *Guiding the Reader to the Next Book,* ed. Kenneth Shearer, 1–20. New York: Neal-Schuman.

Smith, Duncan. 1993. Reconstructing the Reader: Educating Readers' Advisors. *Collection Building* 12, nos. 3–4: 21–30.

———. 1996a. One Reader Reading. In *Guiding the Reader to the Next Book,* ed. Kenneth Shearer, 45–70. New York: Neal-Schuman.

———. 1996b. Librarians' Abilities to Recognize Reading Tastes. In *Guiding the Reader to the Next Book,* ed. Kenneth Shearer, 89–124. New York: Neal-Schuman.

Smith, Duncan, and Suzanne Mahmoodi. 2000. *Talking with Readers: A Workbook for Readers' Advisory.* Ipswich, MA: EBSCO Publishing.

Stephan, Sandy. 1988. Reference Breakthrough in Maryland. *Public Libraries* 27, no. 4: 202.

Tompkins, Jane P. 1981. *Reader-Response Criticism, from Formalism to Post-Structuralism*. Baltimore: Johns Hopkins University.

Wiegand, Wayne A. 1997. Misreading LIS Education. *Library Journal* 112, no. 11: 36–39.

CHAPTER 5

What We Know from Readers About the Experience of Reading

Catherine Sheldrick Ross

This research was supported by a research grant from the Social Sciences and Humanities Research Council of Canada.

In Italo Calvino's wonderful book about reading, *If on a Winter's Night a Traveller,* various characters describe the quality of reading experience that they are looking for:

- "I prefer novels…that bring me immediately into a world where everything is precise, concrete, specific" (1981, 30).

- "The novel I would most like to read at this moment…should have as its driving force only the desire to narrate, to pile stories upon stories, without trying to impose a philosophy of life on you" (92).

- "The novels that I prefer…are those that make you feel uneasy from the very first page" (126).

- "I like books…where all the mysteries and the anguish pass through a precise and cold mind, without shadows, like the mind of a chess player" (157).

- "The novels that attract me most…are those that create an illusion of transparency around a knot of human relationships as obscure, cruel, and perverse as possible" (192).

In that they are on the lookout for books that deliver the reading experiences that satisfy their innermost desires, these imagined readers in Calvino's fiction resemble the real readers that librarians encounter in libraries. Calvino's readers are perhaps unusual in being able to succinctly describe what they most want in leisure reading—concrete images, a piling up of stories, an atmosphere of apprehension, a central narrative consciousness, or whatever. Nevertheless, ordinary readers can tell us a great deal about what they look for in their reading experiences. For more than a decade, my research has focused on talking to readers and on what Stephen Krashen (1993) has called "free voluntary reading"—the reading that people do for pleasure.

To find out about the reading experience of avid readers, I have interviewed 25 readers, and Master of Library and Information Science students interviewed 169 additional readers in successive offerings of my Genres of Fiction and Reading course at the University of Western Ontario. These 194 interviews, which were qualitative and open-ended, were designed to find out how readers themselves experience reading. I wanted to know what readers think reading means to them, how they choose books to read for pleasure, and what elements they look for in satisfying books. This chapter is a summary of findings from this research, some of which has been published elsewhere (Ross 1991, 1995, 1999, 2001; Ross and Chelton 2001).

We know less about the experience of avid readers than we would like to because, until recently, leisure reading has seemed too frivolous to warrant serious academic inquiry. For example, a respected sociological study titled *Maturity in Reading* used a Freudian model to distinguish between two types of reading: "mature reading" was for information and deferred pleasure, whereas "immature reading" was done for immediate pleasure (Gray and Rogers 1964). Lately we have been looking more critically at these socially constructed values that people have taken for granted—values that give priority to reading nonfiction over fiction and to productive reading over reading for pleasure. Readers themselves are familiar with these values even when they reject them. When required to justify to nonreaders the time they spend on reading, avid readers can mobilize these socially approved values in defense of reading. They will say that reading increases their vocabulary, factual knowledge of the world, and literacy skills, all of which are socially valuable because weak literacy skills exclude people from good jobs and full participation in economic, political, and social life. These answers are true (Statistics Canada 1996; Krahn and Lowe 1998; Shalla and Schellenberg 1998) but don't tell the whole story. When probed more deeply, many committed readers interviewed for this study say that reading is a passion that goes beyond skills-training or job preparation. They say that reading is part of their identities; that they are horrified by the prospect of a future in which they couldn't read; and that if they didn't read they wouldn't be the people they are:

> I hate to say that reading is everything, but I think sometimes it's more important than people, and that scares me. It is; it's everything. If I don't have a book, I'm bare. I feel like there's something lacking in my life. I cannot be without something to read. And if it's not a book—if I don't have access to a book (which is fairly rare)—then I'll buy a good magazine. But I have to have something. If I have three or four at one time, that's all the better....[Reading] is part of me. (Jean, age 44, teacher librarian; throughout the chapter the names of interviewees have been changed for anonymity.)

Evidence about the experience of reading for pleasure comes from the transcribed set of interviews conducted with the 194 readers described earlier. The interviewed subjects were not randomly chosen but were deliberately selected as people who read a lot and read by choice. Interviewers were instructed to interview the person of their acquaintance who was most committed to reading for pleasure. Before they conducted and transcribed their interview, the student interviewers were trained in using open-ended questions and follow-up probes and received a set of interview questions to use as a guide for the interview. Using a chronological approach that started with the first thing the reader remembered reading as a child and worked forward to the present, the interviews explored, from the reader's perspective, the whole experience of reading for pleasure, including the following: reading in childhood; ways in which a particular book has made a difference in the reader's life; ways in which the reader chooses or rejects a book; and the reader's idea of the perfect book.

Because the study deliberately focused on committed readers, most of the interviewees studied fell within the 10 percent of the North American population who show up in national reading surveys as "heavy readers"—those who read upward of a book a week (Cole and Gold 1979, 63; Book Industry Study Group 1984, 84). Unlike nonbook readers who read primarily for information, heavy readers tend to say they read for pleasure (Cole and Gold 1979, 61–62). The demographic profile of the interviewees in my study resembled that of "heavy readers," as consistently described in reports of reading surveys based on large-scale national samples. Previous studies conducted in Canada and the United States have found that heavy readers are more likely to be female than male; to be younger rather than older; and to have achieved a higher educational level than the population at large (Book Industry Study Group 1984; Cole and Gold 1979; Gallup Organization 1978; Watson et al. 1980). Of the 194 people interviewed, 65 percent were female and 35 percent were male. Interviewees ranged in age from 16 to 80, distributed as follows: age 16–20 (3.6 percent); age 21–30 (44.8 percent); age 31–40 (18 percent); age 41–50 (14 percent); age 51–60 (11.3 percent); and age 60–80 (8.2 percent). The level of education was generally high.

From Series Book to Genres of Fiction

A fairly consistent pattern emerged in the childhoods of people who later became committed readers. Over and over again these experienced readers mentioned that their parents, siblings, or grandparents read to them as children; that there were many books in their homes; that they received books as gifts; that they went to libraries as children; and that in many cases they had learned to read before starting school. The interviewees generally described a childhood environment that supported reading, making statements such as, "Our family didn't have much money, but I was encouraged to use the library and my parents used the library" or "Both my parents encouraged us to own books and to read" or "There were always plenty of books around the house and someone always willing to read one or two to you or listen while you read one. My life as a child was filled with books" or "We were a reading family" or finally "I came from a reading household…there were always books around….I was praised for being a good reader." The pattern varies from reader to reader, but the key thing is that *something* in their childhood experiences helped these committed readers come to know that reading can be a source of pleasure that one can experience in no other way.

The most avid childhood readers described themselves as omnivorous. They did not in childhood distinguish classics from trash or worthy books from time-wasters but valued books for their ability to give pleasure. They wanted to read without restriction, like Elizabeth, who said, "My reading was always indiscriminate. I just read what I laid my hands on" or Dorothy, who said, "I really was an omnivore. I read almost everything that was available. And I read a lot, so I exhausted the supply of books around me quite quickly." When invited to talk about their childhood reading, more than 60 percent of the interviewed readers spontaneously mentioned having read series books as children (Ross 1995). When libraries refused to stock the series books they wanted to read (series books were considered dangerously seductive—too interesting, too escapist, likely to spoil readers for more solid reading, and so on), these readers simply bypassed libraries. They bought them, borrowed them from friends, or asked for them as presents. As readers outgrew one series, they moved on to other series with older protagonists—from the *Bobbsey Twins* to *Nancy Drew* and the *Hardy Boys*—and then, as reading skill and speed improved, to less formulaic books. Readers frequently mentioned series books, together with books that had previously been read aloud, as the first chapter books that they had succeeded in reading on their own. Reading series books turned out to have been an important stage in the transition to independent reading. Not unexpectedly, for many adult readers, genre books provided the same advantage of familiarity that series books had provided for them as children.

Because genre reading makes up such a large component of pleasure reading, we need to know a lot more about the reading preferences of genre readers. We need to know what they look for in a successful work within a specific genre and how they sort books into different categories. Unfortunately, most of the published research dealing with genres of fiction has focused on the texts and not on the readers of the texts (an honorable exception is Janice Radway's widely praised *Reading the Romance.*) A consideration of genre entered into my study when readers answered questions about what they were currently reading, whether they had favorite genres, and what types of books they did not enjoy and would *not* read. There was of course a significant minority of readers who said that they never read genre books because they considered them to be repetitive and interchangeable. Whereas a nonreader of a particular genre was likely to say that romances (or Westerns, detective stories, or fantasies) were all the same and indistinguishable, veteran genre readers said that they found an enormous range in the quality of books within a specific genre. These experienced readers were able to make numerous discriminations among books of the same genre, differentiating closely among books by noting an individual author's particular handling of elements such as tone, pacing, writing style, character development, and plot elements.

With accumulated knowledge derived from wide reading within a genre, experienced genre readers are able to provide expert evaluations as in David's critique of speculative fiction: "Part of the problem with a lot of science fiction or fantasy is they spend so much time designing the world that there is no time for the characters, or they have one neat idea for the characters and don't know what to do with them after that happens" (age 26, student). Jimmy said that he had come to appreciate Charles de Lint's ability to create "believable female characters, because, especially in horror, I've grown up with a lot of novels where the women have just been around as your blond bimbo stereotype—just there to scream and get victimized. Well, I didn't mind it at first, but…" (age 24, student). Genre readers, like wine aficionados, often become increasingly exacting as their breadth of experience with a genre increases. Horror-reader Terry says that "I look to see if the author can scare me. Not that many authors can" (age 26, student).

Genre readers say they know exactly what reading experience they want at any given time and are often prepared to go to some considerable work to seek out the books they know will provide that experience. Literary critics, who focus on texts rather than on the relationship between book and reader, tend to rank genre books more highly the more unpredictable they are and the more they overturn expected formulaic features of the genre. In contrast, the interviewed readers varied considerably in their desire for a predictable experience versus something unconventional and unexpected. At times predictable is good, as Diane points out, and at other times readers prefer something more challenging and demanding:

> It depends on what I'm looking for. Sometimes I want nothing but escape and then I like a big romance like *The Far Pavilions*. Other times I want something that offers a little intellectual stimulation. Right now I'm reading *The White Hotel* by D. M. Thomas. It's interesting; it's stimulating; it's different...[With *The Far Pavilions*] it's just fun to sit back and let the great romance wash over you and suspend disbelief. And if I'm really tired, I read mystery stories like Agatha Christie. Agatha Christie's for when I'm so tired I can hardly see. (Diane, age 37, social worker.)

Guilty Reading

Readers were keenly aware that some people view pleasure reading as a waste of time or worse. In interviews they sometimes referred to covert reading. Said one member of a book club, "I would read over [doing] anything else. If you went to my house during the day and I wasn't doing anything, I'd be sitting there reading. You feel like you're being caught. [laughter] 'Oh, no, I wasn't on the couch reading. I was really vacuuming!' " In response, another book club reader agreed but said that being in the book club had made all the difference: "You feel guilty. But now I can say to my boyfriend, 'I have to read this book for my book club.' " These readers are conscious of external norms that judge the act of daytime reading as doubly reprehensible: It is nonproductive because reading displaces some other more productive activity such as housework, and it is threatening and antisocial because the reader is enjoying an invisible pleasure that can't be shared. Time spent reading is time taken away from socializing. The reader sometimes wonders whether the claims of the nonbook reader are true: that reading is a barrier to keep the world at bay, a defense, a form of retreat, an escape hatch from the demands of real relationships. (These same criticisms have recently been redirected toward avid Internet users and computer-game players.) Interestingly, studies have consistently found that book readers as a group are far more likely than nonbook readers to participate more in almost every activity except sleeping (Madden 1979). Findings from the Book Industry Study Group study (1984, 71) lead to the conclusion that "Far from being introverted or social outcasts, book readers emerge as well-rounded individuals active in a wide range of social and cultural activities....Book readers are far more likely to socialize (59%) than nonbook readers (41%) or nonreaders (33%)." Despite these research findings, misgivings persist. Debbie noted that "people who don't take as much pleasure as I do from reading can't understand that you would choose to read rather than converse or watch television or listen to the radio":

> Having grown up in a family of readers, I find it perfectly acceptable for people to sit in a room together and to have quiet and everyone to be reading something. Whereas I find people who don't read, they find it upsetting in some way if you're not chatting or watching television or doing some communal activity. And instead you're just choosing to be quiet and read by yourself. They think there must be something wrong....I don't think of [reading] as selfish, but I think it can be something that sets up barriers between people. (Debbie, age 29, copyeditor/journalism student)

Value of Reading in Their Lives

In the interviews, we asked readers, "What would it be like if for one reason or another you couldn't read?" Given the selection criteria for interviewees' participation in the study, we expected them to claim that not being able to read would be experienced as a loss, but the typical response was unexpectedly intense. The majority of committed readers in the study said that being unable to read was unthinkable: "It's a passion. I can't deny it"; "It's a physical need with me to have to read"; "If I were stuck on a desert island without books, I would go crazy"; "My freedom to read is absolutely sacred." Reading for pleasure was so much a part of the reader's identity that, as one reader, Jane, put it, "I wouldn't be me. I wouldn't be the person I am if I didn't read or wasn't able to read. It frightens me to think that something like reading can create you or at least influence who you are so much."

Unlike nonreaders who claim they lack the time to read, the readers in my study said that they *make* time and built opportunities for reading into their daily routines. Although readers set aside certain times and places for reading, a favorite being in bed before going to sleep, many committed readers said that they can and do read anywhere: "I can tuck a book on top of the microwave and hold the pages open with a mixing spoon and read in the kitchen. I can read any place"; "I carry books with me....Reading is for every place—books in the bathroom, books in the bedroom, books by the television, and always in my bag." Daniel, a 49-year-old plant mechanic said, "I take books with me—when I go to a doctor's appointment I take a book with me...or when I take kids to hockey practice or whatever, I have to take a book with me because I know I'm going to have a little spare time to read it."

Readers found it natural and easy to turn to texts as a favored source of information. They used their own life experiences to make sense of texts and conversely used texts to make sense of life in a wide variety of situations. Indeed a defining characteristic of these readers was that reading about a topic, rather than or in addition to asking somebody about it, was a preferred way of learning things. Hence Stella said, "If I find something happening in my life, a high point or particularly low point, my first trip is generally to the library to see if I can read something about it....And if I wanted to learn to do embroidery I'd probably first find a book about it as opposed to asking somebody how to do it." At the time of the interview, Stella was reading gardening books because she was planting a garden; for the two years after returning to the church, she read "lots of books about theology," and when she's "really depressed," she rereads L. M. Montgomery's *The Blue Castle* to cheer herself up. Similarly Diane said:

> I always turn to books for any questions, and I always have. [If a doctor said I had a mysterious disease], I'd go and get a book on it....Part of how I would accept it would be to read everything there was on it....I'd do that with anything that I'd see as a problem. I'd start reading everything I can get on it. I'll start reading a bunch of books around the area and I don't stop reading until I've somehow been reassured....I think it must have something to do with mastery. Until I've got hold of all the information possible, I feel out of control. (Diane, age 37, social worker)

Choosing Books

For avid readers, the process of finding books to read for pleasure encompasses much more than the notion of browsing book stock or searching a catalogue usually evokes. Previous studies of choosing books to read for pleasure, usually based on surveys with preestablished categories of response, tell us how often certain selection strategies occur but not what these strategies mean for the people who perform them. For example, summarizing the results of a survey of 500 fiction borrowers in four different British libraries who were asked how they usually choose novels, David Spiller reported the following responses: author only—11 percent; authors/some browsing—22 percent; equal authors/browsing—36 percent; browsing/some authors—20 percent; browsing only—11 percent (Spiller 1980, 245).

Because library catalogues and indexing systems are currently ill adapted to the task of helping readers find books for pleasure reading (Baker 1986), the experienced readers in my study had to devise their own methods. These methods, we may suppose, are extensions and adaptations of everyday practices that they typically find useful in information seeking. When asked how they go about choosing books to read for pleasure, interviewees typically launched into elaborate descriptions, involving many interrelated considerations. They often started with their own moods at the time of reading and went on to describe how they find new authors or what clues they look for about the books themselves. Notably the systems they described usually depended on considerable previous experience and metaknowledge of authors, publishers, cover art, and conventions for promoting books and sometimes depended on a social network of family or friends who recommended and lent books. Readers drew upon their accumulated knowledge of authors, titles, and genres; memories of what reviewers, friends, or family members have said; clues provided by the book cover and the blurb on the back; and information from sampling the book by reading the opening paragraph or dipping into a few paragraphs at random. Goneril, a 43-year-old service representative, reported, "I look at a book cover and read the little intro, then I usually turn to the middle of the book and read a page, and if it doesn't do anything for me it goes back on the shelf."

In order to be alerted to the existence of new books that will provide the desired reading experience they want, committed readers typically scan their everyday environments for clues. They tuck away in memory or on lists for future use the names of books and authors the read about in magazine and newspaper reviews; books given currency because they have been made into films or television productions; and authors and titles that come up in conversation. Recommendations are important but only from a trusted source with tastes they consider compatible, such as certain reviewers, family members, "friends that know my taste," selected bookstore staff and librarians, and more recently Internet acquaintances. A Stephen King fan, Terry sought out and read a number of the books on Steven King's list of 100 favorite books in *Danse Macabre*. Diane explained how she would typically choose a book by a new author: "It might be by reputation—I've heard about it; it was famous; it was a bestseller….Usually I'll pick up names that I recognize. It's rare that I'll read a book by someone I've never heard of at all." Often readers make lists of books they have heard or read about and, like Diane, "carry these lists in my purse for months at a time looking for books."

The bedrock for choice in pleasure reading is the reader's mood. When asked how he would decide from among his usual reading fare of horror, science fiction, fantasy, detective fiction, or mainstream novels, Terry answered, "The mood I was in. It might depend on what I'd been reading lately. It might depend on the time of day and on whether I'd like to get into something really heavy or something really light." Lorraine, a 27-year-old elementary school teacher speculated, "Maybe that's why I read two or three books at a time. I have to be in a certain mood to read a certain book." Mood was more critical for choosing fiction than for nonfiction. Fiction readers reported that their mood for reading often depended on what else was going on in their lives. When readers are busy or under stress, they often want safety, reassurance, and confirmation and will reread old favorites or read new books by known authors that they can trust. At other times when life is less stressful, they can afford to take more risks in their reading. At such times they may want to be amazed by something unpredictable, and then they might pick books on impulse to introduce novelty into their reading and discover new authors or genres.

The single most important strategy for book selection was to choose a book by a known and trusted author. Said a Salman Rushdie fan, "It's like finding a gold mine and following the vein when you find a good author like that." Nathan said, "I like to read authors. It takes a long time for an author to disappoint me." Second to choosing by author, the next most popular strategy was to use genre to identify the kind of experience a book promised. Readers often used genre in conjunction with author. Typically, a single factor took precedence, and other factors came into play as secondary considerations. A reader might be looking for a mystery story, but the choice of *which* mystery story might depend on the presence of additional elements such as a smart female detective, love interest, a regional setting, or the inclusion of specialty information. Laurie, a 34-year-old student, said that she really enjoyed Barbara Vine's *King Solomon's Carpet,* which was "basically about this guy's fascination with the subway system in London" and allowed her to learn "a lot about different subway systems around the world. I really enjoyed that." For other readers the size of the book is a key factor: "And the third thing I look at [after author and the description on the back cover] is the thickness. I will reject a book even if it's a book by an author that I know if it's a small, little book." In narrowing down choices, readers are strongly guided by what they *don't* want, so that they can quickly rule out whole categories ("nothing too long") and entire genres ("the psychological thriller") .

Once a reader starts to browse within a range of books, then the cover and the clues provided on the book itself become important. Titles are also important—readers said they were drawn both to an unusual, catchy title (in the case of an unfamiliar book) and to a familiar title that they had heard about before. One science-fiction reader, Charles, said, "When you're as genre-specific as I am and read as voraciously as I do, you're looking for some quick identifiers on what's a good book. It'll take me ten minutes to go in [to the science fiction section], get five books, and leave because I'm just so familiar with the genre in general." The most frequently mentioned "quick identifiers" were the cover, the blurb on the back, and the sample page. The sample paragraph or page was often a final test, used as an indicator of the writing style and the level of literary competence the book demanded: "You see a title of a book that sounds interesting, open it up and scan random pages, just to make sure that the writing is at a fairly decent level." The readers we interviewed were emphatic about what they *don't* like in a book and used cues on the book itself as a warning. A feature that strongly attracted one reader equally strongly put another off, but in each case the information was helpful in matching book and reader.

The final factor in book selection involves the reader's calculation of the degree of work the book required. We can regard the likelihood of a reader's choosing a particular book as a ratio of the degree of pleasure the reader expects from the book divided by the degree of effort the reader must expend, physically and mentally, in reading it. Some readers said that they often read "books lying around" or they would "read what's around me" or "books I find at home." Conversely, readers reported being willing to put themselves on waiting lists, special order, or pay hardcover prices to read a book that they expected to yield a high degree of pleasure, such as the latest book by Alice Munro.

The "Perfect Book"

At the end of the interview, we asked readers, "If you could get an author to write the 'Perfect Book' for you, what would it be like? What elements should it include?" Of course, some said that there was no such thing as a perfect book, that the "perfect book" was a stupid concept, or that for them the perfect book was the one they had just read or the one they would like to write themselves. Others pointed out, as David did, that they had different requirements for a perfect book depending on their mood: "There is reading to go with the moment, for entertainment, to get the blood pumping with a good story. And there is reading that you want to reflect on and think about while you are reading it or after you have read it." Siobhan (age 53, librarian) talked about timeliness and receptivity: "Books speak to us at a time and place in our life, in our journey, and what may be the perfect book this year may not be the perfect book next year. I think it depends [on] where we are and what we need in our own lives at that time."

That said, many interviewees, such as Italo Calvino's imagined readers, were actually able to answer the question in considerable detail. Matt's perfect book would "have to have something supernatural in it" and be able to pull him in "in the way nobody but Stephen King has ever pulled me in." He explained, "I'm after the effect rather than the means to the effect. Any way you can scare me is good." Nathan, a 50-year-old English professor said, "I read books to get a certain kind of epiphanal feeling from them—just to get this incredible charge, this energy out of them." Some readers described their idea of the quintessential experience of reading pleasure in terms of a book they had been searching for all their lives, as in this example:

> I know there is a book out there just waiting to be found that would change my life—that would totally change my relationship to my own senses. That's happened to me with some books, where suddenly as a result of this experience you feel things differently. You literally feel, touch things differently, or see things differently. (Mark, age 42, music educator and composer)

For Paul, a 42-year old librarian, the book that comes closest to perfection is Bulgakov's *The Master and Margarita,* which he had read seventeen times. As a child, he had voraciously read fairy tales. As an adult, he said he was "always looking for something that would give me the same experience that I had had as a child—the sense of magic, the sense of wonder, the sense of being out of control, of being sucked into the book whether I wanted to be or not." He was able to recover that sense of magic in Bulgakov's book: "To me, it's more than just a book; it's an entire experience....It's not just a book about magic; it is a magical experience."

Taken together, the interviewees' responses provided overwhelming support for the claim made in Joyce G. Saricks and Nancy Brown's classic *Readers' Advisory Service in the Public Library:* "We have found that most [fiction] readers are usually not looking for a book on a certain subject. They want a book with a particular 'feel' " (1997, 35). To convey the sort of "feel" they wanted, many readers used the shorthand of saying the perfect book would be similar to a specific title:

- "I think *A Winter's Tale* is a perfect book for me."

- "It would be like *A Man Called Intrepid,* which is about William Stevenson."

- "*The Bone People* is a good example of an absolutely brilliant book."
- "It would be like Rosemund Pilcher's *Shell Seekers.*"
- "*French Lieutenant's Woman* came closest to the perfect book other than *Jane Eyre.*"
- "It would be like *Out of Africa.*"

Along similar lines, many said that their perfect book would be a new book written by a favorite author such as Robert Ludlum, Tom Clancy, John Grisham, Stephen King, or Danielle Steel:

- "First of all, I'd probably ask Taylor Caldwell to write it for me."
- "I'd have it based on Poul Anderson."
- "It would be something like Umberto Eco's books."

Sometimes their perfect book would require a whole team of authors:

- "I would have a book written as a collaboration between Mercedes Lackey and Nancy Springer, or even Charles de Lint. Because Nancy Springer has a very poetic way of writing, Charles de Lint makes even the mundane seem magical, and Mercedes Lackey could make a stone cry."

When asked about the elements that the perfect book would include, the readers collectively mentioned many dimensions that they considered important, with different readers having very different requirements. There is an evident similarity between the elements the readers in my study mentioned and Saricks and Brown's "appeal factors," which they identify as pacing, characterization, storyline, and frame (1997, 35–55). From this examination of what readers say they look for in a perfect book, it appears that the ideal index for fiction should retrieve books not on the basis of their subject but on the basis of the appeal factors itemized in the following section. A reader who agrees with statements ALOS is clearly looking for a very different book from the reader who agrees with statements EJNT and so on. The following list is intended to capture a range of response, though clearly not every category is of importance to each reader. As noted earlier, readers' preferences vary depending on their mood and what else is going on in their lives. But at any given time, an individual reader might be able to describe reading preferences by matching three or four of these statements.

Pacing

Action packed vs. leisurely development

A I like a book that I can pick up and I just don't want to put down...For me to be really interested in a book it has to engage me by the very first chapter (Sylvia, age 34, credit collections manager).

B It doesn't seem to be that plot is all that important; where the story is going isn't as important as how it is told or how it gets there (Aldous, age 26, undergraduate student).

Hearing dialogue vs. picturing images

C I often like books with a lot of conversation in them and less description. I'm interested in the way people talk and in hearing different voices (Aldous, age 26, undergraduate student).

D I like really strong images in the books. If I'm reading a book and it actually works—if it's a picture in my head, then that's a big plus for me (Jody, age 18, student).

Kind of Action Represented

Interior vs. exterior action

E I think the characters would be dealing more with a personal conflict than with any outside conflict. Like, they wouldn't be in a war or something like that; they would be deciding what they wanted for themselves. The conflict [would be] within them (Helen, age 21, student).

Weight given to the exploration of ideas and concepts

F I like to see authors explore new ideas in their books. That's one of the reasons why I read science fiction, because they often have different sociological type situations, where society is slightly different. What would it be like if man was on the moon or whatever—that sort of "what if" quite interests me (Evan, age 31, network manager).

Treatment of sexuality

G   I enjoy love and sex in a book (Beverly, age 22, dietitian).

H   If a book has violence or a lot of sex, I won't read it. I don't want a book to upset me or to excite me—other than a quiet excitement. I don't want graphic descriptions. For example, I read *The Color Purple* and I hated it; it was so upsetting. I don't need to read that (Joan, age 31, elementary school teacher).

Characters

Relative importance of characters and plot

I   I think character, usually but not always, is more important than plots. I can stand a book that has a bad plot and good characters better than I can stand a book that has a good plot but lousy characters (Truus, age 40, librarian).

Reader's sense of emotional closeness to, or distance from, the main character(s)

J   I want you to write a novel that makes me feel emotionally close to the main character (Theresa, age 27, MLIS student).

Idealized characters vs. characters that are mixtures of strengths and weaknesses

K   I look for characters that are realistic—not perfect, beautiful, immensely talented and rich people, but sort of realistic characters with human foibles. Growth and development of characters is a good thing, too (Laurie, age 34, student).

Single character vs. complex interrelationships

L   I usually like to see the perfect book have one central character, but I will read books that have multiple-focused characters. I prefer a single character (Evan, age 31, network manager).

M   Well, it would probably have to be definitely centred on relationships between people. And events that would shape their lives and continuity. More than just the one person—maybe two or three generations of people (Mabel, age 64, retired teacher).

The Nature of the World Represented

Realization of the setting

N   I look for a really detailed setting. I don't like just a book that is straight action and no background. I like a book where you can be taken into a different world when you are reading it. It doesn't have to be on another planet; it can be Ottawa. But I want to think that I am *in* Ottawa when I am reading it (Carol, age 25, archaeologist).

O   In *20,000 Leagues Under the Sea,* you know how Jules Verne begins many of the chapters with great long descriptions of what it was like under the water, the colours of the fish, and all that kind of stuff. I didn't even bother reading it. I was interested in what they were doing [in the submarine] as opposed to the descriptions....I'm interested in the story (Maurice, age 57, professional engineer).

Similarity of the imagined setting to the reader's own world

P   Because of their setting, I can't relate to science fiction books as much. They are off on some strange planet somewhere and I can't relate them to my position. Whereas the books I do read, which take place now or in the last century, I can relate to because I can imagine myself being in that situation and doing these things (Henry, age 35, architect).

Q   I want a completely different world where nothing is the same as our world. But if the author was good enough to make it feasible and understandable, then it would be a perfect book (Cliff, age 24, auto mechanic).

Kinds of resolutions and endings

R   That's why I can't read a lot of modern novels because the endings are always sad. Maybe that's why I like Westerns, too, because they always have happy endings....I won't read a book without a happy ending. I've got enough drama in my own life, without any of that (Tom, age 55, professor).

S   The ending doesn't have to be sunshine and butterflies, but it has to be at least resolved. And if I don't feel that it has been resolved at the end or if the book ends unjustly, then I feel cheated (Kelly, age 24, student/artist).

T   I don't like predictable books. I know about a lot of people who look for a predictable format and get comfort from that. But that doesn't appeal to me at all. I want books that are lifelike in presenting the…unpredictability is the wrong word. Life isn't formulaic (Sally, age 40, library assistant).

Sense of felt life

U   There are certain things I demand from a writer. I really like to know that the author is telling me the truth. Not that what they are telling me actually happened, but that it's a true story in the sense that Alice Munro or Edna O'Brien or Eudora Welty or even *The Plague Dogs* are true stories. That the author isn't holding out on me. That the author really feels what he or she is writing about is true (Nadia, age 29, librarian).

Emotional Impact on the Reader

V   I like to read hard-hitting books and I enjoy them, although they may leave me temporarily depressed. I don't want the hero always to win the girl in the end—I can accept the fact that this doesn't happen in real life. I'd rather have it more realistic (Frank, age 54, owner of a moving company).

W   I like a sense of humour and a sense of hope. I *really* do not like books that are cynical and full of despair and that say, "Why bother? Life sucks and then you die." I don't like that. The ending has to have some sort of upbeat hope to it (Truus, age 40, librarian).

X   A lot of books have those ironic endings, where everything looks like it's going along fine and then there's a turn, and you've been fooled. I'm made very uncomfortable by those sorts of books, and I don't read them. In *If on a Winter's Night a Traveller,* the Other Reader says she likes books that made her feel "uncomfortable from the very first page." I don't like feeling uncomfortable from the very first page (Andrea, age 38, librarian).

Demands Placed on the Reader

Y   I was into the classics at one time….But I can't do that much any more because you have to concentrate a lot, and I can't concentrate read after read after read. I don't like having to force myself. If the book doesn't flow easily and interest me, I can't read it. You get a book 300 to 400 pages long and I just can't concentrate or keep up my interest for that long (Daniel, age 49, plant mechanic).

Z   I like a book that doesn't give me all of the information up front, a book that makes me work a bit to read it (Giles, age 44, business development manager).

A fiction classification or a fiction search engine ought to use these twenty-six appeal factors as an intellectual foundation. The subject approach that works to access nonfiction fails to meet fiction readers' needs.

References

Baker, Sharon L. 1986. Overload, Browsers, and Selections. *Library and Information Science Research* 8: 315–29.

Book Industry Study Group. 1984. *1983 Consumer Research Study on Reading and Book Purchasing: Focus on Adults.* New York: Book Industry Study Group.

Calvino, Italo. 1981. *If on a Winter's Night a Traveller.* Trans. William Weaver. Toronto: Lester and Orpen Dennys.

Cole, John Y., and Carol S. Gold, eds. 1979. *Reading in America: Selected Findings of the Book Industry Study Group's 1978 Study.* Washington, D.C.: Library of Congress.

Gallup Organization. 1978. *Book Reading and Library Usage: A Study of Habits and Perceptions.* Conducted for the American Library Association. Princeton: Gallup Organization.

Gray, W., and B. Rogers. 1964. *Maturity in Reading, Its Nature and Appraisal.* Chicago: University of Chicago Press.

Krahn, H., and Lowe, G. S. 1998. *International Adult Literacy Survey: Literacy Utilization in Canadian Workplaces.* Ottawa: Statistics Canada. Catalogue no. 89-552-MIE, no. 4. URL: http://www.nald.ca/nls/ials/monoe.htm (accessed December 26, 2000).

Krashen, Steven. 1993. *The Power of Reading: Insights from the Research.* Englewood, CO: Libraries Unlimited.

Madden, Michael. 1979. *Lifestyles of Library Users and Nonusers.* Occasional papers. University of Illinois Graduate School of Library Science.

Ross, Catherine Sheldrick. 1991. Readers' Advisory Service: New Directions. *Reference Quarterly* 30, no. 4: 503–18.

————. 1995. "If They Read Nancy Drew, So What?": Series Book Readers Talk Back. *Library and Information Science Research* 17, no. 3: 201–36.

————. 1999. Finding Without Seeking: The Information Encounter in the Context of Reading for Pleasure. *Information Processing and Management* 35: 783–99.

————. 2001. Making Choices: What Readers Say About Choosing Books to Read for Pleasure. *The Acquisitions Librarian* 25: 5–21.

Ross, Catherine Sheldrick, and Mary Kay Chelton. 2001. How to Help Readers Choose a Book for Pleasure. *Library Journal*. Forthcoming.

Saricks, Joyce G., and Nancy Brown. 1997. *Readers' Advisory Service in the Public Library,* 2d ed. Chicago and London: American Library Association.

Shalla, V., and Schellenberg, G. 1998. *The Value of Words: Literacy and Economic Security in Canada*. Ottawa: Statistics Canada. Catalogue no. 89-552-MIE, no 3. URL: http://www.nald.ca/nls/ials/words/cover.htm (accessed December 26, 2000).

Spiller, David. 1980. The Provision of Fiction for Public Libraries. *Journal of Librarianship* 12, no. 4: 238–66.

Statistics Canada and Human Resources Development Canada. 1996. *Reading the Future: A Portrait of Literacy in Canada*. Ottawa: Minister of Industry.

Watson, Kenneth F., et al. 1980. *Leisure Reading Habits: A Survey of the Leisure Reading Habits of Canadian Adults with Some International Comparisons*. Ottawa: Infoscan.

CHAPTER 6

The Reader's Altered State of Consciousness

Brian Sturm

> *You get the feeling you're not reading any more, you're not reading sentences, it's as if you are completely living inside the situation.*
>
> Nell (1988b, 42)

> *When I get really involved in reading, I'm not aware of what is going on around me. I concentrate on the people in the book or the movie and react the way they react. The intense concentration is the same in a book or a movie or in imagination as it is in hypnosis. Reading a book can hypnotize you.*
>
> Hilgard (1970, 24)

What happens to us when we read? How is it that we can be "living inside the situation" while our bodies remain slumped in a chair or tucked into bed and our eyes continue to travel across the printed page? The experience is familiar to all readers: the sense of being lost in a book, caught up in the world of the story, taken to another place by the artifice of a narrative. As these phrases suggest, a journey of sorts seems to occur; we are transported to the story world, and for a time, if we are lucky, we are alive within that world. It unfolds for us with a vividness that resembles reality, and when we emerge, we discover ourselves changed, awakened to new possibilities, seeing ourselves and the world with an altered and often refreshed vision.

My purpose here is suggestive and descriptive rather than prescriptive. Although the experience of entranced reading is commonplace, the research on it is scarce and, to some, suspect. Relying, as much of it does, on introspective and subjective accounts—a data source considered unreliable by some behavioral psychologists because it is a private and unobservable *experiential* event rather than a public and observable *behavioral* one (Kimble and Garmezy 1968; Skinner et al. 1984; Watson 1913)—the reading trance remains somewhat shrouded in mystery. Perhaps it should remain so because the magician whose secrets are known becomes a mere purveyor of tricks, however masterfully performed, while the one whose secrets remain holds the key to mystery and enchantment. Although exploration can build understanding and a deeper appreciation of an experience, it can also breed cynicism and disbelief. With that in mind, I will tread gently, for I have no wish to reduce the power of the reading experience; it must remain a uniquely personal journey, different each time as the book, the reader, or the context changes.

The Experience of Story

Roman Jakobsen (1987) describes six factors that verbal communication involves: an *addresser* sends a *message* to an *addressee.* The message requires a *context,* is transmitted through a *contact* or medium, and is formulated in a certain *code* that both communicating parties understand. Applying the first part of this schema to literary theory yields this concept: An *author* writes a *text* for a *reader.* Literary theorists have explored all three of these factors: "Romantic-humanist theories emphasize the *writer's* life and mind as expressed in his or her work; 'reader' theories (phenomenological criticism) [center] themselves on the *reader's,* or 'affective,' experience; formalist theories concentrate on the nature of the *writing* itself" (Selden, Widdowson, and Brooker 1997, 5).

This chapter focuses on the affective approach to literature, which makes the reader's interaction or transaction with the text the subject of attention. Although the text certainly plays an important role in the reading trance and the author's life may add to the reader's understanding of—and hence involvement in—the text, I concentrate on readers' encounters with the printed page and their reactions to those encounters. Louise Rosenblatt (1978, 12) draws a useful distinction between a "text" and a "poem," claiming that the text is what the author creates, whereas the true poem is what the reader creates, using the text as the foundation and adding to it one's personal associations, experiences, images, memories, expectations, perceptions, and the like. "The poem [is] the experience shaped by the reader under the guidance of the text" (ibid.).

Judith Langer (1990, 813) has explored the meaning-making process that readers undergo when encountering a text. She found that readers adopted four "stances" or relations to the text:

- Being out and stepping in

- Being in and moving through

- Being in and stepping out

- Stepping out and objectifying the experience

"These stances," she explains, "are not linear, have the potential to recur at any point in the reading, and are a function of varying interactions between the reader and the text." In the first stance, readers make initial contact with the plot, the characters, and the setting and begin to form a sense of how they interrelate to form a cohesive story. In the second, "readers are immersed in the text world, using both text knowledge and background knowledge to develop meaning." In the third, readers "use their text knowledge to reflect on personal knowledge. They use what they read in the text to reflect on their own lives." In the fourth stance, readers "distance themselves from the text world, reflecting on and reacting to both the content and the experience" (ibid.).

This four-part process is remarkably similar to what listeners experience at oral storytelling events. In another work (Sturm n.d.), I have proposed a model of the storylistening experience that also occurs in four stages, although not necessarily linearly. The listener in a storytelling context moves from the realm of conversation (in which a story is introduced and the dialogic mode of conversation becomes the monologic mode of storytelling) to the Storyrealm (borrowing Young's [1987] word to refer to the time during which listeners begin to actively engage in the unfolding story and the tale begins to "come to life") . The third stage, similar to Langer's second one, is the experience of being immersed in the story; at this point the Taleworld (again using Young's word) is all-consuming, attention is focused on the characters and the unfolding drama, and knowledge of the quotidian world is minimal. In the fourth stage, the listener emerges from this Taleworld back into a similar, though qualitatively different, Storyrealm, and the story takes on the status of a past experience that the listener and storyteller can consider, talk about, and explore as they reenter the realm of conversation.

Perhaps the best illustration of this experience is the movie *The Princess Bride* (1987), in which a young boy unwillingly agrees to listen to his grandfather read him a story. The cinematography follows the progressive immersion of the listener/reader to perfection. At first, one sees the grandfather and the boy on the screen talking of the boy's illness, until the grandfather opens his book and begins to read. After the first few sentences, the camera shows the world of the story, with a young woman riding on horseback across a verdant field, but the sound of the movie is still of the grandfather reading to the boy. As the story begins to unfold in earnest, the characters begin to speak and interact, and the grandfather and the boy disappear entirely. After several minutes of the story coming to life in this way, the boy's voice interrupts the story's flow, and the camera shows the boy and his grandfather once again. This is a momentary break as the child asks a question about the story; and then the grandfather once again begins reading, the camera shows the story, and the characters speak. Throughout the movie, the story is occasionally broken by interruptions by both characters, and in the end, the grandfather closes his book and departs, promising to return the next day to read it again. In a stroke of genius, his parting words mimic one of the character's favorite phrases, and one is left wondering whether the grandfather *was* the story character when he was younger.

All three of these narrative experiences describe moments during which the encounter with the story becomes completely engrossing; the tale seems to absorb all of our conscious attention, and we are caught within the world that is being created for us and by us. Although there is much to explore concerning this entire experience, I wish to focus on those specific moments of utter involvement in the story, when it seems to circumvent the reality of everyday experience and replace it with the unfolding drama of the story. How do we experience these moments, and what kinds of influences augment the experience?

The Neurobiology of Trance

If describing the magic of reading is difficult, describing consciousness is more so. There are as many perceptions of consciousness as there are theorists. The "behaviorists" (Boring 1963; Watson 1913) believe that consciousness must be linked to physiological manifestations, and they explore brain waves, heart rates, galvanic skin responses, and other physiological evidence as indicators of consciousness. "Structuralists" (Battista 1978; Marsh 1977) attempt to categorize aspects of consciousness, trying to map its attributes in the psyche, whereas "functionalists" (Stephen 1979) ponder the utility of consciousness and its value in identity formation and social interaction. "Constructivists" (Goodman 1984) value the independent and uniquely personal nature of consciousness and believe that each person creates or assembles his or her consciousness from the myriad influences and stimuli with which a person comes into contact. Some theorists believe that we can separate consciousness into discrete states that are quantitatively or qualitatively different from others (Tart 1975), whereas others concentrate more on the ever-changing nature of consciousness and try to describe its "flow" (Csikszentmihalyi 1990).

The behaviorist approach to consciousness offers fascinating opportunities for exploring the reading trance, by examining the neurobiology of people while in this trance state, in a way similar to other explorations of trance. Nell (1988b) conducted just such an experiment. He attached electrodes to the forehead, the corners of the mouth, and the platysma (the muscle between the chin and the larynx) of each subject in order to measure the movement of these muscles during reading; he also measured respiration, skin potential, heart rate, and heart period (the interval between heartbeats). Each participant underwent a nine-part experience: five minutes of relaxation with eyes shut; ten minutes and a subsequent fifteen minutes of mild sensory deprivation (translucent goggles and white noise); thirty minutes of ludic, or pleasure, reading followed by five minutes of eyes-closed relaxation; and finally four cognitive tasks to see whether other mental activities would imitate the reading responses. He found that during reading, all of the measures increased over the baseline resting measure with the exception of heart period, which decreased. Although readers claimed that reading was a relaxed and rather passive experience, Nell found that they were actually in a physiologically aroused state. There was also a marked drop in arousal immediately following reading when subjects closed their eyes, and Nell claims that the "delights of bedtime reading may in part be attributed to this precipitous fall in arousal, not only in skeletal muscle but also in skin potential, controlled by the autonomic nervous system" (Nell 1988b, 36–38).

Increased arousal is typical of many trance states. Ritual trance is often induced by rhythmic drumming or prolonged dancing. Roland Fischer (1978) has developed a "cartography" of the conscious states based on the level of arousal associated with each: the hyperaroused (ergotropic) states ending in ecstatic, mystical rapture occupy one-half of a circular continuum, while the hypoaroused (trophotropic) states associated with meditation occupy the other. Interestingly, the two extremes abut, leading to the supposition that the state of consciousness one experiences is similar to whether one arrives there through excitation or tranquility.

Since the late-nineteenth century there has been a growing body of research concerning the two main lobes of the brain (i.e., brain laterality) and the differences in their functioning. The human brain exhibits lateral asymmetry, with the left hemisphere controlling the right side of the body, and the right hemisphere, the left side. Although both hemispheres interact (primarily across the corpus callosum) in stimulus processing, each hemisphere has certain specializations (the neurons in that area of the brain tend to fire more frequently under certain conditions). Richard Restak states:

> To summarize a great deal of research: Things are perceived and analyzed as a whole by the right hemisphere, whereas the left hemisphere breaks things down into their components. The right hemisphere excels at reading maps, working out jigsaw puzzles, copying designs, distinguishing and remembering musical tones, recognizing faces, analyzing other people's emotions via the interpretation of their tones of voice or facial expression (essentially the "reading of body language") , visualizing in three-dimensional space, and other activities involving perceptual-spatial relations. In addition to language, the left hemisphere is involved in all other activities that involve analysis or sequential processing. (1995, 97–98)

Sandra Witelson describes this functional asymmetry in the following way:

> Tasks involving speech production; phonemic discrimination; comprehension of oral and written language; the ability to write; performance of voluntary finger, limb, and oral movements; and the perception of sequences of stimuli are more dependent on left- than right-hemisphere functioning in most people. In contrast, tasks involving the perception of two- and three-dimensional visual and tactual shapes, spatial position and orientation of stimuli, the perception of faces and colors, mental rotation of three-dimensional shapes, the ability to direct attention to both lateral sensory fields, the perception of musical chords and melodies, aspects of the perception of emotional stimuli and prosodic features of speech, and the abilities to dress oneself and construct block models are more dependent on the right hemisphere. (1995, 61)

Barbara Lex explores this specialization in relation to ritual trance states. She, too, explains that the left cerebral hemisphere "functions in the production of speech, as well as in linear, analytic thought and…process[es] things sequentially. In contrast, the specializations of the right hemisphere comprise spatial and tonal perception, recognition of patterns…and holistic, synthetic thought" (Lex 1979, 125). She claims that during certain tribal rituals, the dancing and drumming "drive" or overstimulate the autonomic nervous system (an ergotropic or arousal mechanism), and the repetitive nature of the stimuli impairs left-hemisphere functioning enabling the right hemisphere to dominate "resulting in a gestalt, timeless, nonverbal experience" of total engagement or trance (ibid., 146). The result of this intense arousal is exhaustion, or trophotropic rebound, leading to deep relaxation. Returning to Nell (1988b), although he was not dealing with intense arousal states and exhaustion, he did find that reading involves increased arousal followed by a period of deep relaxation. Perhaps the trance-inducing process of reading mimics that of ritual (the act of reading, after all, is ritualistic and in many ways repetitive and rhythmic) by combining periods of arousal and rest.

Lex's belief that the trance state is characterized by right-hemispheric dominance may also have implications for reading. Waldie and Mosley (2000) mention many studies that implicate the right hemisphere in the reading process. Their own study examined children ages 5–15 and tested them on two tasks: a dual task (how well they could tap a finger of their left or right hand while reading) and a lexical-decision task (how well they distinguished words from nonwords when presented to right or left visual fields). The results of the dual task show more interference with right-finger tapping when the subjects were reading, suggesting that the left hemisphere (which is responsible for the right-hand side of the body) was "needed" for the reading process and therefore disrupted the motor coordination of the right hand; the right hemisphere was not as involved in the reading process, and so the left hand was not as affected. The results for the lexical reading task, however, suggest that for children under ten years of age, word recognition is primarily a right-hemisphere experience but that the left hemisphere predominates for older children. The authors suggest that this age difference may be due to the changing way readers process words as they gain ability: Beginning readers tend to rely on "visual wholes" for pattern recognition (a right-hemisphere strength), whereas more adept readers may switch to "phonological/sequential strategies" that are mediated primarily by the left hemisphere.

This study is suggestive on several fronts: Does the process of reading change when one goes into the reading trance, causing one to recognize words visually (as young children do) and to activate the right hemisphere? Is the gestalt that seems to accompany the reading trance and the ritual trance reminiscent of a particularly childlike way of interpreting the world? Finally, whereas the *process* of reading may be associated with the left hemisphere, could the *pleasure* of reading be associated with the right? Further research will eventually shed light on these issues.

Roberts and Kraft (1989, 326) measured the electroencephalograph (EEG) alpha patterns of boys (ages 6–8 and 10–12) while they read and then discussed their reading. They found that the left hemisphere was most active in younger children as they struggled with the phonetic and syntactic analysis of early reading. The older and more experienced readers, however, showed more bilateral processing (both brain hemispheres): "[A] more advanced stage of reading acquisition is likely to involve increasing use of right-hemispheric processing in collaboration with left-hemispheric processing, rather than a decreasing use of the left hemisphere's linguistic and sequential processing." Ornstein et al. (1979, 401) evaluated the EEG alpha waves of twelve males between the ages of eighteen and forty-five while they read stories and technical reports; their results show a higher activation of the right hemisphere while reading stories than while reading technical reports. They conclude: "[W]hile it is still largely accurate that language is primarily a left hemisphere function, there may be certain aspects of the process of reading that differentially involve the right hemisphere." Finally, Kraft et al. (1980) studied the EEG traces of nine boys and nine girls, ages six to eight, to determine their brain activity during reading and while answering questions about what they had read. The results indicate that the right hemisphere was dominant during the encoding of information (reading) whereas the left hemisphere was dominant during verbal/logical expression (talking about their reading).

Gruzelier (1988) proposes a multistaged process of the brain during hypnosis. At first there is a period of focused attention involving primarily the left hemisphere. There is then a "letting go" period during which the left hemisphere is gradually inhibited, followed by a period of increased right-hemispheric activity. Further stages depend on the nature of the hypnotic induction.

If trance is primarily a right-hemisphere phenomenon and if adult reading is primarily a left-hemisphere phenomenon, then there may be evidence that reading that facilitates trance is a whole-brain activity. Roberts and Kraft's (1989) work seems to suggest this bilateral involvement, and Gruzelier (1988) proposes a sequential activation of the hemispheres. The age changes in hemispheric activity evident in both Waldie and Mosley (2000) and in Roberts and Kraft (1989), although seemingly contradictory, point to research that will shed light on the reading process as it relates to age and reading expertise. The possibilities for further discovery are truly exciting.

A second avenue of inquiry, which no one has pursued to my knowledge with regard to reading and trance, is the measuring of alpha, beta, and theta brainwave activity during altered states of consciousness. Hughes and Melville provide a brief overview of this topic:

> Beta (13–30 Hertz) occurs with strong, excited emotions such as fear, rage, or anxiety, as well as with alert attentiveness, selective attention, concentration, or anticipation (Lindsley, 1952). Brown (1977) has described beta as being correlated with alert behavior, concentrated mental activity such as solving math problems, anxiety and apprehension. Alpha (8–13 Hertz) is associated with a relaxed wakefulness, routine reactions and creative thought where attention may wander and free association is favored (Lindsley, 1952). Brown (1977) has described alpha as being correlated with a generally tranquil, pleasant, almost floating feeling. Theta (4–8 Hertz) occurs with drowsiness, borderline or partial awareness, imagery, reverie and "dream-like states" (Lindsley, 1952). (1990, 180)

Several EEG studies of the brainwave activity of people during meditation and trance have shown marked changes in brainwave patterns. Kasamatsu and Hirai (1969) studied Zen priests and disciples during meditation. They found four stages of brainwave activity: appearance of alpha waves, increase of alpha wave amplitude, decrease in alpha wave frequency, and finally the occasional appearance of rhythmic theta waves. Anand, Chhina, and Singh (1961) studied yogis engaged in *samadhi* (meditation) and found a preponderance of alpha activity and an increase in amplitude even when the yogis appeared relaxed and in a sleeplike state. Das and Gastaut (1955) studied Kriya yogis and noted mainly alpha activity but also a decrease in amplitude of the waves. Banquet (1973) studied practitioners of transcendental meditation and found an increased alpha amplitude and a decreased frequency with occasional bursts of theta waves, much like the findings of Kasamatsu and Hirai (1969). Not all researchers, however, have found a change in brainwave activity during meditation (Bagchi and Wenger 1957; Tebecis 1975). As Schuman (1980, 341) states, "These investigators found *no* consistent or significant difference between meditation and nonmeditation, despite a trend toward increased theta and decreased beta" (emphasis in original).

Hughes and Melville (1990) studied trance channels (people who serve as mediums) and found that during their altered state of consciousness, alpha, beta, and theta waves increased dramatically. Sabourin et al. (1990) took EEG measurements of people during hypnosis and found a marked increase of alpha and theta waves but a decrease in beta waves.

An EEG study of readers of this nature would shed light on the brain-wave activity during reading. Is the experience similar to hypnotic trance with a rise in both alpha and theta (a combined tranquility and imagery) with a decrease in beta (alertness and concentration), or does it mimic the trance channel's experience of heightened brain activity in all three wave patterns? Is it similar to meditation with a concomitant rise in alpha waves? A sense of tranquility and imagery is certainly associated with reading, but evidence of selective attention and anticipation also exists. EEG studies of readers would help categorize the neurologic component of the reading trance phenomenon.

The Experience of Trance

The personal experience of trance, regardless of the induction techniques employed, seems to be fairly constant in general terms; individual differences are, of course, evident, but the self-reports of the trance experience show remarkable consistency. What are the characteristics of the trance experience in its many forms, and how does the experience of readers relate?

In other work (Sturm 2000) I have described some of the characteristics of the storylistening trance. Six were evident in that study: realism, lack of awareness of surroundings or other mental processes, engaged receptive channels, control, "placeness," and time distortion. Realism relates to the sense that the characters or the environment of the story is real or alive. People described this experience as "stories come alive and touch you" or "it's the actual living of the images." Some listeners claimed merely to watch the story unfold around them ("it's like I'm standing here watching, I'm not really part of it"), whereas others were active participants in the story world ("I'm no longer sitting in a tent listening to someone tell a story…I was in those woods, I saw those animals, they were real"). Hilgard (1970, 26) explains that it is "useful to distinguish *character identification* and *empathic identification.* By the first we mean a kind of participation in the action and feeling as though one were indeed one of the characters; by the second we mean participation in the feeling of the story even though the separation of the self from the character is maintained."

The study participants mentioned a distinct lack of awareness of their surroundings. Three different perceptions were evident. For some, the surroundings remained constant and the listener "forgot" to attend to them, simply "didn't notice" them, or consciously "tuned them out." For others, the sense was that the surroundings "disappeared," whereas the third group of listeners felt as though they had left the surroundings and gone somewhere. There was also a full engagement of the listeners' receptive channels. The visual channel was engaged on two levels: the physical visual level, in which listeners watched the storyteller perform, and the mental visual level (visualization), in which they watched the story world unfold. Two aural channels were likewise active: the physical one of listening to the storyteller and the mental one of the Taleworld. Kinesthetic responses to the story were common, from laughing and crying to the subtler frisson of suspense or fear. The emotional channel was also fully engaged as the kinesthetic reactions indicate. These emotions were influenced by the story *telling*, by the *story*, by the *story characters*, by the listener's *memories*, and by the storylistening *experience* as a whole. Some participants also mentioned an emotional connection with the storyteller.

Listeners mentioned a lack or loss of control of the story experience. Although a few mentioned that they actively made an effort to get involved in the story ("I put myself into the story") , most felt they either relinquished control or that control was taken from them. "He made you feel like you were really there" and "I'm kind of taken there or transported there into the story" are examples of this attitude. One participant made a fascinating juxtaposition between willful control and willful lack of control: "I know that I consciously let myself fall into the story." Although the "let myself" implies control, the resulting "fall" implies its lack. Some listeners seem to need to make an effort to reach the point at which the story (or the telling) takes control and carries the listener along, as though one must consciously enter the river before it can carry one away. This may coincide with the left-hemispheric "effort" of the beginning reader and the subsequent right-hemispheric, gestalt experience of the more experienced reader. It also recalls the "willingness" in Coleridge's (1975) "willing suspension of disbelief."

There was also a "placeness" to the story. People constantly referred to being "in" the story. They made claims such as "I feel I'm inside the story; I'm sitting there totally in the story" and "it captivates you into the story." Others described it as "there." "You just kind of get lost there" and "I was just there" are representative expressions. Perhaps it is a feature of the English language, a figure of speech, but the story seems to have a spatial reference for many people; it is somewhere other than their real world, and one often takes a "journey" of some sort (at least metaphorically) to reach the world of the story. This journey could be a metaphor for the induction process of trance, and the spatial quality is certainly consonant with Tolkien's concept of the secondary world.

Finally, listeners mentioned that their sense of time was changed while engrossed in a story. For some, the story seemed to pass faster than chronological time ("time goes pretty quickly when you're in a story; you get into it, and then it's over") , whereas others felt that time passed more slowly (one participant felt that an eleven-minute story had lasted about an hour and a half). There was a further layer added by another listener who claimed that the storyteller's "story seemed very long to me, partly because he went on such a long journey." This idea that the characters' story time influences the listener's perception of time (i.e., the story characters experience fifteen days, and the story feels long, whereas if they experience only one day, the story feels short) bears further exploration. Another intriguing quotation was that "my sense of the passage of time, my subjective sense, was really different; I had kind of an objective sense there too, side by side." If one accepts the listener's feelings of the intense reality of the Taleworld, their multichannel involvement, their perception of being "in" the story, and their lack of awareness of their surroundings, it seems logical that an objective sense of the passage of time would be lacking while they were involved in the story. For at least one of the listeners, there was a dual temporal awareness that seems simultaneous. One could explain this as a sensed simultaneity while in fact the clock time awareness was a moment of noninvolvment in the tale. It could also relate to Hilgard's (1975) claim that hypnotic subjects never fully relinquish conscious awareness; they have a "hidden observer" that does not get involved and that monitors, and perhaps even controls, the various realities they experience. Is there an unfailingly vigilant awareness within us that monitors our experiences like a third eye and draws us back from the Taleworld into quotidian reality?

Many of these same feelings are evident in the literature on reading. W. H. Auden (1967, 84) in his afterword to George MacDonald's *The Golden Key* mentions that "History, actual or feigned, demands that the reader be at one and the same time inside the story, sharing in the feelings and events narrated, and outside it, checking these against his own experiences. A fairy tale like *The Golden Key*, on the other hand, demands of the reader total surrender; so long as he is in its world, there must for him be no other." The dual awareness ("inside and outside"), the lack of control ("surrender") , and the "placeness" of trance ("in its world") are implicated. Tolkien describes it similarly:

> Children are capable, of course, of *literary belief*, when the story-maker's art is good enough to produce it. That state of mind has been called "willing suspension of disbelief." But this does not seem to me a good description of what happens. What really happens is that the story-maker proves a successful "sub-creator." He makes a Secondary World which your mind can enter. Inside it, what he relates is "true": it accords with the laws of that world. You therefore believe it, while you are, as it were, inside. The moment disbelief arises, the spell is broken; the magic, or rather art, has failed. You are then out in the Primary World again, looking at the little abortive Secondary World from outside. (1947, 60)

Michael Benton has pursued Tolkien's idea and developed a three-dimensional model of this Secondary World. The three axes in this model are "psychic distance" (the variable degree of involvement in or detachment from the story), "psychic process" (the variable degree of retrospection or anticipation one experiences when reading), and "psychic level" (the variable degree of conscious or unconscious activity) (Benton 1983, 72). These three axes intersect in space to form the experience of reading, and that point of intersection is constantly shifting as the reader interacts with the text. "The dimensions of the secondary world depend upon shifts that occur upon these planes" (ibid.).

Silverstein mentions the reading experience of his elementary school students (Silverstein 1978, 602). One eight-year-old girl, while reading aloud, suddenly stopped and began turning her head as though watching something. When questioned, she exclaimed that she was watching the ducks, about which she had been reading, waddle across her desk. "On questioning Susan further on whether or not this kind of occurrence bothered her often when she read, she said, 'No. It doesn't bother me much, only when I read slowly. Then the pictures come out and I see them on the book. When I read faster, the pictures don't have time to come out, but instead I see them in my head—and then it doesn't bother me at all" (ibid.). He also found that for many of his students, the words would become blurry and then disappear from the page until a blink would bring them back. This phenomenon seemed to precede a growing intensity of visualization, sometimes to the point of hallucination as just mentioned. "When I read a story book, I can see the events in my mind, just as if I were watching it as a movie," claimed one child, while another said, "[W]hen I read I can actually see in my mind what is going on. It's like a long movie that stops when you stop reading and starts again when you continue on with the story. But this only happens to me with story books, and not with books like reference books" (Silverstein 1978, 604–5).

Erickson (1976) mentions that during hypnosis, the vision can get foggy or blurry or become tunnel vision and that a patient might experience alterations in the color of the background or the size and shape of things. He also mentions the sense of "drifting" that is common in hypnotic induction. Perhaps these experiences are similar to the ones Silverstein's students described.

Gerrig (1993, 10–11) describes the encounter with a "narrative world" as a six-stage process in which the reader is transported into that world:

1. Someone ("the traveler") is transported

2. by some means of transportation

3. as a result of performing certain actions.

4. The traveler goes some distance from his or her world of origin

5. which makes some aspects of the world of origin inaccessible.

6. The traveler returns to the world of origin, somewhat changed by the journey.

Throughout his book, Gerrig explores issues that are reminiscent of the storylistening trance. He mentions that the use of the word *transported* "projects an aura of passivity…[that] accurately encodes readers' descriptions of their experience. The disparity between the passivity of the metaphor and the active complexity of the processes that make the experience of narratives possible suggests that an adequate theory of this domain must concern itself with the illusion of effortlessness" (13). He quotes Iser (1989, 244) on the way in which readers must let their reality fade to be replaced by the fictional reality: "To imagine what has been stimulated by aesthetic semblance entails placing our thoughts and feelings at the disposal of an unreality, bestowing on it a semblance of reality in proportion to a reducing of our own reality. For the duration of the performance we are both ourselves and someone else." Appleyard reiterates this dual sense when he states, "The reader can surrender to the fantasy knowing that it is only a story and that however vivid the sense of involvement is, the listener is always spectator as well as participant and remains in control of the level of involvement" (1990, 40). Although I disagree that, when entranced by a story, one has a sense of control over the process, I also believe that there is a "flicker effect" to being immersed in a story; one "pops in and out" of it quite quickly, and the duration of the trance is rather evanescent. Thus we feel in control because we often emerge from the trance, but while in it, we seem to lose control of the process and are swept along.

Shor maintains that "the reader's fantasy world is an encapsulated unit and it seems totally real….The reader is completely oblivious at the conscious level to the true reality about him" (1970, 92–93). Hilgard argues that what actually happens is that the reader's ego breaks down, decreasing the ability to distinguish between the subjective and the objective, and leading to total immersion in the experience and the feeling of being "transformed or transported by what he reads…swept emotionally into the experience described by the author" (1970, 23). This is similar to the "complete absorption" that is part of Maslow's (1962) understanding of peak experiences. Perhaps the most complete exploration of the reading trance is Victor Nell's work, *Lost in a Book* (1988a). Here he draws together much of the research on imaginative involvement, reading ability, absorption, and dreaming to form a motivational model of the experience of reading (see Figure 12.1). Nell first sets the reading trance in a social context and then explores the component processes of pleasure reading. He then relates reading to dreaming, hypnotic trance, and other consciousness-changing activities, resulting in his motivational model.

The Induction of Trance

Many influences on the ordinary state of consciousness can lead to an altered state. These influences often take the form of rhythmic stimuli that "drive" or "entrain" the conscious mind so that the unconscious rises to the surface and becomes dominant. Events in normal life, such as the passing white lines of the highway, can drop people into a trance (often called "highway hypnosis") quite quickly. Rhythmic flashes of light, such as from a strobe, can induce an altered state, as can rhythmic dancing or drumming (Adrian and Matthews 1934; d'Aquili 1983; Neher 1962). Hypnotic verbal and visual inductions use repetition, rhythm, and a deep sense of trust between hypnotist and patient to ease people into a trance. Distractions or other "startle" phenomena can just as quickly reinstate the normal conscious state. As Fischer (1978) mentions, both activity and passivity can lead to trance.

Milton Erickson (1976, 8), a renowned hypnotherapist, mentions several induction techniques. He claims that truisms (statements that listeners can't or won't refute) help build the trust between the hypnotist and the patient. He feels that internal images are "much more effective [than external ones] in holding attention" and that showing the patient evidence of his entranced state helps deepen the trance (i.e., hand immobility or seemingly automatic movement). He also feels that downplaying distractions and making them seem unimportant helps keep patients in a trance and that helping patients relax and making no demands of them facilitate trance induction.

The hypnotist tries to decrease stimulus input and thereby focus attention on the hypnotist's voice. Hilgard (1970, 255) mentions the work of Kubie and Margolin (1944) and claims that "having described the reduction of sensory input in the usual induction (through immobilization and monotony) they propose that this reduction in sensorimotor channels blurs the ego boundaries of the subject, so that there is a psychological fusion between subject and hypnotist; as this stage is reached the hypnotist's words are confused with the subject's own thoughts." Reading, too, is in many ways a reduced sensory experience. The body is usually still, nearly eliminating its input, and the attention is focused on a small area of the book. The blurring of the hypnotist's voice and the patient's thoughts is reminiscent of the blurring of the author's words and the reader's images. The children who saw the words on their pages disappear and the one who watched ducks cross her desk are perhaps experiencing just this kind of merging of words and experience.

The influences on one's state of consciousness during storylistening are myriad. My work with listeners (Sturm 2000) shows at least sixteen different possible influences that help draw listeners into the Taleworld. One of the most often mentioned influences is the activation of listeners' *memories* by the story. If the story is similar to past experiences or helped recall memories, listeners find themselves more deeply involved in the story that is being told. Other influences include *listeners' expectations* (preconceived notions of what to expect from the event), *personal preferences* (adventure stories told to one who loves them, for example), *physical comfort* (environments that were too cold, too hot, too noisy, etc., made it difficult to become engrossed in the story), *emotional comfort* (one has to be willing to trust the storyteller and put the worries of the day to one side), and the *storyteller's ability* (the preconception that the storyteller is superb facilitated the altered state). Some listeners find that *novelty* (stories they hadn't heard before) helped them become engaged, whereas others found that *familiarity* with the told story did. Several participants mentioned *rhythm*, although the exact rhythm they found entrancing was not discernible. *Occupation* or training is an influence in the sense that a nurse claimed to be unable to "get lost in a story" because she was trained to be vigilant of her surroundings, whereas a participant who was studying shamanic journeying found her entry into the altered state made easier by her training. The *storyteller's involvement* in the story was mentioned as an influence; the teller's involvement seems to be contagious, and a lack of involvement a definite hindrance. *Storytelling style* makes a difference, usually in terms of whether a teller's style matches a listener's expectations or preferences. The *story content* certainly plays a role in bringing listeners into a trance state, as does the development of a *sense of rapport* between the listener and the teller. Two other influences that were mentioned, though infrequently, were *recency* (the most recent story was reported to be the most entrancing) and *humor* (some people found the funny stories the most engaging).

Many of these influences are also plausible influences on the reading trance. Physical discomfort would certainly decrease the likelihood of involvement in the story, as would emotional discomfort and a conflict between the listener's expectations of the book and the actual experience. Novelty and familiarity could exert a similar influence on the reader, as the anticipation of reading a new book or rereading an old favorite should help involve the reader. The content of the book and the reader's expectations would have an impact on the reading experience similar to the storytelling one, and the rhythm in the text (while certainly different from that of speech or drumming), if identifiable, might influence a reader as much as a listener.

Other influences at work in reading can certainly help a reader enter an altered state of consciousness. Fletcher, Hummel, and Marsolek suggest that the "causal structure of a narrative controls the allocation of attention as it is read" (1990, 239). This causality within the text seems to give coherence to the story events, thereby leading to greater comprehension. Gerrig (1993) mentions the following "participatory responses" of readers as they interact with a text: hopes and preferences (for the direction of the plot and the results of characters' actions), suspense (this occurs when a reader lacks knowledge about the outcome of an event that has significant consequences), and replotting (the reader plays with multiple possible outcomes). All of these strategies, while focused on the reader's responses, are potential influences on one's state of consciousness. Brewer and Lichtenstein (1982, 480) draw on the work of Berlyne (1971) and suggest that "enjoyment is produced by moderate increases in arousal ('arousal boost') or by a temporary sharp rise in general arousal followed by reduction of the arousal ('arousal jag'), and if both processes operate together enjoyment is produced by both the rise and the subsequent drop in arousal ('arousal-boost-jag')." This is reminiscent of the drop in brainwave activity immediately following reading, and it may be part of the reason for the pleasure people associate with reading and the abandon with which they engage in it.

Conclusions

Hypnosis, storylistening, and reading, even though they surely differ in terms of the forms of induction and the methods of precipitating trance, may be similar experiences of altered states of consciousness. Many of the characteristics of these altered states are qualitatively similar, and the influences that help alter one's state of consciousness seem comparable. Although I have suggested possible connections, detailed research is needed to explore the phenomena associated with this reading trance. Behaviorists will continue to explore the physiological correlates of reading, and as the data grow, we may be able to find more relationships among these various trancelike experiences. Structuralists will help map the boundaries of these secondary worlds, and constructivists will further our understanding of the reader's role in creating the reading experience. In the meantime, readers will continue to curl up with a good book, and regardless of whether science advances their understanding of the experience, they will still revel in "the ease with which we sink through books quite out of sight, [and] pass clamorous pages into soundless dreams" (Gass 1970, 27).

References

Adrian, E. D., and B. H. C. Matthews. 1934. The Berger Rhythm: Potential Changes from the Occipital Lobes in Man. *Brain* 57: 355–84.

Anand, B. K., G. S. Chhina, and B. Singh. 1961. Some Aspects of Electroencephalographic Studies in Yogis. *Electroencephalography and Clinical Neurophysiology* 13: 452–56.

Appleyard, J. A. 1990. *Becoming a Reader: The Experience of Fiction from Childhood to Adulthood.* Cambridge: Cambridge University Press.

d'Aquili, Eugene. 1983. The Myth-Ritual Complex: A Biogenetic Structural Analysis. *Zygon* 18: 247–69.

Auden, William H. 1967. Afterword. In *The Golden Key*, ed. George MacDonald, 81–86. New York: Farrar, Straus & Giroux.

Bagchi, B., and M. Wenger. 1957. Electrophysiological Correlates of Some Yogi Exercises. *Eletroencephalography and Clinical Neurophysiology* supplement 7: 132–49.

Banquet, J. P. 1973. Spectral Analysis of the EEG in Meditation. *Eletroencephalography and Clinical Neurophysiology* 35: 143–51.

Battista, J. R. 1978. The Science of Consciousness. In *The Stream of Consciousness: Scientific Investigations into the Flow of Human Experience*, ed. K. S. Pope and J. L. Singer, 55–90. New York: Plenum Press.

Benton, Michael. 1983. Secondary Worlds. *Journal of Research and Development in Education* 16: 68–75.

Berlyne, D. E. 1971. *Aesthetics and Psychobiology.* New York: Appleton-Century-Crofts.

Boring, Edwin G. 1963. *The Physical Dimensions of Consciousness.* New York: Dover.

Brewer, W. F., and E. H. Lichtenstein. 1982. Stories Are to Entertain: A Structural-Affect Theory of Stories. *Journal of Pragmatics* 6: 473–86.

Brown, Barbara. 1977. *Stress and the Art of Biofeedback.* New York: Bantam Books.

Coleridge, Samuel Taylor. 1975. *Biographia Literaria.* New York: Dutton.

Csikszentmihalyi, Mihalyi. 1990. *Flow: The Psychology of Optimal Experience.* New York: Harper and Row.

Das, N. N., and H. Gastaut. 1955. Variations de l'Activité Electrique du Cerveau, du Coeur, et des Muscles Squelettiques au Cours de la Méditation et du l'Extase Yogique. *Eletroencephalography and Clinical Neurophysiology* 6: 211–19.

Erickson, Milton. 1976. *Hypnotic Realities.* New York: Irvingston.

Fischer, Roland. 1978. Cartography of Conscious States: Integration of East and West. In *Expanding Dimensions of Consciousness*, ed. A. A. Sugerman and R. E. Tarter, 24–57. New York: Springer.

Fletcher, C. R., J. E. Hummel, and C. J. Marsolek. 1990. Causality and the Allocation of Attention During Comprehension. *Journal of Experimental Psychology: Learning, Memory, and Cognition* 16: 233–40.

Gass, William H. 1970. *Fiction and the Figures of Life.* New York: Alfred A. Knopf.

Gerrig, Richard J. 1993. *Experiencing Narrative Worlds: On the Psychological Activities of Reading.* New Haven, CT: Yale University Press.

Goldman, William. 1998. *The Princess Bride.* Produced and directed by Rob Reiner. 98 min. Twentieth Century Fox Film Corp. Videocassette.

Goodman, Nelson. 1984. *Of Mind and Other Matters.* Cambridge: Harvard University Press.

Gruzelier, J. 1988. The Neuropsychology of Hypnosis. In *Hypnosis: Current Clinical, Experimental, and Forensic Practices,* ed. M. Heap, 68–76. London: Croom Helm.

Hilgard, Ernest. 1975. *Hypnosis in the Relief of Pain.* Los Altos, CA: W. Kaufman.

Hilgard, Josephine R. 1970. *Personality and Hypnosis: A Study of Imaginative Involvement.* Chicago: University of Chicago Press.

Hughes, Dureen J., and Norbert T. Melville. 1990. Changes in Brainwave Activity During Trance Channeling: A Pilot Study. *The Journal of Transpersonal Psychology* 22: 175–89.

Iser, Wolfgang. 1989. *Prospecting: From Reader Response to Literary Anthropology.* Baltimore: Johns Hopkins University Press.

Jakobson, Roman. 1987. Linguistics and Poetics. In *Language in Literature,* ed. Roman Jakobson, 62–94. Cambridge, MA: Belknap Press.

Kasamatsu, Akira, and Tomio Hirai. 1969. An Electroencephalographic Study on the Zen Meditation (Zazen). In *Altered States of Consciousness: A Book of Readings*, ed. Charles T. Tart, 489–501. New York: John Wiley.

Kimble, G. A., and N. Garmezy. 1968. *Principles of General Psychology*, 3d ed. New York: Ronald Press.

Kraft, R. Harter, et al. 1980. Hemispheric Asymmetries During Six- to Eight-Year-Olds' Performance of Piagetian Conservation and Reading Tasks. *Neuropsychologia* 18: 637–43.

Kubie, L. S., and S. Margolin. 1944. The Process of Hypnotism and the Nature of the Hypnotic State. *American Journal of Psychiatry* 100: 611–22.

Langer, Judith. 1990. Understanding Literature. *Language Arts* 67: 812–16.

Lex, Barbara. 1979. The Neurobiology of Ritual Trance. In *The Spectrum of Ritual: A Biogenetic Structural Analysis*, ed. Eugene d'Aguili, 117–51. New York: Columbia University Press.

Lindsley, Donald B. 1952. Psychological Phenomena and the Electroencephalogram. *Electroencephalography and Clinical Neurophysiology* 4: 443–56.

Marsh, Caryl A. 1977. A Framework for Describing Subjective States of Consciousness. In *Alternate States of Consciousness*, ed. N. E. Zinberg, 121–44. New York: Free Press.

Maslow, Abraham. 1962. *Toward a Psychology of Being.* Princeton: Van Nostrand.

Neher, Andrew. 1962. A Physiological Explanation of Unusual Behavior in Ceremonies Involving Drums. *Human Biology* 34: 151–60.

Nell, Victor. 1988a. *Lost in a Book.* New Haven: Yale University Press.

———. 1988b. The Psychology of Reading for Pleasure: Needs and Gratifications. *Reading Research Quarterly* 23: 6–50.

Ornstein, Robert, et al. 1979. Differential Right Hemisphere Involvement in Two Reading Tasks. *Psychophysiology* 16: 398–401.

Restak, Richard. 1995. *Brainscapes.* New York: Hyperion.

Roberts, Theresa A., and R. Harter Kraft. 1989. Developmental Differences in the Relationship Between Reading Comprehension and Hemispheric Alpha Patterns: An EEG Study. *Journal of Educational Psychology* 81: 322–28.

Rosenblatt, Louise. 1978. *The Reader, the Text, the Poem: The Transactional Theory of the Literary Work.* Carbondale: Southern Illinois University Press.

Sabourin, Michel E., et al. 1990. EEG Correlates of Hypnotic Susceptibility and Hypnotic Trance: Spectral Analysis and Coherence. *International Journal of Psychophysiology* 10: 125–42.

Schuman, Marjorie. 1980. The Psychophysiological Model of Meditation and Altered States of Consciousness: A Critical Review. In *The Psychobiology of Consciousness*, ed. Julian M. Davidson and Richard J. Davidson, 333–78. New York: Plenum.

Selden, Raman, Peter Widdowson, and Peter Brooker. 1997. *A Reader's Guide to Contemporary Literary Theory*, 4th ed. New York: Prentice Hall.

Shor, R. E. 1970. The Tree-Factor Theory of Hypnosis Applied to Book-Reading Fantasy and to the Concept of Suggestion. *International Journal of Clinical and Experimental Hypnosis* 18: 89–98.

Silverstein, Samuel. 1978. A Report on Reading. *Academic Therapy* 13: 601–5.

Skinner, B. F., et al. 1984. Skinner: Canonical Papers. *Behavioral and Brain Sciences* 7: 473–701.

Stephen, Michele. 1979. Dreams of Changes: The Innovative Role of Altered States of Consciousness in Traditional Melanesian Religion. *Oceania* 1: 3–22.

Sturm, Brian. 2000. The Storylistening Trance Experience. *Journal of American Folklore* 113: 287–304.

———. n.d. Lost in a Story: Modeling Storytelling and Storylistening. In *Storytelling: Interdisciplinary and Intercultural Perspectives*, ed. Irene Blayer and Monica Sanchez. New York: Peter Lang. In press.

Tart, Charles T. 1975. *States of Consciousness.* New York: Dutton.

Tebecis, A. K. 1975. A Controlled Study of the EEG During Transcendental Meditation: Comparison with Hypnosis. *Folia Psychiatrica et Neurologica Japonica* 29: 305–13.

Tolkien, J. R. R. 1947. On Fairy-Stories. In *Essays Presented to Charles Williams*, 38–89. Oxford: Oxford University Press.

Waldie, Karen E., and James L. Mosley. 2000. Developmental Trends in Right Hemispheric Participation in Reading. *Neuropsychologia* 38: 462–74.

Watson, J. B. 1913. Psychology as the Behaviorist Views It. *Psychological Review* 20: 158.

Witelson, Sandra F. 1995. Neuroanatomical Bases of Hemisphere Functional Specialization in the Human Brain: Possible Developmental Factors. In *Hemispheric Communication: Mechanisms and Models*, ed. Frederick L. Kitterle, 61–84. Killsdale, NJ: Lawrence Erlbaum.

Young, Katherine Galloway. 1987. *Taleworlds and Storyrealms: A Phenomenology of Narrative.* Dordrecht: Martinus Nijhoff.

PART II

Advisory Services in Public and School Libraries Today: The State of the Art

Introduction to Part II

The second part of this book examines the state of the art in advisory services in public and school libraries. An understanding of the present level of service is helpful in identifying both areas of strength and areas that need further improvement. The section begins with an examination of advisory services in the two most familiar environments—public and school libraries—and then looks at the resources that readers' advisors employ in their service to customers, from the more traditional print resources to indirect resources to Internet resources.

In Chapter 7 Anne May reports on research that she and colleagues at the Queens College Graduate School of Library and Information Studies conducted. They used the nonintrusive methodology that Shearer and others employed to explore how readers' advisory transactions were carried out in a public library system in New York. May examines the role of the readers' advisor in the interaction with library patrons, the extent to which comprehensive readers' advisory interviews were conducted, and the tools used by readers' advisory staff. Unfortunately, May finds that many librarians seemed uncomfortable with the requests for advice. She reports that comprehensive readers' advisory interviews rarely took place, that staff almost never asked questions regarding the appeal of specific titles, and that the advisors often seemed reluctant to use readers' advisory tools to satisfy patrons' queries. Just as other researchers in this area, May finds much need for improvement in the readers' advisory transactions that she and her colleagues experienced.

Chapter 8 by Carol Doll focuses on advisory services in school library media centers. Doll reminds us that the school media center functions within the school community and that advisory is part of the curriculum support role media specialists play. Doll finds many opportunities to work with teachers and students to suggest specific titles appropriate for the curriculum or for enjoyment. She outlines a wide range of advisory techniques, including storytelling, booktalks, reading aloud, creating bibliographies, and providing individual guidance, and she also identifies a number of resources to support these activities, from general and specialized bibliographies to electronic resources.

The focus of Chapter 9, by readers' advisory guru Joyce Saricks, is on the types of advisory tools available to librarians and the ways in which staff members can incorporate those tools in the provision of readers' advisory services. Saricks also goes beyond the tools to suggest how librarians can learn to use interviewing skills, in addition to reference resources, to create what she calls "truly satisfying conversations about books with readers." The emphasis, as with many other authors in the book, is on understanding the relationship between readers and their books and building on that relationship to strengthen the services that librarians provide.

The readers' advisory resources and services that public librarian Nora Armstrong discusses in Chapter 10 are indirect, or what Armstrong calls "nonmediated." Like Doll, Saricks, and Johnson, Armstrong outlines a rich array of resources and services that librarians can use to enrich the experiences of their customers, including displays, booklists, bookmarks, and library programs that emphasize books and reading. Even though these methods of promotion exist, Armstrong is also aware of the challenges and discusses these as well.

Finally, in Chapter 11, Roberta Johnson looks at Internet resources of interest to readers' advisors. As Johnson points out, the last four years have seen the Internet become a very useful tool for practicing readers' advisory, and she provides a tour of resources that answer patron requests, provide information on authors and their works, and assist with collection development. Johnson's wide-ranging tour includes Usenet news groups, electronic mailing lists, and a host of Web sites. Johnson focuses not only on the resources but also on how library staff might use them to meet the specific readers' advisory goals of the library.

As with Part I of the book, Part II presents both cause for concern—the evidence May finds that many readers' advisory interactions are less than satisfactory—as well as cause for hope—the rich array of resources and services that Doll, Saricks, Armstrong, and Johnson outline and the ways in which these can help librarians enrich the relationships with their customers.

—R.B.

CHAPTER 7

Readers' Advisory Service: Explorations of the Transaction

Anne K. May

The majority of library users turn to their libraries in search of recreational reading materials (Berry 1993; Fialkoff 1997). However, these patrons are not always treated well. Although many libraries claim to provide adult readers' advisory, in actuality, such reading guidance is often elusive. In fact, many users do not realize that it is even proper or realistic to elicit reading suggestions from staff. Moreover, libraries oftentimes do not make users aware that such a service is available.

The landscape of the public library is changing. With the Internet and other electronic sources becoming ubiquitous in the home and office, it is likely that more and more patrons will fulfill their information needs without ever setting foot on library premises. In fact, one commentator has already noted that the circulation of nonfiction books is declining nationwide (Smith 2000b). Because leisure pursuits are still the most common rationale for public library visits in this information-centric age, it makes sense for libraries to court their most important constituency—recreational readers. One way to fulfill this mission would to be to renew the emphasis on providing readers' advisory services.

Historical Backdrop

Readers' advisory programs have vacillated in popularity over the years. The service traces its origins to the late nineteenth century and reached its zenith in the 1920s and 1930s. In its beginnings, it was an all-encompassing adult education plan. Advisees met with specially designated librarians who prescribed works aimed at morally uplifting the participants. Pleasure reading was not within its scope—in fact, fiction works were widely derogated and treated as suspect. Instead, the general goal of early readers' advisory services was the self-improvement of patrons. During World War II and its aftermath, there was no longer an impetus for readers' advisory services. A full work force with little leisure time may have led to the service's decline, and library directors adopted the stance that every librarian should be capable of performing this function, not just the designated advisors.

In recent years a resurgence of interest in reading guidance has occurred. However, the contemporary incarnation of readers' advisory no longer has the same didactic emphasis. Instead, its aim is to facilitate readers in fiction selection—matching readers with books to read for pleasure. Library staff usually do not attempt to reform patrons' reading choices. The lynchpin of modern reading advisory practice is that readers need not apologize for their literary tastes (Herald 2000).

This readers' advisory renaissance has a practical " how-to" bent with the aim of improving the skills of those providing advice. Much of the literature concerns itself with the tools they might employ, the methods of conducting the readers' advisory interview, staff training, and the promotion of the service to public library patrons (American Library Association, Readers' Advisory Committee 1997; Chelton 1993; Saricks and Brown 1997). But simply because instructional resources are accessible does not necessarily mean that staff members are effectively implementing reading guidance. Despite the availability of professional materials, many librarians still regard the readers' advisory interchange as a daunting undertaking. Research has found that seldom is the experts' advice on how to conduct a readers' advisory transaction fully realized. A recent editorial lamented the woebegone state of this particular library service and asked, "Why are we so bad at reader's advisory?" (Fialkoff 2000) The writer used pejorative terms such as "mediocre" and "abysmal" to report on the current state of the art. The profession must take the printed models and move them beyond the page and into actual practice. At a Public Library Association preconference in 2000, Duncan Smith, organizer of the preconference, urged public librarians to dedicate themselves anew to becoming readers' advisors and offered a twelve-step program for those taking the pledge (Smith 2000b).

Research Into the Readers' Advisory Transaction

The need to reinvigorate readers' advisory services is uncontestable. Change must begin with the way that library personnel approach the interchange between staff member and patron. There has been a paucity of research illuminating the reader's advisory transaction from the adult user's point of view. Indeed, reading guidance has been perceived as a self-evident task, one that is easy to perform. Such a misconception has crippled inquiry: "Research on the subject of assisting readers to find what they want has been rare, even while questions abound and the consequences are important to the field" (Shearer 1996b, 182). Although there have been trailblazing studies on the reference transaction interchange, few have focused on its readers' advisory corollary. Exceptions include Shearer's study "The Nature of the Readers' Advisory Transaction in Adult Reading" (Shearer 1996a) and a master's project titled "An Investigation of Readers' Advisory Transactions in Nassau County (NY) Public Libraries" (Lackner, May, Miltenberg, and Olesh 1998; May, Olesh, Miltenberg, and Lackner 2000). Both endeavors were informed by the qualitative studies of reference encounters (Crowley 1985; Durrance 1989; Dewdney and Ross 1994; Gers and Seward 1985).

In his work Shearer takes pains to differentiate the readers' advisory interchange from that of its reference counterpart. He defines the readers' advisory transaction as "an exchange of information between two people with the purpose of one person's suggesting text for the other's later reading interest to one of them....The text suggested in the transaction is expected to meet a recreational, emotional, psychological, or educational need" (Shearer 1996a, 3). Readers' advisory is distinguishable from reference in that the successful conclusion of the former neither results in the provision of a fact or missing data nor attempts to fill a known gap in an otherwise complete knowledge framework. "The success of a readers' advisory transaction is reflected in a reader discovering a book...which is enjoyable, entertaining, stimulating, mind stretching, and eye-opening; it is in the realm of the subjective" (ibid.).

Shearer's research took place between 1992 and 1994, at which time a group of North Carolina Central University graduate students visited various county, independent municipal, and multicounty (regional system) public library settings predominately in North Carolina and posed as readers' advisees. The student researchers completed questionnaires in which they described the resulting transactions and rated the staff members on the basis of their knowledge, professionalism, and attention to the patrons' requests. In his narrative report of the best and worst encounters, Shearer addressed issues such as the educational qualifications of the advisors and the congeniality of the various interactions.

In Shearer's study, the librarians rarely referred to professional tools. Although staff members mentioned the catalog in passing, they made no concerted or systematic effort to consult professional materials or employ electronic finding aids, according to the narratives. In large measure, staff members made off-the-cuff suggestions. Although much advice was predicated on the personal knowledge of a particular staff member, consultations among colleagues did occur. An advisor who did not read black fiction sought out a fellow staff member to ascertain African-American authors. In another episode, three people gave input on a follow-up to *The Color Purple*.

Despite the acknowledged differences between readers' advisory and reference interactions, the findings of Shearer's work mirror many of the concerns of researchers in the reference arena. The following aspects were problematic in many of the encounters:

- The lack of identifying cues by which patrons could identify professional librarians

- The choice of a majority of staff members to accept the user's initial question at face value and omit a reference interview

- Search failure following unmonitored referrals

- The omission of follow-up questions in the majority of transactions (Shearer 1996a)

Nassau County Study

Shearer's explorations served as the inspiration for a Master's project conducted by four graduate students of the Queens College Graduate School of Library and Information Studies: Catherine Patricia Lackner, Anne K. May, Elizabeth Olesh, and Anne Weinlich Miltenberg. Our study, titled "An Investigation of Readers' Advisory Transactions in Nassau County (NY) Public Libraries," investigated whether actual practice in public libraries replicated the terms of engagement for model readers' advisory encounters set forth by the experts. To this end, each of the fifty-four independent community libraries or library districts of Nassau County (which abuts New York City and has a population of approximately 1.3 million) was visited by one of the researchers posing as a readers' advisee.

Methodology

The study encompassed the following research questions:

- What was the role of the readers' advisor in his or her interaction with library patrons?

- To what extent did the designated library personnel conduct a comprehensive readers' advisory?

- What professional tools did readers' advisory personnel utilized?
- Would the advisor query the advisee about her personal domains of reading?
- Would the advisor ask the advisee about a book she had read and really enjoyed?
- Would the readers' advisor elicit the elements of appeal of a particular book or genre?

(Another research question involved the manner and extent of passive readers' advisory service. For a report on these findings, see May, Olesh, Miltenberg, and Lackner 2000.)

Each researcher was provided with a script for the library visit (Figure 7.1) and an extensive worksheet to fill out at the completion of each readers' advisory encounter (Figure 7.2). These materials were carefully designed to elicit qualitative research findings in answer to the research questions.

Upon entering each library, each researcher positioned herself in the fiction stacks and waited to see whether a librarian or other staff member would approach offering assistance. Saricks and Brown (1997) called for libraries to be proactive and station personnel in the fiction area to aid patrons. In only one instance did a staff member approach a researcher; at all other times, the researcher had to initiate contact with a librarian to ask for reading guidance. The advisee sought out the point of service closest to the library's main entrance and asked, "Is there a librarian who can help me find a good book?" After being directed to the appropriate staff member, the investigator restated the purpose of her visit. She then observed and evaluated the quality of service using the criteria of experts such as Mary K. Chelton (1993), Catherine Sheldrick Ross (1991), Joyce G. Saricks (1997), Kenneth Shearer (1996a, 1996b), and Duncan Smith (1993).

Script for Library Visit

i. Enter library and proceed to fiction stacks. Roam about for 5 minutes. Are you approached by staff member offering assistance? Pose the inquiry described in step iii.

ii. If not approached by the staff member in step i, proceed to point of service nearest main entrance to library. Ask at desk if there is a librarian who can recommend a good book

iii. Ask staff member in fiction or individual to whom you are directed in step ii if s/he knows of a good book. Does s/he conduct a readers' advisory interview? Does s/he ask you what you last read and enjoyed? If so, offer up *Memoirs of a Geisha*. If not,

Continued on next page

keep track of what this individual asks and try to interject the aforementioned title. Does s/he dismiss you and point you toward the stacks?

If asked why you liked *Geisha*, here are suggested answers:

(a)   it was well written and absorbing

(b)   it was historical and informative

(c)   it gave insight and knowledge into a world off limits and not well known

(d)   it was escapist fare but more substantial than junk reading

(e)   the characters were well developed

(f)   it was a good story mainly populated by women

iv.   If asked what you read and like, say you read eclectically—fiction, historical fiction, biographies, and mysteries. You just want to be entertained but do not read garbage.

v.   Take note of advisor's attitude. Is s/he inconvenienced by query, impatient, etc., or is s/he generally happy to be of assistance? Does s/he get sidetracked and attempt to help other patrons while attending to you?

vi.   Does advisor utilize readers' advisory tools? Does s/he instruct you in their use?

vii.   Does s/he consult with other colleagues?

viii.   Does s/he proffer booklists or bookmarks for your use?

ix.   Does s/he suggest or recommend?

x.   What titles does s/he enumerate? Does s/he booktalk or summarize the works?

xi.   Does s/he come with you to the stacks for retrieval?

xii.   Think about your general satisfaction with the transaction. Rate advisor on attitude, attentiveness, and nature of his or her response.

Figure 7.1: Script for Library Visit

Sample Library Worksheet

Area of Study	Finding	Description or Comments
General Information		
Date and time of visit	11/9/98 1:20 pm	
Size of library (small, medium, large)	small	
Size of population served	small	
Activity level of library during visit	slow	
Fiction Stacks		
Was a staff member stationed in the stacks?	no	Library is so small that the reference desk is situated close to the fiction stacks.
Did s/he approach you?	no	
What was the method of approach?		
Readers' Advisory		
What locational point of service did you approach to ask for a "good book"?	circulation	
What was the attitude of the respondent?	friendly	
Where were you directed?	reference	

Continued on next page.

Area of Study	Finding	Description or Comments
Did the staff member conduct a formal readers' advisory interview?	no	Reference desk attendant wore a tag identifying her as a librarian. She asked what I read—mystery? Reply: "I read everything." I was pointed to a display of critically acclaimed first works—she told me to pick one (FYI: This display was in a 2-sided carrel near the entranceway—the side hosting the display was not obvious upon entry). I returned and said: "What else do you suggest?" She posed no questions and I offered up *Geisha*. The librarian said she hadn't read it and by the time it would get to her off the reserve list she'd be old and gray (now she's in her 30s or 40s). She walked me to the new fiction and started pulling works off the shelves. She asked if I read Cornwell or Mott Davidson (mystery writers). I had previously explained that I was looking for more literary works. She handed me *Cave Dweller* (Dorothy Allison) and *Mannequin* (J. Robert Janes). The latter she said was set in France. She said she read Ian Rankin and liked his mysteries and pulled his latest off the shelves.
Did s/he ask: • What book you read last and enjoyed? • Why you enjoyed that book?	no	
• Which genres you typically read? • What types of books/ stories you enjoy?	yes (didn't use term *genre*)	Asked what I read but ignored answer that I wasn't particularly interested in mysteries.
Did s/he consult with other staff members during the course of advisement?	no	

Area of Study	Finding	Description or Comments
Did s/he employ readers' advisory tools? Which ones? Were you instructed in the use of these tools?	no	
Did s/he make a suggestion or a reading recommendation? How was the suggestion phrased? Which titles were suggested? (enumerate) Were the suggested titles booktalked or summarized?	yes no	First I was steered to a display titled "Best First Novels Chosen by LJ as Novelists Worth Watching" and told to choose a book. I returned and insisted on additional aid. Cornwell and Mott Davidson were mentioned in passing. I was handed *Cave Dweller*, *Mannequin*, and the new Rankin. Rankin was recommended based on the librarian's personal reading preference. *Cave Dweller* and *Mannequin* were handed over with the comment "How about…?" The mystery writers were mentioned as possibilities.
Were you given any booklists, bookmarks, annotated bibliographies, etc.? (enumerate)	no	
Describe the attitude and attentiveness of the advisor. Did s/he attend to you exclusively or conduct other business with other patrons and colleagues?	 I was attended to exclusively.	The librarian seemed a bit bothered by my request and somewhat dismissive. First she pointed me to the display—but I persisted and insisted upon additional service. I only got the attention I ultimately received because I refused to be deterred. I checked out two titles and the circulation clerk queried: "What are you doing here so far from your home library?" She remarked something to the effect: Why would you come here? You're a patron of a much larger institution.

Continued on next page.

Area of Study	Finding	Description or Comments
Calculate the time spent with you.	5 minutes	
How busy or taxed was the point of service rendering RA?	untaxed—I was only patron	
Promotion/Passive RA		
Were there any posters or fliers advising patrons of the availability of RA?	no	
Were there any posters or fliers advising patrons of book clubs or literary discussion groups sponsored by the library?	no	Oprah's Book Club Selections posted by dictionary stand
Shelving: • Were books shelved by genre? • Interfiled with genre spine labels? • Shelved by interest categories?	yes	Separate shelving: mystery and romance Interfiled works with spine labels: sci-fi, western, and additional romance novels
Was a bestseller list posted? Where?	yes circulation	
Were readers' advisory tools kept accessible by the fiction stacks?	no	
Were there any displays/exhibits of books by category or special* interest?	yes	Display of critically acclaimed first works (inconspicuously located); cart of Spanish fiction (sign in foyer referring to these works)

Area of Study	Finding	Description or Comments
What handouts were available for patrons? (e.g., bookmarks, booklists, annotated bibliographies, etc.) From which point of service were they displayed and/or distributed?	yes	Bookmark bibliography (no annotations) of fiction re: engineers and engineering (located among community handouts at circulation desk)
Does the library subscribe to NoveList or other readers' advisory databases for the use of patrons on premises?	not mentioned	
Does the library post a Web page?	yes	
Are readers' advisory services mentioned on Web page?	no	
Are there links to other readers' advisory resources?	no	
Does the library enable patrons to utilize readers' advisory tools (e.g., NoveList) online?	no	

Figure 7.2. Sample library worksheet

For purposes of this study, all advisees read *Memoirs of a Geisha* by Arthur Golden and stated that it was the most recent book they had enjoyed. This title was chosen because it represented the author's only extant fiction. The multicultural nature of the work gave rise to the possibility of ethnic steering: Would staff recommend only novels with Asian themes or with Asian authors, or would they launch a full-fledged readers' advisory interview?

Each investigator also gauged the attitude and patience of the readers' advisor with her query. Under consideration was whether the readers' advisor devoted his or her attention to the investigator or became distracted by other patrons and colleagues. The researchers examined how the advisor went about the transaction: Did he or she consult with colleagues, use professional tools, or employ any other methodology? The advisees noted whether the staff member suggested a range of titles, leaving the matter of choice to the patron , or whether the advisor recommended titles and foisted them on the patron.

Findings

Despite the geographic difference and a time differential of four years, our study supports many of Shearer's findings. In most instances, it was not readily apparent whether the person fielding the request held an MLS degree. Personnel wore no tags that identified their academic credentials; in only five facilities did staff wear name tags or sit by signs marked "librarian on duty." In most instances, investigators could only attempt to discern the professional from the paraprofessionals by explicitly asking whether the specified staff member was a librarian.

The response by staff to the reading guidance query varied. Reactions ranged from delight to trepidation to bafflement to downright dismissal of the request for a good book. In some instances, advisees were welcomed with remarks such as "You've come to the right place" or "I'm so excited to find someone who reads." But in other locations, the personnel were simply unreceptive. For instance, one reference librarian remarked, "That's a tall order," when asked for a "good read." The manner and body language of particular staff members conveyed irritation. Their attitude proclaimed that the demand was atypical and somewhat inconvenient. In certain encounters, the researchers received the message that the reference desk was to be consulted only as a last resort. One staff member asked an advisee why she had not looked at new fiction or consulted the *New York Times Best Seller List* before enlisting the staff member's aid. Another staff member summarily dismissed a researcher and told her to consult the Cardex (which turned out to be the OPAC), while yet another staff member referred a researcher to a display of acclaimed first works.

Many librarians and paraprofessionals seemed uncomfortable with our requests for advice. One librarian remarked, "You know, this is the query the reference desk dreads," and another muttered under her breath, "I hate this question." In several cases, clerks or library aides were far more eager to help investigators than their professional counterparts. In a facility that had no full-time librarian, a staff member approached an advisee in the fiction stacks and offered assistance. Four clerks cheerfully aided her for at least fifteen minutes. At the conclusion of the interchange, one clerk remarked, "Wasn't that fun?" In at least three encounters, the circulation clerks provided suggestions about authors or titles that were comparable to those the reference librarians suggested. Moreover, in each instance, these staff members continued to assist the advisees even after they had been referred to the reference desk.

Our study and those of Shearer and his colleagues have found no compelling reason why readers' advisory work must be the exclusive domain of librarians:

> [W]e have at this time, no evidence that readers' advisory work must be conducted by professionals. Their performance does not seem better on average, than nonprofessionals. To be sure, the worst transactions were conducted by nonprofessionals, but so were some of the very best. (Shearer and Bracy 1994, 457)

In fact, certain librarians referred the advisees to circulation clerks because the aides were more voracious readers or because the paraprofessionals recalled information that the librarians could not remember.

The formal comprehensive readers' advisory interview as the experts envisioned was not fully performed at any of the Nassau County encounters. Unlike the Shearer researchers, we did not immediately ask for a book "like" a designated title. Instead, we initially asked for "a good book" and waited for the staff member's response. In the vast majority of transactions (80 percent), personnel probed our general domains of reading. They asked questions such as "What kinds of books do you read?" or "What kinds of books do you like to read?" However, in only one instance did a staff member ask an investigator what exactly it was about the types of books she read that brought her enjoyment.

As in Shearer's research, staff members almost never asked questions on the appeal of works. They never probed into which elements were critical to our selection or appreciation of fiction. At one large library, a staff member said that a reading recommendation would depend on what authors the advisee read, yet she never specifically asked the advisee which writers she followed. The "ice breaker" question ("What was the last book you read and enjoyed?") was posed on only two occasions. And even in these two interviews, staff members failed to elicit further information regarding the specifics of the book's appeal.

All too often library personnel remarked on their own reading preferences instead of listening to their clientele. Comments included: "I only read Mary Higgins Clark," "I only read mysteries," or "I only read nonfiction to keep up with the reference desk." Such responses underscored the evidence that many staff members were under the misapprehension that in order to recommend a particular genre, they had to read in that genre. Even more problematic were statements by certain personnel that they didn't read or they "hadn't the time to read."

In many instances, the advisor's inquiry into the patron's reading tastes was perfunctory. Frequently the staff member opened the interview by asking, "Do you read mysteries?" before mapping the advisee's other domains of reading. This is contrary to model practice. Each readers' advisory transaction should center on the client. Of paramount importance are the *reader's tastes, values, and wants.* Although we spoke of reading eclectically, on many occasions the advisors suggested as suitable selections the types of works they themselves were enamored of. Although many staff members made appropriate recommendations, these reflected the staff members' own reading preferences rather than a professional approach to answering the query, "What do I read next?" In one of the most outlandish encounters of the study, a librarian who read primarily nonfiction suggested a book on the Shroud of Turin as a successor work to *Geisha.*

Just as in the Shearer study, we had to take the initiative by providing information that a formal readers' advisory interview should have elicited. In the great majority of transactions, we cued the advisors by offering *Memoirs of a Geisha* as the last book read and enjoyed. Only one librarian rose to the task and asked, "What was it that you exactly liked about the book?" Others commented instead, "I haven't read it," or "I've heard of it," or "You're unlikely to find another novel as well written." In every episode, it was incumbent upon us to elaborate upon the novel's merits. We commented on the literary nature of *Geisha* and our desire for well-written fiction with a female protagonist. Our investigators also emphasized an interest in works with a multicultural focus or works featuring women in exotic locations. What we asked for was a window into a world that was foreign to the advisees' everyday experience.

The majority of the staff members we consulted did not unthinkingly recommend books by Asian authors or with Asian motifs as follow-ups to the Golden work. Nonetheless, they suggested many books with Asian or Asian-American protagonists, such as *Snow Falling on Cedars*, *Middle Son*, and *Still Life with Rice.* But other encounters were not so satisfactory and evidenced a ritualized, almost knee-jerk reaction to the query. At one library, the staff member's only recommendation was James Clavell, author of *Shogun.* During another exchange, the reference person retorted, "I suppose you've read all of Amy Tan," and at yet a different library, the librarian declared, "Well, there's always Pearl Buck." Certain librarians took an alternate tack and recommended female authors who depicted female protagonists, such as Fay Weldon, Olivia Goldsmith, and Anne Tyler, without heeding the multicultural component of the request.

The list of suggested or recommended titles and authors was many and varied. Surprisingly, there was little duplication among the works and authors proffered by the fifty-four libraries. Mentioned as possible reading selections were 134 different titles from *All Over but the Shoutin'* to *Yellow Raft in Blue Water* (see Figure 7.3). Two advisors even promoted *Geisha* before the investigator could interject that it was the last book read. Sixty separate authors were championed, from Alice Adams to Fay Weldon (see Figure 7.4).

Consultation was frequent, and book recommendations were often a collegial enterprise. Staff members called in others to help them, and on certain occasions personnel chimed in their ideas without even being solicited. In several encounters, bystanding patrons added their commentary to the ongoing interchange.

Much of the time (44 percent of all transactions) titles were plucked from the new fiction racks. At one library, volumes were foisted upon the patron with the librarian taking the attitude, "I know what's good for you," and limiting the researcher to her two handpicked selections. At another facility, the librarian responded to the initial inquiry for a good book by exclaiming, "I can help you." Without even launching an interview, she pulled *The Poisonwood Bible* by Barbara Kingsolver off the shelf. When the researcher asked for additional choices, the librarian responded, "What's wrong with this?" Some staff members suggested titles on the basis of their popularity among their library's clientele, while others relied on book reviews in proposing titles. One idiosyncratic librarian recommended the works of Judy Blume because he knew and liked her as a person. A few advisors used an amalgam: personal experience, popularity, and critical acclaim as benchmarks for their recommendations. In large measure, staff relied on their own intuitive knowledge to the exclusion of all other methodologies in fielding requests for book suggestions.

Titles Suggested/Recommended As a Follow-up to *Memoirs of a Geisha.*

Title	Author	Number of Suggestions/ Recommendations
Cold Mountain	Frazier, Charles	7
Snow Falling on Cedars	Guterson, David	4
Black and Blue	Quindlen, Anna	3
Divine Secrets of the Ya-Ya Sisterhood	Wells, Rebecca	3
Paradise	Morrison, Toni	3
Summer Sisters	Blume, Judy	3
The Most Wanted	Mitchard, Jacquelyn	3
A Monk Swimming	McCourt, Malachy	2
Breath, Eyes, Memory	Danticat, Edwidge	2
Charming Billy	McDermott, Alice	2
Evening Class	Binchy, Maeve	2
Memoirs of a Geisha	Golden, Arthur	2
Snow in August	Hamill, Pete	2
Stones from the River	Hegi, Ursula	2
The Color of Water	McBride, James	2
The God of Small Things	Roy, Arundhati	2
The Midwife	Courter, Gay	2
Visitors	Brookner, Anita	2
Women of Brewster Place	Naylor, Gloria	2
A Lesson Before Dying	Gaines, Ernest J.	1
A Patchwork Planet	Tyler, Anne	1
A Perfect Crime	Abrahams, Peter	1
A River Sutra	Mehta, Gita	1
A Thousand Acres	Smiley, Jane	1
All Over but the Shouting	Bragg, Rick	1
Angela's Ashes	McCourt. Frank	1
Angels in a Harsh World	Bradley, Don	1
Apaches	Carcaterra, Lorenzo	1
Are You Somebody?	O'Faolain, Nuala	1
Bastard out of Carolina	Allison, Dorothy	1
Black Leopard	Voien, Steven	1
Breaking News	MacNeill, Robert	1
Bridget Jones' Diary	Fielding, Helen	1

Title	Author	Number of Suggestions/ Recommendations
Brimstone Wedding	Vine, Barbara	1
Cambridge	Phillips, Caryl	1
Circle of Friends	Binchy, Maeve	1
Collector of Hearts	Oates, Joyce Carol	1
Corelli's Mandolin	De Bernieres, Louis	1
Damage	Hart, Josephine	1
Damascus Gate	Stone, Rogert	1
Darkness Falls	DelVecchio, John	1
Death at the Crossroads: A Samurai Mystery	Furutani, Dale	1
Dinner at the Homesick Restaurant	Tyler, Anne	1
Empire of the Sun	Ballard, J. G.	1
Europa	Parks, Tim	1
Firebird	Graham, Janice	1
Flowers in the Blood	Courter, Gay	1
Foreign Studies	Endo, Shusaku	1
Greatest Generation	Brokaw, Tom	1
Green City in the Sun	Wood, Barbara	1
Hacks	Wren, Christopher S.	1
Herb and Lorna	Kraft, Eric	1
Hill Towns	Siddons, Anne Rivers	1
Homecoming	Plain, Belva	1
Homeplace	Siddons, Anne Rivers	1
In the Deep Midwinter	Clark, Robert	1
In the Time of the Butterflies	Alvarez, Julia	1
Inn at Lake Devine	Lipman, Elinor	1
Kagami	Kata, Elizabeth	1
Kowloon Moon	Theroux, Paul	1
Ladder of Years	Tyler, Anne	1
Lenoir	Greenhall, Ken	1
London	Rutherford, Edward	1
Lovers and Friends	Marechetta, Camille	1
Mannequin	Janes, J. Robert	1
Middle Son	Iida, Deborah	1

Continued on next page.

Title	Author	Number of Suggestions/ Recommendations
Miracle Cure	Palmer, Michael	1
Mirage	Khashoggi, Soheir	1
Mommy Dressing	Gould, Lois	1
Mona in the Promised Land	Jen, Gish	1
Moon Cakes	Louie, Andrea	1
My Heart Laid Bare	Oates, Joyce Carol	1
Native Speaker	Lee, Chang-Rae	1
On Gold Mountain	See, Lisa	1
On the Occasion of My Last Afternoon	Gibbons, Kaye	1
Once upon the River Love	Makine, Andrei	1
Out of Nowhere	Mortman, Doris	1
Past Caring	Goddard, Robert	1
Possession	Byatt, A. S.	1
Princess: A True Story of Life Behind the Veil in Saudi Arabia	Sasoon, Jean	1
Ramses Series	Jacq, Christian	1
Reign of the Favored Women	Chamberlin, Ann	1
Rise of the Euphrates	Edgarian, Carol	1
Serenity of Whiteness	Hong, Zhu	1
Seventh Heaven	Hoffman, Alice	1
Shining Through	Isaacs, Susan	1
Short History of a Prince	Hamilton, Jane	1
Smilla's Sense of Snow	Hoeg, Peter	1
Spending	Gordon, Mary	1
Spring Moon	Lord, Bette Bao	1
Still Life with Rice	Lee, Helie	1
Stone Diary	Shields, Carol	1
Switcheroo	Goldsmith, Olivia	1
Tai-Pan	Clavell, James	1
Tell Me Your Dreams	Kingston, Maxine Hong	1
The All-True Travels and Adventures of Lydie Newton	Smiley, Jane	1

Title	Author	Number of Suggestions/ Recommendations
The Beekeeper's Apprentice	King, Laurie R.	1
The Book of Blam	Tisma, Aleksandar	1
The Chimney Sweeper Boy	Vine, Barbara	1
The Country Ahead of Us, the Country Behind	Guterson, David	1
The Dieter	Sussman, Susan	1
The Essence of the Thing	St. John, Madeleine	1
The Fifth Queen	Ford, Ford Maddox	1
The First Eagle	Hillerman, Tony	1
The Fourth Estate	Archer, Jeffrey	1
The Game of Kings	Dunnett, Dorothy	1
The Handmaid's Tale	Atwood, Margaret	1
The Holder of the World	Mukherjee, Bharati	1
The Hundred Secret Senses	Tan, Amy	1
The Joy Luck Club	Tan, Amy	1
The Kindness of Women	Ballard, J. G.	1
The Kitchen God's Wife	Tan, Amy	1
The Last Hostage	Nance, John	1
The Lazarus Child	Mawson, Robert	1
The Liar's Club	Karr, Mary	1
The Lives and Loves of a She-Devil	Weldon, Fay	1
The Midwife's Advice	Courter, Gay	1
The Pagoda	Powell, Patricia	1
The Poisonwood Bible	Kingsolver, Barbara	1
The Secret Book of Grazia dei Rossi	Park, Jacqueline	1
The Shell Seekers	Pilcher, Rosamunde	1
The Stillest Day	Hart, Josephine	1
The Street Lawyer	Grisham, John	1
The Troublesome Offspring of Cardinal Guzman	De Bernieres, Louis	1
The Undertaker's Widow	Margolin, Phillip	1
The Vampire Armand	Rice, Anne	1
The Voyage of the Narwhal	Barrett, Andrea	1

Continued on next page.

Title	Author	Number of Suggestions/ Recommendations
The Wind-up Bird Chronicle	Murakami, Haruki	1
The Woman Warrior	Kingston, Maxine Hong	1
Tripster Monkey: His Fake Book	Kingston, Maxine Hong	1
Tuesdays with Morrie	Albom, Mitch	1
Two for the Devil	Hoffman, Allen	1
White Mare's Daughter	Tarr, Judith	1
Yellow Raft in Blue Water	Dorris, Michael	1

Figure 7.3. Titles suggested/recommended by library staff as a follow-up to *Memoirs of a Geisha*.

Authors Suggested/Recommended As a Follow-Up to *Memoirs of a Geisha.*

Author	Number of Suggestions/ Recommendations
Cornwell, Patricia	4
Siddons, Anne Rivers	3
Carr, Caleb	2
Clavell, James	2
Davidson, Diane Mott	2
Goldsmith, Olivia	2
Kingsolver, Barbara	2
Mahfouz, Najib	2
Mitchard, Jacquelyn	2
Quindlen, Anna	2
Weir, Alison	2
Adams, Alice	1
Auel, Jean M.	1
Blume, Judy	1
Brookner, Anita	1
Brown, Sandra	1
Buck, Pearl	1
Conroy, Pat	1
Cussler, Clive	1
Dereske, Jo	1
Dickens, Charles	1

Author	Number of Suggestions/ Recommendations
Forsythe, Frederick	1
Fraser, Antonia	1
George, Elizabeth	1
Gibbons, Kaye	1
Godwin, Gail	1
Gordon, Mary	1
Greene, Graham	1
Gregory, Philippa	1
Hillerman, Tony	1
Hoffman, Alice	1
Holt, Victoria	1
Howatch, Susan	1
James, P. D.	1
King, Laurie	1
Kingston, Maxine Hong	1
Lord, Bette Bao	1
MacMillan, Terry	1
Matthiesen, Peter	1
Mayle, Peter	1
McCullough, Colleen	1
Meyers, Annette	1
Michener, James	1
Morris, Mary McGarry	1
Morrison, Toni	1
Parks, Tim	1
Perry, Anne	1
Perry, Thomas	1
Piesman, Marissa	1
Plain, Belva	1
Quick, Amanda	1
Ragen, Naomi	1
Rankin, Ian	1
Renault, Mary	1
Rendell, Ruth	1
Rice, Anne	1
Rolvaag, O. E.	1
Tan, Amy	1
Tyler, Anne	1
Weldon, Fay	1

Figure 7.4. Authors suggested/recommended by library staff, without regard to specific titles, as a follow-up to *Memoirs of a Geisha*.

It also appeared that the advisors were reluctant to resort to professional tools to satisfy the readers' advisory query. Only 46 percent of the librarians employed such tools, and most often the online catalog was the tool of choice, which the librarians employed in three ways: to locate titles and /or authors with whom staff members were familiar, to find "related titles," or to conduct a keyword search. In several instances, personnel used the OPAC to determine whether Golden had written another book. Beyond this, few staff members utilized any other print or electronic readers' advisory resources, and they consulted no Web sites whatsoever with readers' advisory content. But even when they employed tools, they provided no bibliographic instruction. Instead, staff members tended to search the OPAC or use other resources without offering a minimum of education or even mentioning the name of the tool to the researcher. This practice continued even when the advisee explicitly asked the staff member for instruction.

In forty-eight instances, researchers received the advisor's undivided attention. There was a minimum of competing distractions inasmuch as the visits took place when libraries were relatively quiet. In the majority of libraries, staff members accompanied the investigator to the stacks to retrieve the reading matter. In one library, a staff member excused herself without explanation and did not return for more than five minutes. The researcher was in a quandary as to whether to stay or go. The librarian eventually returned with four titles collected from the older fiction shelves. In certain encounters, the advisors remained at the service desk and pointed the patron in the direction of the new stacks, the OPAC, or the print catalog.

The time spent in each encounter varied. In 92 percent of the interactions, the time spent with the librarian ranged from less than five minutes up to fifteen minutes. In most instances, the interchange was over once the books were recommended. But on rare (two) occasions, the researchers engaged in extended dialogues with the advisors. In these instances, the patron and librarian shared their likes and dislikes and discussed the various emotions that particular titles evoked.

The amount of effort that library staff members expended on behalf of the query differed markedly. Some suggested one or two books or authors and made no further contributions. In general, the majority of staff members tried to render assistance. But as the preceding anecdotes show, their expertise and confidence varied considerably. Regardless of the personnel's knowledge of specific titles and/or authors or their reliance on memory or use of professional tools, almost all investigators left each library with reading matter. The vast majority of the time, the staff suggested titles and left it to the patron's discretion to accept or reject these selections. It has been deemed far less threatening to talk with a reader and suggest a range of books than to take the responsibility for recommending something the advisor thinks is appropriate (Saricks and Brown 1997). At only four libraries were no titles suggested whatsoever. At one facility with no full-time librarian on the premises, the clerk on duty ended any and all discussion with, "Sorry, I can't help you," after admitting she hadn't read *Geisha*.

The degree of affability of staff members varied also. At one large library, a staff member who refused to be of assistance apologized for not being able to help. In contrast, an adult services librarian who devoted much time and effort to reading guidance was remorseful about not being able to do more. Certainly personnel who were pleasant and well meaning made a more favorable impression than those who seemed burdened and put off by the request for advice. If the researchers perceived condescension or irritation in the encounter, they considered the readers' advisory transactions unsatisfactory, regardless of the suitability of the suggested materials. This finding replicated Shearer's results—the attitude and congeniality of the advisors were more important to advisees than the appropriateness of the selected titles. "The problems exhibited in the least successful transactions…have much more to do with inappropriate business etiquette (such as not acknowledging a waiting patron's presence) than subtleties relating to advisory transactions" (Shearer and Bracy 1994, 457).

Surprisingly, only three of the persons consulted asked the investigators to return and tell them how they liked the suggested works. This observation of little follow-through was also consistent with Shearer's work. One of the librarians interested in establishing an ongoing dialogue was the person who foisted two and only two books on one of the researchers. Another was a professional who emoted a consuming love of books. She suggested works that she had read and savored and praised the advisee for being a reader. This transaction epitomizes how the readers' advisory interchange may exist as a forum in which to display an unabashed adoration of books. Says Shearer, "Reading is such a solitary activity that readers have few opportunities to express why they like what they like; the expression of recollected reading pleasure and the sharing of that pleasure with the staff appears to enhance user satisfaction—satisfaction with both the staff member who asks the question and listens attentively to the answer and also with the library" (Shearer 1996a, 18). But in stark contrast, another librarian warned, "Don't blame me if you don't like the book."

Conclusions

In this information-centric age, one must reemphasize a fact that remains constant: recreational reading is still the most common rationale for public library visits. "Leisure, hobby and self-improvement" items make up the majority of circulated materials (Berry 1993), thus indicating an important role for readers' advisory services in all public library systems. It appears from the Nassau County library visits that many of the public libraries have retreated from this mission. In fact, our study found no formal institutionalized readers' advisory protocol among the observed encounters. Rather, its findings "underscored that a nonmethodical, informal and serendipitous response was the norm to a patron's request for a 'good read.' This [was] an approach that at times, serve[d] patrons brilliantly but more often offer[ed] unprofessional and unsatisfactory service" (May, Olesh, Miltenberg, and Lackner 2000, 43). It is a sentiment with which Shearer would certainly agree. Despite the differences of time and place between the two studies, both groups of researchers had remarkably similar experiences.

Whither readers' advisory? Our research and that of Shearer highlight long-existing problems in the delivery of this service. However, both qualitative studies were exploratory in nature and did not entail systematic, repeated visits with each library. In general, we based our findings on random samples involving one or two of each facility's staff members. The readers' advisory service we received was dependent on the person we consulted and perhaps that person's disposition on a particular day. Nonetheless, we discerned certain overall trends.

In order to follow up these trends and investigate new, related avenues and issues, additional research involving more extensive fieldwork is needed. In this manner a more accurate picture may emerge of the way reading guidance is facilitated among the public libraries in North Carolina; Nassau County, New York; and all across our nation.

Whether the provision of readers' advisory has improved since the two studies is questionable. Certainly, recent articles indicate that our public libraries need to expend more effort in this arena (Fialkoff 2000; Smith 2000a). The profession can and must do better. Public library staff members must take the pledge and recommit themselves to providing better readers' advisory service. What better place to begin than with a revitalized readers' advisory transaction? Libraries must do more than pay lip service to experts such as Chelton, Ross, Saricks, Shearer, and Smith. Their tenets must be put into action. We owe our most important constituents, the recreational readers, at least that much.

References

American Library Association, Readers' Advisory Committee, Collection Development Section, Reference and User Service Association (RUSA). 1997. Readers' Advisory Reference Tools: A Suggested List of Fiction Sources for All Libraries. *Reference Quarterly* (Winter): 206–9

Berry, John C. III. 1993. Most People Come for the Fun of It. *Library Journal* 118 (October 15): 6.

Chelton, Mary K. 1993. Read Any Good Books Lately?: Helping Patrons Find What They Want. *Library Journal* 118 (May 1): 33–37.

Crowley, Terrence. 1985. Half-Right Reference: Is It True? *Reference Quarterly* 25 (Fall): 59–68.

Dewdney, Patricia, and Catherine Sheldrick Ross. 1994. Flying a Light Aircraft: Reference Service Evaluation from a User's Viewpoint. *Reference Quarterly* 34 (Winter): 217–30.

Durrance, Joan. 1989. Reference Success: Does the 55 Percent Rule Tell the Whole Story? *Library Journal* 114 (April 15): 31–36.

Fialkoff, Francine. 1997. Reader's Advisory. *Library Journal* 122 (March 15): 48.

———. 2000. A Plea for Reading. *Library Journal* 125 (May 15): 74.

Gers, Ralph, and Lillie Seward. 1985. Improving Reference Performance. *Library Journal* 110 (November 15): 32–35.

Herald, Diana Tixier. 2000. *Genreflecting,* 5th ed. Englewood, CO: Libraries Unlimited.

Lackner, Catherine Patricia, Anne K. May, Anne Weinlich Miltenberg, and Elizabeth Olesh. 1998. *An Investigation of Readers' Advisory Transactions in Nassau County (NY) Public Libraries.* Master's project, Graduate School of Library and Information Studies, Queens College, Flushing, NY.

May, Anne K., Elizabeth Olesh, Anne Weinlich Miltenberg, and Catherine Patricia Lackner. 2000. A Look at Reader's Advisory Services. *Library Journal* 125 (September 15): 40–43.

Ross, Catherine Sheldrick. 1991. Readers' Advisory Service: New Directions. *Reference Quarterly* 30 (Summer): 503–18.

Saricks, Joyce G. 1997. Readers' Advisory Training: Why and How. *Booklist* 94 (November 15): 544–45.

Saricks, Joyce G., and Nancy Brown. 1997. *Readers' Advisory Service in the Public Library*, 2d ed. Chicago: American Library Association.

Shearer, Kenneth. 1996a. The Nature of the Readers' Advisory Transaction in Adult Reading. In *Guiding the Reader to the Next Book*, ed. Kenneth Shearer, 1–20. New York: Neal-Schuman.

———. 1996b. Reflections on the Findings and Implications for Practice. In *Guiding the Reader to the Next Book*, ed. Kenneth Shearer, 169–83. New York: Neal-Schuman.

Shearer, Kenneth D., and Pauletta B. Bracy. 1994. Readers' Advisory Services: A Response to the Call for More Research. *Reference Quarterly* 33 (Summer): 456–59.

Smith, Duncan. 1993. Reconstructing the Reader: Educating Readers' Advisors. *Collection Building* 12, nos. 3–4: 21–30.

——. 2000a. *Talking with Readers: A Competency Based Approach to Readers Advisory Service*. Reference and User Service Association (RUSA) (December 2000) [Preprint].

——. 2000b. *Librarians and Libraries: Growing Readers' Advisory Services in the New Century*. Presentation at the Readers' Advisory Preconference of the Public Library Association, Eighth National Conference, Charlotte, NC.

CHAPTER 8

Advisory Services in the School Library Media Center

Carol A. Doll

Introduction

The fundamental distinctions between readers' advisory services in a school library media center and readers' advisory elsewhere arise from a single, but important, difference: the setting. A school library media center functions within, and is always part of, a school community. This context, which brings both challenges and rewards, is unavoidable. And school library media specialists must, first and foremost, function as members of that school community.

The main function of a school is to educate youth to become tomorrow's adults. The media specialist works with teachers, administrators, students, and parents toward that goal. By collaborating with teachers to develop and deliver the curriculum, the media specialist enhances that curriculum with information literacy skills. By working with administrators to develop and maintain a quality school library media program, the media specialist provides a foundation for the curriculum. By teaching and leading students, the media specialist helps to develop lifelong learners. This job can be overwhelming, frustrating, and infinitely rewarding.

Readers' advisory is one of the many professional skills that the media specialist employs to educate students. This skill has long been recognized in the national standards, including those for 1998, *Information Power: Building Partnerships for Learning*, which addresses readers' advisory in this way:

> Library media programs are justly proud of their long tradition of providing reading, listening and viewing guidance to students and others in the learning community. Strong and imaginative activities that promote reading have always been a staple of program offerings, and over the years, the program's focus has expanded to promote critical viewing and listening skills as well. These core abilities of reading, viewing, and listening, along with writing and communication, form the basis for developing information literacy skills that are basic for today's students. Through its promotion of the pleasure and fulfillment to be derived from using various media for both information and recreation, the library media program educates and encourages the school community in the uses of all communication tools. (American Association of School Librarians and Association for Educational Communications and Technology 1998, 66)

Because of the unique setting, the library media specialist who performs readers' advisory must take into account the needs of the teachers he or she works with and the demands of the school curriculum. Readers' advisory takes place when a student searches for recreational reading or reading for school assignments. It also takes place when a teacher comes in search of material to use with a specific class or lesson. All youth librarians, in both schools and public libraries, actively work to promote reading—both recreational and educational.

Characteristics of Readers' Advisory in Schools

The most important influence on readers' advisory within the school is the curriculum. The curriculum provides the structure, goals, and objectives of teaching and learning. Consequently, the media specialist builds a collection to support this curriculum, and the media specialist does much of her readers' advisory work within a curriculum-based collection.

Ideally, in the school setting the media specialist collaborates with teachers to integrate the media center resources into lesson plans and throughout the curriculum. This partnership provides the media specialist with opportunities to promote books and reading as well as to build information literacy and research skills. (A helpful resource for learning about collaboration theory is *Interactions: Collaboration Skills for School Professionals* by Friend and Cook [1996].)

A multitude of resources that feature literature-based activities and lessons is available to both teachers and school library media specialists. These resources are useful when designing particular lessons. For example, the school library media specialist and a teacher may be planning a U.S. history lesson about pioneer life and westward expansion. Together they work to identify titles proven to appeal to many young readers, such as Patricia MacLachlan's *Sarah, Plain and Tall.* They might also add alternative titles—Gary Paulsen's *Mr. Tucket* and Elvira Woodruff's *Dear Levi: Letters from the Overland Trail,* to name a few. Besides knowing the collection, knowing the curriculum, and understanding student reading preferences, the school library media specialist must be creative and flexible enough to make multiple connections between literature and learning.

Also, to be more effective at reader's advisory, the media specialist can take time to learn about the reading preferences of students, which she can do by speaking directly with them. Professional reading (e.g., journal reviews) and informal surveys can bolster the media specialist's knowledge and provide additional information.

Today some schools are implementing resource-based instruction, whereas others use whole language reading instruction. Occasionally schools abandon traditional textbooks completely and use library books for almost the entire curriculum. Sustained Silent Reading (SSR) or a similar program for nondirected silent reading for both students and teachers is a part of the school day in some places. The media specialist can take advantage of these and other opportunities to share library materials with teachers and students. For instance, the media specialist may want to offer booktalks in the media center on a variety of titles popular among students and then leave with the teacher a book cart filled with multiple copies of those titles.

Because of the media specialist's unique role in the school, he or she has in many ways a captive audience for readers' advisory. There is the potential for every student in the school to be in the school library media center, possibly numerous times, during the school year. When collaborative planning occurs between media specialists and teachers and when they integrate media center resources into the resulting lesson plans, students must often come to the school library media center for instruction or materials. This creates a unique opportunity to reach students who would not come voluntarily. With skillful matching of resources to students, even reluctant readers return for more. For example, *The Outsiders* by S. E. Hinton, a title guaranteed to appeal to reluctant readers, works well for high school discussions of social class prejudices.

Because the media center is located in the school and therefore normally follows the school time schedule, students often do not have access to the collection, facilities, or personnel after school hours and on weekends. In addition, many school libraries have limited budgets and collections. Therefore, many students also use public library facilities. Public librarians often visit schools, especially for booktalks. Media specialists and public librarians can work together to provide the best services possible to students and teachers.

Readers' Advisory Techniques

Within the school setting, the media specialist applies traditional readers' advisory methods, while attempting to also meet the demands of the curriculum. The media center can provide book displays, reading lists, bookmarks, topical bibliographies, and book clubs in the same way that public libraries do. Although there is no mystery to readers' advisory in the school setting and no techniques have been developed specifically for the media center, the media specialist often works actively to promote reading and books. She does this by applying professional knowledge about literature, students, teachers, and the curriculum to the collection. The following techniques for building an appreciation of literature may be especially useful to the school library media specialist.

Reading Aloud

Many of us have fond memories of listening to adults read us stories when we were young, often before we could read for ourselves. Reading and sharing stories is a marvelous way to build the love of stories and prepare young children for reading. Jim Trelease's *The Read-Aloud Handbook* (1989) offers techniques to enhance this activity and tips for selecting titles to use for read-alouds. The bibliographies of suggested titles (appropriate for all ages) are a good reference for both beginning and experienced readers. In *Books Kids Will Sit Still For*, Judy Freeman also gives advice on reading aloud (Freeman 1990). More important, she includes extensive bibliographies of recommended titles separated by grade level. She also makes the point that you may not need to read the entire book; sometimes a chapter or two is enough.

But read-alouds are unfortunately too often abandoned once children learn to read on their own. The popularity of recorded books gives evidence that some people never outgrow the joy of listening to a story read aloud, and older students—even adults—have much to gain through listening to literature. The story that is shared aloud builds listening skills and naturally leads into related learning activities such as writing and discussion.

By working together, teachers and the media specialist can identify and develop topics to cover in specific lessons. Then they can select appropriate titles for reading. A high school art class could enjoy several versions of *Cinderella* as they study the variety in illustration and the various page layouts involved in creating picture books. Sixth-graders may enjoy listening to the work of Nathaniel Hawthorne or Cynthia Rylant, who are both good writers. Early elementary students enjoy listening to some of the many folktales and fairy tales available in picture books. Listening to the stories improves language and listening skills, can spark students' imaginations, and often leads them back to the books.

Storytelling

Nothing builds the love of story like storytelling. It is the most ancient form of literature and speaks to our primal human need for stories. Like read-alouds, storytelling is often relegated to primary grades and young listeners, when in fact storytelling appeals to people of all ages. In the purest form, storytelling consists of a teller, an audience, and a story. The storyteller stands in front of the audience and in a straightforward manner, without props or dramatics, narrates the story. When done in this way, teller and listeners together create a special moment that no other reader's advisory or sharing technique realizes. (And in some situations it is an advantage to be able to maintain sustained eye contact with the students.)

Listening to stories, like listening to read-alouds, increases language and comprehension skills (Peck 1989, Nelson 1989, Reed 1987). Storytelling can be part of the services the media specialist offers either directly or indirectly, through guest tellers. Media specialists, teachers, or guest storytellers can also teach storytelling techniques to upper-elementary, middle, and high school students. Such instruction is legitimately part of most school curriculums, where students should learn how to speak in public.

Storytelling often uses folktales and legends, particularly to strengthen the multicultural curriculum. But many other sources are also suitable. For example, urban legends are very popular with teens. A good source for them is the scholarly work by Jan Harold Brunvand (1981), which includes numerous tales for retelling.

Although the idea of standing in front of a class telling a story may intimidate some, anyone can be a good storyteller. A number of books are available to guide both beginners and those with more experience. The best for the traditional approach to storytelling is *Storytelling: Art and Technique* (Greene 1996), which offers solid guidance in all aspects of storytelling from story selection to story preparation to story delivery. Extensive bibliographies suggest additional professional titles for further study and stories for all ages suitable for telling. Any of the three editions (the first two done with Augusta Baker) of *Storytelling: Art and Technique* would be valuable for any storyteller.

For those who work with young children, Margaret Read MacDonald has developed a more interactive storytelling technique especially appropriate for that age. In the *Storyteller's Start-Up Book* (MacDonald 1993), she offers suggestions for finding, learning, and telling stories. MacDonald presents a method for learning stories that takes less time than the approach advocated in *Storytelling: Art and Technique*. MacDonald includes twelve stories that storytellers have used successfully with young children.

By planning together, the media specialist and teachers can identify stories that are both appropriate for telling and that meet the needs of teachers and students. For example, they might use a mystery to develop critical thinking and problem-solving skills. With any age student studying Native Americans, stories from the individual tribes could be shared orally in the way of Native tellers. For upper-elementary grades, some of the satires of traditional fairy tales, such as *The True Story of the Three Little Pigs* (Scieszka 1989), could strengthen the classroom curriculum by inspiring students to write their own version of the tale. Urban legends would be suitable for a high school speech class as one model for delivering a speech.

The New York Public Library has published *A List of Stories to Tell and Read Aloud* (New York Public Library 1990). This list contains titles that library storytellers have used successfully with children. In addition, subject and cultural indexes facilitate finding stories for particular topics such as food, plants, winter, Tibet, Native Americans, or Jewish culture.

Not all school library media specialists have the time or the desire to be storytellers. In that case, it is often possible to identify others who are willing to tell stories to students. Contact a local university, college, or community college. Often faculty in education or library and information science know about storytelling and can identify local storytellers. Staff members at the local public library may also be able to suggest people.

Readers' Theater

In readers' theater, students enjoy the drama of a story while participating in telling the tale. Unlike traditional drama, readers' theater does not require participants to learn lines, wear elaborate costumes, or create complicated sets and props. Instead, using a script, students assume roles and read their lines in an informal group. Some readers' theater scripts are based on traditional folktales, fractured fairy tales, true stories, historical events, or literary classics.

Again, one can tailor this technique to curriculum needs. It is easy to see how a readers' theater performance on the signing of the U.S. constitution, for example, might complement a history lesson, making it come alive for students.

Although readers' theater is especially useful with older students whose reading skills have been developed, other sources (for example, *Multicultural Folktales: Readers Theatre for Elementary Students* by Barchers [2000]) are specifically for beginning readers. Students can even create their own readers' theater scripts, basing them on a book they have read for a class assignment. However students use them, readers' theater scripts provide an effective way to actively involve students in reading while building comprehension and oral presentation skills.

Booktalks

Most young adult librarians, children's librarians, and media specialists are aware of the value and power of booktalking. Basically, booktalking is an infomercial for books and other materials. The media specialist should work with the teachers to identify pertinent topics, such as the environment, mysteries, or the American Revolution. Then the media specialist, using her knowledge of the students and the materials in the school library media center collection, selects specific titles to present. Both fiction and nonfiction titles can be appropriate, and booktalks work best with students who can read independently.

A good booktalk will start with an introduction that prepares students to listen. Then the media specialist showcases specific titles, flowing smoothly from one to another. The media specialist may choose to discuss many titles briefly or a few titles in more depth. She may emphasize the plot, character, or mood; the book itself often suggests an appropriate approach. The intent is to share enough of the book (or audio or video recording) with listeners to entice them into reading the entire book.

Joni Bodart (1980) produced several books and one video on booktalking. In the first book, she presents complete information about preparing for, delivering, and evaluating booktalks. The later pages contain sample booktalks for specific titles. (Although Bodart has subsequently published several more books with sample booktalks, her first volume is still the most helpful for learning how to prepare booktalks.)

Another good source of information about booktalking is the chapter "Booktalking: Don't Tell, Sell" in Patrick Jones's manual on working with young adults in libraries (Jones 1998). Jones is very successful at working with young adults, and his advice is practical. Appropriately, his main emphasis is how to design the booktalk to "hook" listeners.

One of the most helpful short pieces on this topic is the article by Mary K. Chelton titled "Booktalking: You Can Do It" (Chelton 1976). This is quite valuable for the concise, useful guide it gives to potential booktalkers. Among the practical tips, she reminds booktalkers not to wait until the last minute to prepare, to carefully state the title and author of each book, and not to oversell average books. Although the article addresses public librarians who might be visiting schools, the content is equally appropriate for media specialists.

Anne Guevara and John Sexton (2000), also public librarians, share their experiences in booktalking to middle school students. Their work has dramatically increased the communication and cooperation that occurs between their public library and the local media specialists and teachers. One technique Guevara and Sexton have found especially useful is to prepare a bookmark-style bibliography listing the titles they have discussed. The booktalker gives this bookmark to the students, the teachers, and the media specialist (or the public librarians, when school personnel give the booktalk).

By collaborating with teachers to develop lesson plans, the media specialist will find many opportunities to use booktalking with students. Booktalking can alert students to some of the gems of the collection and may even make the required reading more enjoyable. In a high school literature class, a booktalk featuring classics of British literature such as *Wuthering Heights* may help students understand the book's appeal. For upper-elementary students studying Colonial America, a booktalk could make them more aware of the wide array of historical fiction and fact available to them. Junior high students may have a different view of the environment and be ready to start work on reports after a booktalk emphasizing that topic.

As in public libraries, booktalking in the school library media center is a good way to let students know how much fun reading can be.

Author Visits

Meeting the author or illustrator of a favorite book can be a thrilling experience for a young reader. Although few (if any) schools have the resources to fly J. K. Rowling in from England, many more affordable options are available to the media specialist. Finding local authors or illustrators to visit, e-mailing them, or setting up a virtual visit on the Internet are just some of the creative ways to connect young readers with professional writers or artists. (Publishers will sometimes arrange for an author or illustrator to visit the school when they are on tour to promote their latest book.) East (1995) provides all the information you need to plan and execute a successful author or illustrator visit from the initial decision to invite someone to the final thank-you letter.

Schools with Internet access can also take advantage of the many online author and illustrator resources now available through publishers, book clubs, and booksellers (for example, Penguin Putnam Young Readers Web Site [URL: http://www.penguinputnam.com/yreaders/index.htm, accessed February 2001], where color photos, booktalks, and activities accompany author and illustrator biographies). For those who lack Internet access, the traditional approach of writing to popular authors and illustrators or focusing on student favorites in author/illustrator studies can be effective as well. *Terrific Connections with Authors, Illustrators, and Storytellers: Real Space and Virtual Links* (Buzzeo and Kurtz 1999) offers guidance in connecting with and creating meaningful links between bookpeople and children and young adults.

As with the techniques discussed previously, author and illustrator visits can certainly enhance the curriculum. Many publishers now provide curriculum guides to go along with their books. For example, after a visit from Deborah Hopkinson and reading her book, *Birdie's Lighthouse*, students built their own papier-mâché lighthouses, complete with rocks at the base and flashing lights (Buzzeo and Kurtz 1999). (Note: These curriculum guides contain valuable information and can be very useful, but they are also intended to sell the author's work.) Some authors and illustrators have Web sites and have also created curriculum guides to accompany their books (for example, Jan Brett's home page, URL: http://www.janbrett.com [Accessed February 2001], features craft projects and cyber-postcards to send to friends by e-mail). Working together, media specialists and teachers should turn up more possibilities for curriculum connections in science, math, social studies, art, music, or language arts.

Book Clubs

Book clubs provide young readers an opportunity to interact freely with each other by discussing a book all of them have read. Book clubs may be either a part of the curriculum or an individual enrichment activity for volunteer students. In the simplest format, the school library media specialist selects a book for the club, students read the book, and then all attend a meeting and share their opinions of the work. The media specialist must be prepared to both initiate and guide discussions. Usually she compiles a list of questions before the book club meets. It may also be necessary to provide multiple copies of the titles selected for reading.

The Association for Library Service to Children guidelines for book clubs provides basic information for starting and running a book club. Often one of the most challenging tasks for the school library media specialist is leading the discussion. Setting rules for student interaction (such as asking children to wait until the end of the meeting to tell whether they liked the book) and generating a list of questions before the meeting help the discussions go more smoothly. Based on her personal experiences, Ward gives tips and practical suggestions for school media specialists who want to start a book club (1998).

Creating Bibliographies

School library media specialists often prepare lists of suggested or recommended titles that both match a specific topic and are appropriate for a specific set of students. Bibliography topics may be related to the school curriculum and grow out of collaboration between teacher and media specialist, or a teacher or student may suggest them, or they may result from the school library media specialist's knowledge or interests. Useful in many ways, the lists may be formatted as a bookmark to encourage reading or as part of a bulletin board display.

When the media specialist compiles these lists, one of the first sources to consult to supplement personal knowledge is the card catalog or automated catalog for the school library media center. The main advantage of this is that the titles are already in the collection. The local public library is another source that is accessible to students and teachers, too. With sufficient lead time, the school media specialist can consult professional tools to identify specific titles to buy. The purchasing cycle often takes three to four weeks or more, so it is important to plan ahead.

Individual Guidance

One of the joys that many media specialists experience is the opportunity to talk to excited students about a book, a video, or an audiotape they have enjoyed. Some students readily share such experiences; others may be more reticent. They may share excitement about the story, awe over the recognition of self or situation in the title, or wonder about some new knowledge. Too often in schools, the main emphasis is on the lesson, and it is possible to miss this kind of excitement. But such opportunities will arise even in the midst of a very busy schedule.

The readers' advisory interview is discussed in other chapters of this book, but one should note that the key to successfully guiding students in their reading is to ask questions sensitively and listen to their answers carefully. In Chapter 14 Angelina Benedetti offers insightful suggestions on how to prompt teens to share their reading preferences, and many of these methods would be equally effective with younger students. Of course, if the book is part of an assignment, the school library media specialist must also draw upon her knowledge of the collection and curriculum.

Knowledge of children's and/or young adult literature and knowledge of children and young adults form the foundation for recommendations. Also, listening to the individual student to determine what sparked excitement is important. By blending these three things together, the media specialist can match titles and students. As with most skills, the media specialist will become more proficient with practice. Listening to students and getting feedback after they have read recommended titles offers the media specialist additional clues as to what to recommend next and what the student generally enjoys. Furthermore, by listening to the students, she may learn about other titles to read herself or to recommend to others. The joy of reading can be contagious, and individual readers' advisory is one way to spread the contagion.

It can be especially challenging (and rewarding) to do individual readers' advisory with young adults. Tom Reynolds, a young adult librarian in Edmonds, Washington, shares specific suggestions on relating to teenagers (Reynolds 1998). He makes the point that readers' advisory should be a collaborative activity—both reader and librarian should be working together to find the right book for the reader.

The following sources for identifying specific titles are useful for providing individual guidance. In addition, discussing books with other professionals (either in person or on a listserv) can elicit titles. However, most individual guidance is spontaneous. In this case, the media specialist works more effectively when she herself has read and enjoyed the books she recommends to students. That is why it is so important for her to know the collection. Some professionals keep a quick reference file with selected details about specific titles to help in making recommendations to students. By talking with students about current interests and activities, one can identify subjects for future purchases and reading.

Identifying Specific Titles

Media specialists have numerous tools that can help identify specific titles for readers' advisory. Because this chapter deals with readers' advisory for students from kindergarten through twelfth grade, obvious sources are those for children and/or young adults. The chapter also includes sources for adult titles because some high school students will be reading science fiction, fantasy, romance, or other adult genres.

General Bibliographies

Some standard, retrospective bibliographies list titles appropriate for school libraries. They are arranged in Dewey classification order. More important for readers' advisory, indexes offer subject access. The H. W. Wilson catalogs (*Children's Catalog, Middle and Junior High School Library Catalog*, and *Senior High School Library Catalog*) list only books. *The Elementary School Library Collection: A Guide to Books and Other Media* (Winkel n.d.) includes audiovisual and electronic media, too. The titles they list have been reviewed and are recommended for use with students. Most of the listings are in print and available for purchase at the time the bibliography goes to press. At the same time, the listings are generic (i.e., suggested for "Anywhere, U.S.A.," and may not meet the needs of a particular school).

When looking for suggested titles on a particular subject, such as earthquakes, dinosaurs, or Dr. Martin Luther King Jr., these retrospective bibliographies can help identify possible titles quickly. For example, the eighth edition of *Middle and Junior High School Library Catalog* (published in 2000) lists four nonfiction titles on earthquakes: *Shake, Rattle, and Roll: The World's Most Amazing Volcanoes, Earthquakes, and Other Forces* by Spencer Christian; *Earthquake Game: Earthquakes and Volcanoes Explained by 32 Games and Experiments* by Matthys Levy and Mario Salvadori; *Earthquakes* by Sally M. Walker; and *Plate Tectonics* by Alvin Silverstein, Virginia Silverstein, and Laura Silverstein Nunn. In addition, the catalog also suggests two fiction titles: *Quake!* by Joe Cottonwood and *PaperQuake* by Kathryn Reiss.

Some of the titles may already be familiar to the media specialist. If not, she can locate them in the school library media center, in a public library, or through interlibrary loan for personal examination.

Specialized Bibliographies

One of the best sources for subject access to children's picture books is *A to Zoo: Subject Access to Children's Picture Books* (Lima 1993). This work indexes thousands of picture books under topics such as fire engines, kites, and cats. This is a very complete subject access to a large number of quality children's picture books.

The Bookfinder (Dreyer 1977) offers unique subject access to children's books that deal with the issues of growing up. In addition to topics such as migrant workers and twins, the bibliography includes developmental issues such as revenge, avoiding responsibility, and homesickness. The content of the first three editions has now been reworked into *The Best of Bookfinder* (Dreyer 1992).

Some bibliographies are designed specifically for readers' advisory services. Among the most useful are the Genreflecting Advisory Series. The series suggests specific titles as "good reads." It also covers series fiction titles. Media specialists might wish to consult *Genreflecting* (Herald 2000) for work with high school students, *Teen Genreflecting* (Herald 1997) for middle school or high school students, or *Junior Genreflecting* (Volz, Scheer, and Welborn 2000) for upper-elementary and middle school students. Among the genres they include are romance, science fiction, adventure, and historical fiction. These bibliographies separate historical fiction recommendations into lists by century. There are also genre-specific titles in the series that provide more detailed coverage of individual genres.

Every year the young adult librarians of the New York Public Library revise their list of recommended books for young adult readers (New York Public Library n.d.). It is consistently one of the best bibliographies available for media specialists working with high school students. It lists fiction and nonfiction titles covering almost every topic imaginable. One of the strengths of the bibliography is that it is compiled by librarians working directly with young adults on a daily basis.

Electronic Sources

Access to electronic readers' advisory tools, such as NoveList and What Do I Read Next? is often limited by the media specialist's budget. However, a subject search of the Internet using the term "readers' advisory" results in 3,000 to 5,000 hits. Obviously, this is a topic of interest to people working with books and libraries. A few of the most useful sites are listed here. You could explore and find sites you like better than these, but the following sites would be a good beginning.

Some professional organizations maintain Web sites than can be useful for readers' advisory. Two divisions of the American Library Association (ALA) have committees that review and recommend materials for students. The Association for Library Service to Children (ALSC) has won numerous book awards (including the Caldecott, Newbery, and Coretta Scott King awards) and some media awards. The Young Adult Library Services Association (YALSA) has committees that generate lists of best books and media for young adult readers and annually bestow the Printz award. Both ALSC and YALSA post these lists and award winners on their respective Web sites. By following links through the divisions, you can access both through the ALA Web site (URL: http://www.ala.org [accessed December 26, 2000]).

Among the Web sites on children's and young adult literature in general, the one David Brown maintains at the University of Calgary is particularly good. He provides discussion boards, quick references, and multiple links to authors, stories, and resources for teachers, parents, storytellers, and (implicitly) media specialists. This site is a good source for lists of titles that have won Canadian and other international awards (URL: http://www.ucalgary.ca/~dkbrown/index.html [accessed December 26, 2000]).

Many public libraries have Web sites with readers' advisory links for children, young adults, and adults. The Inland Library System is a three-county system in southern California serving San Bernardino, Inyo, and Riverside counties. Their readers' advisory page features links to recommended sites, including Amazon.com. Their listing was taken from a workshop handout that the Metropolitan Cooperative Library System in Los Angeles uses (URL: http://www.inlandlib.org/reference/readers.htm [accessed December 26, 2000]).

Ann Chambers Theis maintains Overbooked, a Web site for "ravenous readers." It includes multiple links for genre fiction, reviews and reviewing, and what to read next. Separate pages are available for children's and young adult readers' advisory (URL: http://www.overbooked.org [accessed December 26, 2000]).

The Salt Lake County library system has one Web page for children's books and one for teen books. Both pages provide extensive lists and links for award winners, book lists, series books, authors, and book-related items. Although a few links mandate a Salt Lake County library card for access, many links are open to the general public (URL: http://www.slco.lib.ut.us [accessed December 26, 2000]).

LM_NET is a listserv devoted to school library media programs. It has several thousand subscribers, many of whom are currently media specialists. This is a very active list, with about 100 messages per day. Many of the postings deal with problems or concerns related to the daily activities in schools or school library media centers. It is not unusual for someone to ask list members for help in identifying titles to use with students. Recent postings have solicited suggestions for picture books to use with high school students, titles for students who liked the Harry Potter books, and historical fiction for a specific time period. LM_NET listserv protocol asks the questioner to post a compilation of answers received. This makes it possible to locate these lists for readers' advisory purposes by searching the archives at URL: http://askeric.org/Virtual/Listserv_Archives/LM_NET.html (accessed December 26, 2000).

Conclusion

One of the greatest joys for school library media specialists is to share their love of literature with students. They have many opportunities to work with teachers and students to suggest specific titles appropriate for the curriculum and for enjoyment. Storytelling, booktalking, reading aloud, and individual reading guidance can all promote reading and books in the school setting. With interest in readers' advisory burgeoning and the wealth of new readers' advisory tools available, we are now better equipped to perform reader's advisory in schools. Let's get kids excited about reading, listening, and viewing!

References

American Association of School Librarians and Association for Educational Communications and Technology. 1998. *Information Power: Building Partnerships for Learning.* Chicago: American Library Association.

Association for Library Service to Children. 1981. *Programming for Children's Book Discussion Clubs.* Chicago: American Library Association.

Barchers, Suzanne I. 2000 *Multicultural Folktales: Readers Theatre for Elementary Students.* Englewood, CO: Libraries Unlimited.

Bodart, Joni Richards. 1980. *Booktalk! Booktalking and School Visiting for Young Adult Audiences.* New York: H. W. Wilson.

Brunvand, Jan Harold. 1981. *The Vanishing Hitchhiker: American Urban Legends and Their Meanings.* New York: W. W. Norton.

Buzzeo, Toni, and Jane Kurtz. 1999. *Terrific Connections with Authors, Illustrators, and Storytellers: Real Space and Virtual Links.* Englewood, CO: Libraries Unlimited.

Chelton, Mary K. 1976. Booktalking: You Can Do It. *School Library Journal* 22 (April): 39–43.

Dreyer, Sharon Spredemann. 1977. *Bookfinder: A Guide to Children's Literature About Interests and Concerns of Youth Aged 2–18.* Circle Pines, MN: American Guidance Service.

———. 1992. *The Best of Bookfinder: A Guide to Children's Literature About Interests and Concerns of Youth Aged 2–18.* Circle Pines, MN: American Guidance Service.

East, Kathy. 1995. *Inviting Children's Authors and Illustrators: A How-to-Do-It Manual for School and Public Librarians.* New York: Neal-Schuman.

Freeman, Judy. 1990. *Books Kids Will Sit Still For: The Complete Read Aloud Guide.* New York: R. R. Bowker.

Friend, Marilyn, and Lynne Cook. 1996. *Interactions: Collaboration Skills for School Professionals*, 2d ed. White Plains, NY: Longman.

Greene, Ellin. 1996. *Storytelling: Art and Technique*, 3d ed. New Providence, NJ: R. R. Bowker.

Guevara, Anne, and John Sexton. 2000. Extreme Booktalking: YA Booktalkers Reach 6000 Students Each Semester!" *VOYA* 23 (June): 98–101.

Herald, Diana Tixier. 1997. *Teen Genreflecting.* Englewood, CO: Libraries Unlimited.

———. 2000. *Genreflecting: A Guide to Reading Interests in Genre Fiction*, 5th ed. Englewood, CO: Libraries Unlimited.

Hopkinson, Deborah. 1997. *Birdie's Lighthouse.* New York: Atheneum.

Jones, Patrick. 1998. *Connecting Young Adults and Libraries: A How-to-Do-It Manual*, 2d ed. New York: Neal-Schuman.

Lima, Carolyn W. 1993. *A to Zoo: Subject Access to Children's Picture Books*, 4th ed. New York: R. R. Bowker.

MacDonald, Margaret Read. 1993. *The Storyteller's Start-up Book.* Little Rock, AK: August House.

Nelson, Olga. 1989. Storytelling: Language Experience for Meaning Making. *The Reading Teacher* 42 (February): 386–90.

New York Public Library. 1990. *A List of Stories to Tell and Read Aloud*, 3d ed. New York: New York Public Library. [Order from Office of Branch Libraries, The New York Public Library, 455 Fifth Avenue, New York, NY 10016.]

———. n.d. *Books for the Teen Age.* New York: New York Public Library. (Order from the Office of Branch Libraries, The New York Public Library, 455 Fifth Avenue, New York, NY 10016.)

Peck, Jackie. 1989. Using Storytelling to Promote Language and Literacy Development. *The Reading Teacher* 43 (November): 138–41.

Reed, Barbara. 1987. Storytelling: What It Can Teach. *School Library Journal* 34 (October): 35–39.

Reynolds, Tom. 1998. Connecting with the Young Adult Reader: A Reader's Advisory Strategy. In *Young Adults and Public Libraries: A Handbook of Materials and Services*, ed. Mary Anne Nichols and C. Allen Nichols, 107–21. Westport, CT: Greenwood.

Scieszka, Jon. 1989. *The True Story of the Three Little Pigs.* New York: Viking.

Trelease, Jim. 1989. *The Read-Aloud Handbook.* New York: Penguin.

Volz, Bridget Dealy, Cheryl Perkins Scheer, and Lynda Blackburn Welborn. 2000. *Junior Genreflecting.* Englewood, CO: Libraries Unlimited.

Ward, Caroline. 1998. Having Their Say: How to Lead Great Book Discussions with Children. *School Library Journal* 44 (April): 24–29.

Winkel, Lois, ed. n.d. *Elementary School Library Collection: A Guide to Books and Other Media, Phases 1, 2, 3.* Newark, NJ: The Bro-Dart Foundation.

CHAPTER 9

The Best Tools for Advisors and How to Integrate Them into Successful Transactions

Joyce G. Saricks

Those of us fortunate to be working librarians during this readers' advisory renaissance understand how much the unprecedented wealth of tools available to us—in electronic and print forms—has enhanced our skills and knowledge. Never have we had so much information at hand to help us answer readers' requests for "good books" or books on particular topics or books that meet their specific reading requirements. Although we use these tools extensively in preparing to work with readers—in creating lists and displays to share with readers and in exploring genres and subgenres to increase our own understanding—many of us still have difficulty using these tools effectively with readers. Even though at times we can readily incorporate the use of reference tools into the interview, as when a reader asks a factual question, on other occasions (seeking a "good book," for example) our efforts may feel stilted, and neither we nor the reader finds the inclusion of tools in the interaction satisfying or helpful.

Sharing with patrons the wealth of information at our fingertips has often proved complicated. This chapter discusses the types of tools, both commercially and locally produced, available to librarians, explores ways in which we incorporate tools in the readers' advisory interview, examines possible barriers to their successful use, and suggests ways in which we learn to use both our interviewing skills and reference resources to create truly satisfying conversations about books with readers, setting up the long-term relationships on which readers' advisory thrives.

We should never lose sight of how fascinating—and how much fun to use—these tools can be. If we enjoy using them ourselves, we can readily see how important it is to share them with readers. Just as we share the pleasure of good books that meet our readers' needs, so we should share the enjoyment and satisfaction that exploring these interesting resources provides. Long ago I admitted to being an index junkie. The more indexes or access points a reference tool provides, the happier I am using it. I love to explore new reference tools, reading about authors I know and discovering new ones. Indexes that link authors or types of books send me on lengthy and satisfying searches as I pursue leads to discover new authors—and new ways to use a particular tool. Needless to say, I am not the only one who enjoys "playing" with reference tools in this way, and it behooves us to remember that because many readers share this same pleasure, we should make an effort to introduce them to the tools as well. In my experience readers are often amazed at the range of resources we have to help them find books in their favorite genres or information about their favorite authors. Sharing these resources, showing readers new tools, and explaining how to use them should be a natural part of our interactions, whether we turn to them to answer a question or simply present them to readers as resources.

What Are Readers' Advisory Reference Resources?

What do I mean by readers' advisory reference resources or tools? These resources come in many forms—print, electronic, and even human. Any book that discusses authors and their books can be used as a readers' advisory resource, as can titles that discuss genres and subgenres and provide us with useful lists of authors and titles within these categories. Most libraries already own many tools that are valuable in providing readers' advisory. An evaluation of the reference collection and circulating 800s often reveals a broad range of books that serve as valuable readers' advisory reference sources, and one can identify and create a collection without increased funding. Many libraries own copies of *Genreflecting* or *What Do I Read Next?* and their various offspring. Electronic resources may be commercial, such as NoveList (URL: http://novelist.epnet.com [accessed December 26, 2000]) and *What Do I Read Next?* (URL: http://www. galenet.com/servlet/WDIRN [accessed January 5, 2001]), or freely available on the Web, such as Amazon.com, Bookbrowser.com, the Kent

District Library's *What's Next? A List of Books in Series* (URL: http://www.kentlibrary.lib.mi.us/whats_next.htm [accessed December 26, 2000]), and more [See Chapter 11 for more discussion of electronic resources.

Review journals increasingly make excellent readers' advisory resources. It is interesting that more and more reviews try to place books and authors within genres or in comparison to others that might appeal to the same reader.[1] Genre overviews, aimed at readers' advisory librarians, appear with regularity in *Booklist,* as do columns on romance in *Library Journal,* and on inspirational fiction—often an area in which reviews are more difficult to find—in both *Booklist* and *Library Journal.* Genre-specific journals, *Romantic Times* and *Locus,* for example, expand our horizons with reviews we might not otherwise discover and with articles of interest to readers' advisors and fans alike. The problem with using review journals as reference sources is that it is difficult to keep track of the material that appears in them. Do we ask permission and post articles, columns, or reviews for readers so that we can advertise and circulate them? Do we then keep files of useful articles? Or if we remember an interesting article on the author a reader is asking about, do we search for the citation using indexes? Most of us simply lose track of this vast amount of information. We may remember something from an article or review, but we are less likely to keep the material available for future consultation.

Do not forget the value of other staff and even readers as reference resources. What staff and patrons tell us about what they have read and what they have read and heard about authors and genres can also help expand our own knowledge. Hearsay is a valid source of information in the readers' advisory interview. If we have not read a book, we still feel comfortable sharing another reader's comments. Readers' advisory is a collaborative activity, with readers and librarians sharing their knowledge of and pleasure in books and reading. Even though we do not purposefully designate a staff member as a genre expert, we know the value of consulting the fan of a genre. Certainly the success of Fiction_L,[2] the popular readers' advisory mailing list, is due in part because librarians recognize its value as a reference source, a group of more than a thousand readers who may be able to answer our questions.

Readers' advisory librarians also make a practice of creating their own tools, taking information from all these sources and assembling it into a form designed to help readers. Every bookmark and booklist we create is a readers' advisory reference resource, one that our patrons cherish, because it reflects a concise list of materials available in this library, on a particular subject or theme. If we receive a lot of requests for legal thrillers, we create a list to hand out, rather than taking every patron through every possible reference source and creating individual lists each time the question arises.

We keep lists at our desks as well, collecting information on frequently requested topics and eventually producing something tangible to share with readers. Displays are also reference resources. We create displays that reflect the interests of readers at our libraries. We find the books through our own knowledge, suggestions from other readers, and standard print and electronic tools. We use these published, commercial tools on a regular basis to create other resources, often smaller universes of books that are easier for readers to browse.

When we first started doing readers' advisory seriously at my library in the early 1980s, *Fiction Catalog* was the premiere source of subject access to fiction. How times have changed! Not only are there more, and certainly more sophisticated, commercial readers' advisory resources that provide similar access, but a query on almost any topic posted on Fiction_L will produce dozens of appropriate titles in a matter of hours. We certainly cannot use lack of resources as an excuse for not providing full and diverse displays on interesting, popular topics or bookmarks and booklists on almost every topic our readers request.

Why Are Readers' Advisory Tools Important?

Readers' advisory reference tools serve three main purposes in addition to providing answers to the factual questions we receive daily at our service desks: They make legitimate our service and the questions we receive, they serve as memory joggers when our minds go blank, and they expand our memory. First, having a collection of resources and consulting them to answer readers' questions or to research on our own make readers' advisory service more legitimate in the eyes of some users, librarians, and administrators. The popular belief is that if there is a source to consult, these questions about fiction are just as important and quantifiable as any reference question. Even though readers' advisory is not "just like" reference, tools are valuable in that they reinforce the reference function for fellow librarians and administrators, who may need convincing that readers' advisory is a legitimate service. Patrons benefit, although perhaps subconsciously, from the understanding that they have asked a "real" question, if we consult a reference tool to answer it.

I think the other purposes are even more important. On many occasions we consult tools, not to find an answer, but simply to get our minds working so that we can find an answer. Looking at a reference source, like walking to the stacks, gets our minds working. We come across a title or an author, and this reminds us of something else that is even more appropriate in answering a patron's query. I have always said there is a magic in books; they know when we are desperate, and handling them jumpstarts our brains.

The same is true with readers' advisory reference sources. They often provide the stimulus that brings appropriate suggestions to mind. Looking up information using a reference tool focuses our minds on something other than what we cannot consciously remember; it frees our minds to make the connections that lead to useful suggestions.

Finally, as Duncan Smith has pointed out for years in his inspirational workshops, readers' advisory reference tools provide librarians with added memory. They expand our personal databases and help us offer more possibilities. We cannot read everything, and most of us cannot remember even a fraction of what we have read. Not only do these reference tools introduce us and readers to far more titles than we would encounter through our own reading, they also offer us the comfort of a safe haven, a place we can look and expect to find something that will help the reader standing in front of us. They often provide lists of authors and titles, and, based on our experience, we can identify those that are most appropriate to the question. Readers' advisory tools are not designed to replace librarians; they offer possibilities that we can help readers interpret and explore.

How Do We Use Tools in the Readers' Advisory Interview?

How we incorporate tools into the readers' advisory interview is not as straightforward as it is in the traditional reference interview. In the latter we turn automatically to reference resources; no question is correctly negotiated unless the sources we consult are cited. The outcome is usually a single correct answer, identified in an authoritative source and presented to the patron as a fait accompli. Readers' advisory transactions, on the other hand, tend to be more flexible. In fact, readers' advisory interviews are conversations about books, and the pattern they follow does not consistently reflect an established formula but depends on input from both patron and librarian. Conversations allow us more flexibility in the way we communicate with the patron and answer questions. Whether we turn immediately to readers' advisory reference resources depends on several factors: our interpretation of what the reader asks, our knowledge of areas of interest, and how the reader reacts as we offer material. We base the way we interact on the manner in which we read these signs. Thus, if in this conversation, I discover that a patron is interested in—or might enjoy—a genre I read regularly, I may be more comfortable simply going to the shelves to discover suggestions. My personal knowledge provides enough depth so that I can offer a range of titles and let the reader choose. On the other hand, if the reader has read extensively in a genre I am not especially familiar with, I may recognize early on that I need the expanded memory and knowledge that reference tools afford. Consulting sources and introducing them to this reader are the next logical steps. Incorporating sources in this conversation can fit comfortably into the pattern.

Although we cannot easily define readers' advisory questions, they seem to fall within four basic types: those that request factual information (for example, all titles by an author, the next book in a series, or the series that features a particular character), those that seek reading suggestions within a particular genre or subgenre, those that require authors similar to an author read and enjoyed, and those who are simply looking for a good book to read. Obviously these overlap, and we are often not certain what type the reader has asked because readers are often not certain themselves until we explore their needs in more depth in the readers' advisory interview. However, examining each type and the ways we might incorporate tools to help answer helps us understand better how we can use tools in the readers' advisory interview.

When readers ask us reference-type questions—the author of a series featuring a particular character, or the titles of a series in order, or even a list of mysteries set in Seattle—we readily turn to reference sources and offer the reader the information as well as an introduction to a potentially useful source. We all have favorite sources we turn to in order to answer these questions, and as we consult them, we introduce them to readers, allowing them to see a collection of resources they might also browse through or consult on their own. However, the interaction does not end there; the next step is to go to the shelves to find the books. Here, the interview may change and veer in any of a number of directions: The reader may find a book and leave satisfied; the reader may have read all of that series and want something similar; or the reader may have read all by that author and be tired of it, seeking instead something quite different. What else might that person read? As in reference, even the most straightforward-sounding query may lead in other, more complex, directions before the patron leaves with books in hand.

Other readers ask for reading suggestions in a particular genre. They may identify the genre—I have often had readers' requesting suggestions in the mystery or fantasy genres by name—or they may talk about authors they enjoy and ask, not for books "just like" those authors write, but for other titles within the genre. Here again we can often turn comfortably to reference sources, especially if the reader asks about a genre with which we are not as familiar. We may consult *Genreflecting* (Herald 2000)—or other genre-specific titles in the *Genreflecting* series—for example, to determine whether it covers the genre or subgenre, as these tools offer excellent descriptions. Is this the kind of book the patron seeks? If so, which authors does the resource list? We go from lists to the stacks, helping readers discover books they might be in the mood to read. On the other hand, we may be familiar with the genre, and in the stacks, we might be able to select and describe a number of titles or authors, again allowing the reader to make choices about which books to take. The reader may have asked for a type of book popular at the library, one for which we have developed our own annotated booklist. We share that with the reader, too, using it to supplement commercial reference tools and our suggestions in the bookstacks. All these become elements in this ongoing conversation about books and reading.

Related to these readers are students who come to the desk with an assignment to read on a particular topic or a book set in a particular time period. They trust us more if we can turn to the reference tool first, before we give them the book that is most accessible and easiest to read or that meets all their other stated and unstated requirements. If we pull that information off the tops of our heads, it may not seem good enough for a class assignment. This is the time to consult the books.

Readers seeking authors "just like" others they have enjoyed present us with a more difficult task. Unfortunately, there seems to be no reference tool sophisticated enough to discover what the reader enjoys about a particular author and then to make appropriate suggestions of other authors. Providing an answer to this kind of question requires excellent interviewing skills, perceptive interpretation of the nuances in the reader's responses to suggested titles or types of fiction, an intuitive grasp of what the reader is really requesting, and a knowledge of the collection at hand. However, readers' advisory tools do help us conduct this type of interview and offer possibilities. Personally I distrust those sources that offer long lists of authors "just like" someone else. What elements of the author's writing and appeal are they comparing? Subjects? Style? I much prefer sharing an electronic source such as NoveList, which, although the matches are limited to similar subjects, allows the librarian and the reader to see and choose what to match. For example, a patron might look at a Tom Clancy title and choose, from among the headings that describe Clancy's books, "adventure," "suspense," and "techno-thrillers" as those that represent what the patron enjoys. Selecting these categories results in a list of twenty-three titles that match all three elements—and a much longer list of matches of one or more of those subjects. Readers, once they discover this kind of source, can move from author to author and heading to heading, exploring possibilities.

Examples of print sources that offer similar access are those created by Jean Swanson and Dean James, *Killer Books: A Reader's Guide to Exploring the Popular World of Mystery and Suspense* (Swanson and James 1998), and *By a Woman's Hand: A Guide to Mystery Fiction Written by Women* (Swanson and James 1996). Although they include a selection of authors covered only in the mystery and suspense genres, Swanson and

Dean often offer suggestions of additional authors to read, in each case including the appeal aspect they are matching. For example, at the end of the article describing Susan Isaacs, this paragraph suggests possibilities for further reading: "Readers who have enjoyed the work of Isaacs might try the suburban sleuths created by Valerie Wolzien and Jill Churchill. Those looking for witty satire might try the works of Sarah Shankman and Sharyn McCrumb" (Swanson and James 1996, 115). We librarians often use these print and electronic sources to create our own lists of authors whom fans of a favorite popular author might enjoy. The key, of course, is that none of these lists provides exact answers for readers. They simply offer possibilities readers might try on their own or after consultation.

In addition, readers who ask for "good books" or recommendations of something to read are often reluctant to consult reference sources or even to allow us to do so. They appreciate personal suggestions, not lists from reference sources. (And if we provide a list to answer a question, the patron's first question is usually, "Which ones have you read?") For this reader, consulting a reference tool creates far too much fuss; he becomes uncomfortable if we make a production out of answering his question. He is not certain that the question is legitimate, and he certainly does not want to advertise his inability to find a book on his own. Although he has asked the most difficult question we encounter, we know even if we had tools sophisticated enough to help us answer this, such a patron will likely not be pleased if we immediately start looking in books or databases for suggestions.

This type of question underlines the nature of the readers' advisory interview as a conversation about books. We talk with readers generally about books that they have read and enjoyed. Are they in the mood for that or something different? Many readers enjoy this opportunity to talk about books that have given them pleasure or met a particular need in their lives. We go from their comments to suggestions—from the print and electronic tools or perhaps from the displays or booklists to the shelves and possible book suggestions.

Readers simply looking for something to read are often put off if we turn immediately to a reference source rather than automatically making suggestions or at least going to the bookstacks to talk about books. Luckily, browsing in the stacks often stimulates our memory of something that might work. Then we might suggest that, if the reader has a little time, she try this new resource. Readers are unlikely to discover reference tools and use them on their own. Offering them as part of our routine in handling questions means they may also eventually become comfortable using them on their own and in conjunction with the interview.

For example, I had a reader chatting at the desk, wondering whether she had read all of Maeve Binchy's books. She liked Binchy a lot; did I think there might be some she hadn't read? This was clearly a request for me to accompany her to the stacks to determine which of Binchy's books were in. I took along our bookmark, "While You're Waiting for Rosamunde Pilcher's *Winter Solstice*" because I knew Binchy was suggested as a possibility for readers wanting Pilcher's book. Perhaps one of the other authors would work for this reader, too.

Needless to say, the reader had read all Binchy's books, so we started down the bookmark list with Barbara Delinsky. Walking through the stacks—a time of inspiration for patrons and librarians alike—she commented that she had grown up in Montana and really liked books about the West. We sidetracked to NoveList, selected some titles set in Montana, and left it printing while we picked up another booklist on display—"Murder in Mountain Standard Time." She liked the setting but not the idea of mysteries (although she left clutching the bookmark). In the meantime we talked about time periods. Because the stories did not have to be contemporary, I also gave her an author I thought she might find as accessible as Binchy but who writes of women in the historical West: Jeanne Williams. From the NoveList printout, we also selected an Ivan Doig novel, so she left with two books and three lists (a bookmark, an annotated booklist, and a printout from an electronic source). She came back the next week to tell me how much she liked the author I had given her—and luckily she remembered the name because I did not even remember the transaction—and we found her more of Williams's books. She would be away for a few weeks, she warned me, but she would be back for more. All and all it was a successful interview, and even though the author she wanted to read more of came from my own reading experience, I am not certain I would have thought of her without the intervening activities: walking in the stacks, referring to lists we had created (using readers' advisory reference tools), and working with a reference tool to create a list aimed at the reader's specific interests.

What Problems Do We Encounter Using Tools?

Although the previous discussion reflects ways in which we might regularly incorporate tools in our readers' advisory interviews and how some of us do, there are also problems, perceived barriers to using reference sources. A number came to light as the result of a survey I posted on Fiction_L on October 27, 2000.

One problem is our perception that many readers do not expect us to turn to resources to answer their queries. Some even expect us to have read and be able to recall details from all the fiction in the library. Others indicate that any "trouble" needed to discover the answer is unnecessary; their question is not that important. Just as readers often do not think they have asked a real question, they do not expect to find books or electronic sources that might help. On the other hand, more than one librarian suggested that by offering reference tools we might seem to be passing patrons off to books rather than providing the personal service that is the hallmark of readers' advisory. Balancing the personal attention with the more structured use of resources is clearly problematic.

Another issue is that complex electronic resources require training for us to use them comfortably with readers. If we and our staff are not comfortable using them and if we have not explored the range of materials we can find in them, we are less likely to share them with patrons. The same applies to print resources. We are much more likely to share a source we are familiar with and have explored on our own—or one in which we have previously found answers. Staff training would help all of us, and one librarian commented that better instructions for the electronic tools, or perhaps training for patrons at her library, would make them more useable and more frequently consulted. All responded that they wished they and their staff used available resources more effectively in working with readers.

Placement of reference materials can also pose a barrier. For example, one respondent reported that most of the readers' advisory is done at the circulation desk, yet the commercial tools are in the reference department. Unless readers are lured to the reference area to continue their inquiries or provided with locally produced materials that advertise the additional resources available, they are certainly not benefiting from the library's resources. Even if the books are nearby, they may be in a reference section that seems intimidating and uninviting. Even more problematic is the necessity of a computer to access electronic resources. These may be available only at the service desk, or there may be one or two computers throughout the library that provide access to this and many other resources.

What Strategies Easily Increase the Use of Tools?

One of the most important elements of the readers' advisory interview, regardless of whether we use reference resources, is that we are offering possibilities and seldom precise, single answers to queries. Librarians who are accustomed to acting as go-betweens, helping readers evaluate the material provided by tools or by suggestions, incorporate tools more readily into their interactions with readers. Our job is not to turn a patron loose with a reference book or electronic resource and leave him to his own devices, although we may certainly get him started, leave him to browse, and then return to help sort out the material discovered. Readers' advisory tools greatly expand the material we can offer a reader, but readers still benefit from the skills of the trained readers' advisor who can help evaluate the material found.

Another strategy is to place readers' advisory reference tools in proximity to the fiction collection, making them available in an area where patrons are comfortable exploring them. Chairs and tables where readers can sit and browse create an atmosphere conducive to enjoyable explorations. However, it also helps to advertise their presence. In the survey one librarian commented that she highlights two popular mystery reference resources, *Detecting Men* (Heising 1998) and *Detecting Women* (Heising 1999), for example, by placing signs in the mystery collection directing readers to their reference collection. They serve as a reminder that there are reference books to consult and/or browse, sources of interesting information for the fan. Electronic tools readily available on computers are certainly inviting to patrons, who might come across them by serendipity. Increased visibility of tools and the products we create using them—bookmarks, booklists, and displays—enhance their usability.

Once they discover readers' advisory reference sources, many readers love them and return to use them again and again. Readers come to the desk regularly, asking to see that book we used to find mysteries set in Chicago or that computer program that had the plot summaries and allowed them to match books with similar subjects. And, with increasing frequency, they request a reprint of the list of books in a particular series. They admit we printed it last week or earlier this week, but they left it at home. Although introducing readers to tools may sometimes remove librarians from the equation of helping them find satisfying books to read, the tools also provide another way in which readers make a connection with librarians as they share what they have discovered.

What Are the Best Tools?

The best readers' advisory reference tools are those we are most comfortable using, those that open the collections to readers and librarians alike. They may be print or electronic resources, commercial or locally produced, but they are the ones we use most frequently for our own searches and to help patrons. Based on our staff and clientele, these may differ widely among libraries. We all have our favorites, and as patrons become more familiar with what is available, they develop their own favorites as well.

Should we be concerned if tools are not part of every interaction? In readers' advisory work, the emphasis is on the interaction, on the process. Through the interview, we discover what the reader seeks and we offer suggestions from what we know or what we discover using reference tools. Neither print nor electronic technology is sophisticated enough to allow for the nuances implicit in most readers' advisory interviews. Tools serve as adjunct members in the interaction, not the focus they often become in reference interviews.

On the other hand, it seems clear that all of us could benefit from discovering ways to include these tools more frequently in our interactions with readers. As we use tools, we expand readers' knowledge and our own. The more we use the tools, the more we learn about how they can help us and the range of information available. We need to develop conversational gambits that lead naturally to reference sources. We might say, as I have, "If you're like me, you'll enjoy browsing through these, too. But come and talk with us; tell us what you like about the books you found as well as the tools you used."

In introducing patrons to tools, we should remember to offer our assistance as intermediaries. Have we really helped a fan of legal thrillers if we simply provide a list of fifty authors and titles to explore? Of course not. Our expertise allows us to help narrow that list, either by choosing other search terms or by offering our own knowledge of the authors or titles listed. Although tools are useful when they open readers to the possibilities available, too many possibilities are no better than none at all. And how can we rely solely on reference sources to answer that mom who is looking for fantasy books for her two young teenage boys? No list will take into account the mother's concern about finding titles without too much sex, but a librarian as intermediary can help limit lists and reassure the parent.

What might we do to make better use of these tools to enhance our readers' advisory interviews and service? Certainly sharing them with readers whenever appropriate helps. One of our goals as readers' advisors is to create a long-term relationship so that readers are comfortable coming back over and over, no matter what they have in mind to read. With these readers especially, it is a good idea to make them aware of the possibilities. They may not always want to talk with us. Where else might they find some suggestions? Do we make bookmarks and booklists readily available to patrons? Do readers know that there are books that explore genres and subgenres, that provide fascinating information about authors and their books, that suggest similar authors? Is everyone on our staff comfortable using these tools? Staff awareness and comfort are almost as important as that of patrons. We are less likely to offer tools that we are uncomfortable using or have never successfully used ourselves, so training should certainly be a priority.

Readers' advisory work is done best by sensitive listeners who can read the nuances in readers' responses to suggestions and techniques. It is not surprising that these are likely the best on our staff at integrating tools into interviews and knowing when that may not be the best direction to pursue. The best readers' advisory service provides trained staff who interact intelligently in these conversations about books with readers. No matter how much we read, we can never keep up with the diverse reading tastes of all those who use our library; we collect reference tools to help us expand our own knowledge and to provide the best possible service to readers.

Notes

1. A good example is Bill Ott's review of Robert Littell's *Walking Back the Cat*. He writes that in this book "you'll find a fine mix of Tony Hillerman atmosphere, le Carre psychology, and RossThomas plotting" (Ott 1997, 1967). Those comparisons help us place the title and give us clues on how to describe both book and author to readers.

2. To subscribe to Fiction_L, send an e-mail message to requests@ maillist.webrary.org with *one* of the following commands in the subject or body of the message:

    subscribe fiction_l (to subscribe to the regular list)

    subscribe digest fiction_l (to subscribe to the digest)

    Within an hour you should receive the Fiction_L welcome message. If you do not receive it or if you have questions about the list, please contact Natalya Fishman, Fiction_L manager, at fladmin@webrary.org.

References

Heising, Willetta L. 1998. *Detecting Men: A Reader's Guide and Checklist for Mystery Series Written by Men*. Dearborn, MI: Purple Moon Press.

———. 1999. *Detecting Women: A Reader's Guide and Checklist for Mystery Series Written by Women,* 3d ed. Dearborn, MI: Purple Moon Press.

Herald, Diana Tixier. 2000. *Genreflecting,* 5th ed. Englewood, CO: Libraries Unlimited.

Ott, Bill. 1997. Review of *Walking Back the Cat,* by Robert Littell. *Booklist* 93 (May 15): 1567.

Swanson, Jean, and Dean James. 1996. *By a Woman's Hand: A Guide to Mystery Fiction Written by Women,* 2d ed. New York: Berkley Books.

———. 1998. *Killer Books: A Reader's Guide to Exploring the Popular World of Mystery and Suspense*. New York: Berkley Books.

CHAPTER 10

"No, Thanks—I'd Rather Do It Myself": Indirect Advisory Services

Nora M. Armstrong

Think about the last time you went to the video rental store: You may have gone in with a definite idea of the movie you wanted to see, but maybe you didn't have a specific title in mind. You just knew you were in the mood for a certain kind of story. When you walked in, large posters greeted you, advertising the latest arrivals, which were arranged in their own section. The store was organized into different areas: action/adventure, comedies, family films, kids' videos and games, and so forth. There might have been a display area featuring staff favorites or a seasonal theme. You may have found a catalog or perhaps even a computer terminal through which you could browse to identify all the movies of your favorite director or actor. Somewhere near the checkout register there was probably a board alerting you to the movies that were going to be released in the near future. Popcorn, candy, and sodas were available for purchase right near the registers—impulse-buy items, located where they would sell most effectively. As you left you might have picked up a flyer full of short blurbs about new releases, whetting your appetite and urging you to keep coming back so you could enjoy all those marvelous stories. Even if you didn't rent exactly the movie you'd come in for, the odds are that you did not leave that store empty-handed. And most likely, you did not ask any of the staff for help—there was enough information available to you as it was.

Guess what? The same thing happens in libraries. We do offer nonmediated assistance to our users. Short of buying refreshments at the checkout desk (although with the rising popularity of coffee shops attached to libraries, even this is changing), people can enter a library today in search of a story and walk out with one—be it in the form of a print or e-book, videocassette, DVD, or book-on-tape—to satisfy their needs or desires, all without asking a single staff member for help.

There are many reasons that someone in search of a story at the library does not seek direct help from staff members. It may be that he already knows exactly what he wants and is able to find it himself. More often, however, he may be unsure of exactly what he's looking for. It is also remotely possible that he is already aware of the tools and aids available to help him in his quest. Then there is the pervasive attitude (in the profession as well as among the general public) that questions concerning recreational reading/listening/viewing are less serious than strictly informational queries and are therefore unworthy of the staff's attention and time (Shearer 1998). Nevertheless, the mere fact that a member of the public has chosen to enter the library makes him just as much a client as if he walked up to any service point and asked for assistance, and we have an obligation to serve his need. What are librarians doing to help this person in his search, short of direct mediation?

This is a quick overview of the current state of what can be called, for want of a better term, indirect advisory services—that is, anything short of a one-on-one transaction between library staff and users that helps those users find their way to the next enjoyable narrative experience. Some may be tempted to think of these techniques as passive, but there is nothing passive about them; indeed, many of them are labor-intensive, even if the work that goes into their creation and implementation is not immediately obvious to the casual eye. Many of them have to do with effective marketing of library collections, whereas others address the more social, interactive aspects of the narrative experience and its aftermath. Some work; some do not. But "doing something is more effective than doing nothing" (Chelton 1993, 35). As the growing interest in advisory services over the last ten years or so demonstrates, more and more librarians are electing to do something.

The techniques and tools that library staff members use are remarkably similar to those found in a video store or, for that matter, a bookshop. They include displays, printed lists, notices of upcoming releases, and finding aids in both print and electronic formats. Like bookstores, libraries also host story-centered events, such as author appearances and book discussion groups. A relatively new addition to the library repertoire is the creation of adult reading programs, long a staple in children's departments, but only now being deployed to reach grown-ups. Some libraries are even offering customized service, using a reader profile that tailors a list of materials to the individual patron. Using a combination of tools and techniques increases the likelihood that library users in search of a story will leave the building satisfied.

The most obvious method of indirect assistance is to build displays of materials and to place them at strategic points in the library, where patrons are most likely to see them. They need not be elaborate or fancy, nor should they be so large that their size is daunting to the viewer. The most difficult step in creating a display is deciding on a theme and location and maintaining it once it has been put up.

The two most logical places for displays are at the entrance to the library itself and near the collections. A popular entrance-area display is a new-book shelf, where users can browse the latest additions to the collection. Another is the returns cart; this gives the visitor the opportunity to see what others have been reading and perhaps feel "safe" in choosing from those titles. (A British study showed that up to 50 percent of circulation in the authors' library came from the books on returns carts [Van Riel and Fowler 1996].) The fact of a book's newness or of its recent return is the only unifying factor in these kinds of displays.

For displays near the collections, librarians usually work from a more definite theme, and these can come from anywhere. Many of them are seasonal in nature: holidays, seasons of the year, designated months (such as women's history month or Black history month), or a current event such as an election or the World Series. A display can highlight a certain genre or subgenre of literature—for example, cozy mysteries or nonfiction survival stories. Some of the most ingenuous themes for displays come from one's colleagues, near and far. I gratefully acknowledge the contributions of the members of the Fiction_L listserv, an e-mail loop dedicated to reader's advisory. In my two years on the list, I have been amazed and delighted at their collective wisdom, creativity, and generosity. An example of all three qualities is a list compiled for a display of nonfiction men's adventure stories—"Manly Men Doing Manly Things Manfully." Fiction_L rocks!

Some displays incorporate more than one kind of material: "Seen the Movie? Read the Book" is a common theme. One of the best recommendations is to place a book truck of older books in plain sight with a sign reading, "Good Books You May Have Missed" (Saricks and Brown 1989).

Another location for displaying materials is on the endcaps of the stacks; this is a very easy way to show off items. It gives the browser the chance to see the cover of the book, to pick it up and flip through it, and decide whether she wants to take it home with her. This kind of display need have no theme and is easy to maintain; staff members merely keep an eye on the endcaps and refill them when they are empty.

How big are these displays? A standard recommendation is that they be made up of at least twenty-five but no more than fifty items (Baker 1999). If there are not enough materials, the user may bypass the display altogether; if there are too many, the user may feel overwhelmed by the number of items to choose from. The best practice is to keep the display stocked, but not overstocked. Leaving one or two spaces purposely empty helps to send the message that taking an item out is allowed. More than once a patron has asked me whether it is okay to do so. The answer is always, "Absolutely—that's why they're there."

Some displays are intrinsically ongoing, such as the new-materials shelf, but others are meant to stay up for a limited amount of time. The most effective displays stay up for two to four weeks. Any less, and regular users may miss them; any more, and they may seem like permanent fixtures that garner less than the desired amount of attention (Baker 1999).

Booklists and Bookmarks

The creation of booklists and bookmarks is another way librarians can help their customers find stories that appeal to them. These do not need to be elaborate or overlong; something as simple as posting the bestseller lists from the *New York Times*, *Publishers Weekly*, or *USA Today* is a common practice. Many libraries keep lists of Oprah's Book Club titles on hand, and *Booklist* regularly runs a feature of "After Oprah" read-alikes that many librarians print out and distribute.

Patrons widely use and appreciate read-alike lists of any kind. Someone who enjoys cozy mysteries, for example, will be glad to see a list of authors and titles that are similar to those she's already read and liked. Providing her with a list of this kind is an effective way to help her find a story that satisfies her tastes. Such a list can be created in conjunction with building a thematic display, then kept on hand, periodically updated, and available for patrons. Librarians also customize ready-made lists: When the Modern Library published its list of "best fiction of the twentieth century," some librarians used it as the basis for a display and created bookmarks with all the titles, marking all those that their library systems owned.

Subscribing to book-oriented periodicals is another common practice. Magazines and newspapers such as *Publishers Weekly* and the Sunday editions of the *New York Times* and the *Washington Post* are chock-full of reviews and articles about books and the book industry and are valuable resources for library customers. *Library Journal* and *Booklist* are useful not only to library staff but also to their patrons for news and reviews. *Book*, a monthly magazine aimed at the recreational reader, contains reviews and information about books and authors. And rest assured, if it's been reviewed in *People*, customers will seek it out! These sources examine not just print books but audiobooks and videos, too, and *Publishers Weekly* now includes regular reviews of e-books.

A number of genre-specific periodicals focus on customers interested in specific kinds of stories. Science fiction and fantasy readers can rely on reviews published in a magazine such as *Locus*, which enjoys a solid reputation for reliable, informed opinions. *Romantic Times* is a good source for romance readers to find out about forthcoming books in that field. A significant advantage of having this kind of resource available is the lack of (perhaps inadvertent) sneering or condescension toward a specific genre that may be apparent in more mainstream publications. The genre fan is assured that the creators of the magazine are not going to look down their noses at the fan's tastes and that the information is reliable because the writers and editors understand the appeal and conventions of the genre in question.

Aside from periodicals, librarians rely on printed guides to literature. With the burgeoning interest in advisory services, this is a growing field, and it seems that every issue of *Library Journal* or *Booklist* contains a review of at least one new title. An article in the 1996 Winter/Spring issue of *Reference Quarterly* lists an exhaustive bibliography of these resources at three levels of completeness: core, expanded, and comprehensive. It has served as the basis for many librarians to develop an advisory reference collection (Readers' Advisory Committee, Collection Development Section, RUSA 1996).

One of the most helpful practices is to place these printed materials as close to the collection as possible. A common practice is to situate a service desk near the fiction stacks, for example, where the staff keeps a copy of *What Do I Read Next?* (a guide to genre fiction that is published biennially), as well as the quinquennial *Fiction Catalog* and its annual supplements. Keeping these materials out where the public can see and look at them, perhaps with a sign to indicate this, is a way to encourage their use. There's a trick involved, though: Library users are not necessarily accustomed to seeing, let alone using, the tools for finding a good story in a library. It is the job of the library staff to arrange these materials so that their visitors know about them and feel comfortable using them. Some libraries feature them on a table or shelf at the entrance to the stacks so that they are hard to miss. A small display of relevant periodicals in this space is also helpful.

In order to keep track of their own reading, many library staff members keep a reader's notebook for themselves or their department, a simple and easy way to remember the books they have read and their general impressions of them. This is also a very useful tool for clients if the staff puts the notebook out where the public can leaf through it. Title, author, date of publication, a very short synopsis, and an indication of whether the reader liked the book—this is all the information necessary for the browser. The amount of interest something as easy as this can generate is surprising—and gratifying.

There are electronic resources that patrons can use on their own, too. Now that most libraries have automated catalogs, it is not uncommon to find a computer catalog terminal—or several of them—near the collection. Patrons are then able to determine for themselves whether the library owns the materials they are interested in borrowing. As well, the overwhelming majority of libraries are now connected to the Internet, and numerous sites are devoted to helping people find a good story; some are available by subscription, but many more are free. Without discussing the merits of these, it is important to mention them because they are such a valuable resource, and letting customers know about them is a good practice. A list in the form of a small flyer or bookmark that customers can take away with them lets them know of sites that they might not otherwise have learned about. Some sites have created their own bookmarks and will provide them to libraries for the price of postage.

If the library has access to an online subscription service (for example, NoveList or the electronic version of *What Do I Read Next?*), placing a computer terminal with an Internet connection near the collection, with a short set of instructions for accessing and using the service, proves helpful to patrons. This way they can do their own searching if they like. Providing a direct link or icon on the screen to a free megasite such as Amazon.com or IMDB (a movie database, URL: http://www.imdb.com [accessed December 26, 2000]) helps them make use of these resources. (I wonder how much more likely a patron reluctant to ask for advisory help would be to request assistance in using the catalog or a PC terminal. My experience is that if the question is technology-related, people are much more likely to ask for help. Again, I believe this speaks to patrons' perception of the "frivolousness" of questions about recreational reading.)

In order to help patrons find and enjoy a story, librarians are developing a new kind of tool, the reader profile. This is a short questionnaire that the patron can fill out and give to the staff; the questions include the all-important "Tell me about a book/movie that you enjoyed," as well as other questions designed to help identify elements that appeal to the patron (genre, location, characters, setting, etc.). Armed with this information, staff members then use the tools at their disposal and build a customized list of materials likely to meet the patron's tastes. Although this involves mediation on the part of library staff, I include it in the list of indirect advisory services because of the minimal contact between the patron and the librarian—indeed, if the patron wishes, they may never meet face-to-face in this kind of transaction. The patron can even choose to use a false name. Imagine a little gray-haired grandmother who does not wish the world to know of her penchant for reading grisly true-crime stories, and the appeal of such a service becomes more apparent.

Programs Centered on Books and Reading

One of the most visible and popular methods of providing indirect advisory services at libraries is programming centered on books and reading. These include book discussion groups, author appearances, and reading clubs. A well-publicized event draws the public into the library and (we hope) affirms for them the legitimate role of stories in their lives.

Book discussion groups, often called book clubs, have been a staple of library service for many years, and there are a few standard operating models. The club may be a group that reads and discusses Oprah books and read-alikes or one that meets to talk about literary fiction of the recent past. Some groups work from a specific list of readings, such as those the Great Books Foundation prepares. The club may be a genre-based group, concentrating on mysteries, science fiction, or romance. In some cases, participants do not have to read the same books; they merely come together to talk about what they have read since the last time the group met.

Interest in book clubs with multicultural themes is growing. For example, the San Diego Public Library runs a program called "Borders and Bridges/Puentes y Fronteras" and provides materials for discussion in both Spanish and English. The Cumberland County Public Library in Fayetteville, North Carolina, has for a number of years hosted the "Opened Gates" program, highlighting writings of African-American authors; the Topeka and Shawnee County Public Library in Kansas runs a similar group, as well as another whose theme is "Native American Classics." Certainly dozens more such programs exist in libraries across the country, and the demand for them will only grow as the nation becomes more appreciative of its own cultural diversity.

Whatever the unifying theme of the group, some common ground rules can help ensure its successful operation. The library staff sees to it that information about the meeting time and location for the group receives adequate publicity, perhaps through the library's calendar of events or a notice published in the local paper. Staff also makes certain that a sufficient number of copies of the material are available for all potential participants to read and discuss (for this reason, most groups avoid current bestsellers: Demand for the material from the general public is too high at that moment). If the readings are relatively short, as is often the case with Great Books discussions, staff may keep a supply of photocopies on hand for interested parties. Many librarians will ask the group what they want to read or have them choose from a list of titles; some groups choose their readings six months or a year in advance. This helps the librarians ensure availability of the materials, either through purchase or arranging for interlibrary loan well in advance of the time the group will use them.

Before the group meets, some librarians engage in a bit of background research into the author and/or the circumstances behind the writing of the book. Although this is not strictly necessary, many club members appreciate knowing a little more about the "story behind the story." This knowledge can add a level of enrichment to the discussion. In addition, it is the librarian's responsibility to prepare or find a series of questions to focus the discussion once the group meets. Finding these lists is much less difficult a task than it used to be. They often appear on publishers' Web sites and can be printed out and distributed beforehand so that participants can think about the questions as they are reading. In the case of older or classic literature, a librarian may even turn to a study guide such as *Cliff's Notes* to get ideas for questions or discussion points.

When the club meets, the librarian starts the discussion with an observation or question and then steps back to let the members express their opinions and impressions. This does not mean, however, that the facilitator does nothing. This person has the task of keeping the discussion focused on the reading and of ensuring that all members have the opportunity to participate without one or two people dominating the meeting. This sometimes requires great tact and diplomacy and brings all of a librarian's customer-service skills into play. It is worth the effort, though, and is essential to the successful operation of the group. Letting everyone know that their ideas are welcome and that there are no right or wrong answers in this setting is one of the keys to making the club a success.

A recent innovation in book-centered programming is the adult reading club, modeled after popular children's reading clubs. This kind of program tends to be more flexible than a formal book club because there is no set meeting time and no set list of books participants must read. All that they must do is come into the library to pick up a reading club packet at the start of the program, read (or listen to) the prescribed number of books in the prescribed period of time, and return the form—a reader's log, for example—that indicates which books they have read. Although some programs of this type require that club members read from several genres, there is no list of titles they must complete—they can read anything in the specified genres. Most programs also encourage but do not require participants to write short, anonymous reviews of what they have read. These reviews serve as another advisory tool for other participants, and they make an effective display at the end of the program as well.

A reading club like this usually offers incentives—in the form of small premiums and prizes that local businesses donate—for people to participate. Eligibility for each of these is dependent on the level of participation or the number of books the participants read or listen to. Aside from obtaining the premiums—something small such as a coffee mug or a brass-plated bookmark—staff members also prepare the program materials, which include a flyer explaining how the club operates, a reader's log, and book review forms. Printed publicity materials consist of flyers and posters for distribution in the library and the community. A common practice is to create another flyer with the names of all the businesses that have donated prizes and to send one to each business with a thank-you letter at the end of the program. This kind of program benefits everyone involved: The businesses get some free publicity, the library attracts more users, and readers feel rewarded for doing something they like to do.

The Seattle Public Library offers a unique program, "If All Seattle Read the Same Book." This is a several-day-long event that takes a multimedia approach. The chosen book is made widely available in both libraries and bookstores, and the public radio station broadcasts a reading of it as well. The author then appears on a radio call-in show and engages in a dialogue with the public about the work. Again, everyone benefits from the event: Bookstores sell books, people tune in to the radio station, the author gets publicity, the library circulates books, and the readers' involvement in the story is deepened.

The mutually beneficial relationship among readers, writers, and libraries is perfectly mirrored in library-sponsored author appearances. The library is glad to host such events, especially if the author is well known: Good turnout for such an event is almost guaranteed. For their part, most authors have a deep appreciation for libraries—not just for their role in increasing the authors' readership but also for the practical help the authors themselves have found at their own libraries over the years. The association among these parties is natural.

An author appearance can fall into one of several categories: an isolated event, one of a series of periodically offered programs, or part of a larger event, such as a festival of literature-centered programs offered over a short period (Sager et al. 1998). Local authors, perhaps not so well known, may agree to appear and talk to interested parties about their books and the craft and business of writing. Some libraries develop a series of genre-oriented programs, whereby published authors in a variety of genres are invited to come to the library and discuss their specific genres. Depending on their specific policies, each library can make an author's books available for sale; obviously, the willingness of the library to allow for this increases the chance that authors will take part in the events. Both of these types of programs are usually open to the public with no registration or sign-up required.

Such is not usually the case when the event in question features a very well known author. Because of space limitations, tickets to such an appearance may be a necessity; often they will be free and provided for by a Friends of the Library group, who may be paying the author's honorarium. Sometimes the fee is paid for through a grant or a library endowment fund; in any case, the policies of many libraries preclude charging the public for events held there.

This sort of appearance is more common in larger library systems, which enjoy the funding and publicity mechanisms necessary for such events. Often it is part of a larger program, such as the Novello Festival, sponsored by the Public Library of Charlotte and Mecklenburg County in North Carolina, which has hosted such well-known authors as Steven Ambrose and Pat Conroy. Another example is "New York Is Book Country," an annual celebration of books and the book industry held in the publishing district in Manhattan. Denver is the site of the annual Rocky Mountain Book Festival, and Nashville hosts the ALA-sponsored Southern Festival of Books, which draws many southern authors, some just starting, others well established in their careers. If the library lacks the wherewithal to put on or participate in such a major event, even the isolated appearance of a solid mid-list author is often a big hit in the community. Moreover, when the author is from the area, this adds to the popularity of the event.

Appearances such as these go a long way to enhance the library's positive reputation in the community and to reinforce in the public's mind that the library is a safe place for them to visit when they need or want a narrative experience to enrich their lives. All the techniques and tools discussed in this chapter are designed and implemented with this goal in mind: People need stories in their lives, and the library can help them fulfill that need, whether the help they seek is provided person-to-person or more indirectly.

Challenges

In spite of all the innovative techniques and tools librarians use to deliver indirect advisory services, a number of challenges do exist, and these tend to be elements outside the control of front-line library staff. Many library buildings are older, and their physical layouts are not conducive to effective marketing of the collections they house. Aside from moving the stacks around, if the building itself is difficult to work with, arranging the collection in an effective manner is a genuine challenge.

Not all collections are inherently browsable, either. While many fiction collections have been "genrefied," that is, divided into sections by genres, this is by no means a universal practice. Indeed, in larger systems some branches may be genrefied, while others are not. Staff shortages may mean that a collection has not undergone comprehensive weeding in some time, leading to overcrowded shelves of books that can overwhelm the casual browser.

One area where libraries are letting their users down is in the classification and cataloging of many popular materials, more specifically mass-market paperback books. In some instances, these "more ephemeral" materials receive only the most basic, stripped-down treatment from technical-services departments, with a stripped-down entry into a part of the catalog that is often inaccessible to the general public. How prudent is it for a library to buy a book and then not allow the public—the book's owner and its intended audience—to know of its presence in the library, without a lot of effort on the part of the user? The argument can be made that cataloging is an expensive, time-consuming task, and in these days of ever more scarce resources some sacrifices must be made. Still, a bare-bones catalog entry, accessible to the public, should not be out of the question (Hood 1996).

Perhaps the biggest challenge in creating a comprehensive approach to advisory services is the necessity of winning over administrative support, which will allow the library to devote resources of staff and material to such an effort. When the library's director and board of trustees understand and appreciate the importance of recreational reading/listening/viewing in the lives of the institution's core users, half the battle is won. When the library staff knows it has administrative backing, the task is made much easier.

In the hazy recesses of their minds, most library-school graduates re-call at least hearing of the five rules of library science put forth by S. R. Ranganathan: books are for use; every book has its reader; every reader has his/her book; save the time of the reader; the library is a growing organism (Bakewell 1986). We can change the wording slightly and apply these same rules to modern-day advisory services. The materials in our collections are for use, be they print or e-book, or a story delivered in another medium. Every story has its receptor, and every person has his or her story. By all means, save the time of the user, and as our collections grow and change, our libraries grow, too.

When we talk about advisory services, it's likely that two of these laws will spring immediately to mind: that is, "Every story its receptor; every person his/her story." But the other three are equally applicable. We want to save the user as much time as possible, not leave her to wander the stacks, discouraged and frustrated in her search for the next good book or tape or movie. We want the materials in our collections to be used. And we want to impart to users that the library they are visiting is growing and dynamic, responsive to their needs and wants, in recreational as well as informational pursuits. We need to let them know there are good stories waiting for them at the library—all they have to do is come in and look around.

References

Baker, Sharon L. 1999. *Marketing Library Collections*. Presentation at the Readers' Advisory Section of the Public Library Association's biennial symposium, Chicago.

Bakewell, K. G. B. 1986. Ranganathan, Shiyali Ramamrita. In *ALA World Encyclopedia of Library and Information Services*, 2d ed., 690–92. Chicago: American Library Association.

Chelton, Mary K. 1993. Read Any Good Books Lately? Helping Patrons Find What They Want. *Library Journal* 118 (May): 33–37.

Hood, Anna Kathleen. 1996. Grace Under Pressure: Public Relations, Readers' Advisory, and Fiction-Friendly Collections. *Mississippi Libraries* 60 (Winter): 103–6.

Readers' Advisory Committee, Collection Development Section, Reference and User Service Association (RUSA). 1996. Readers' Advisory Reference Tools: A Suggested List of Fiction Sources for All Libraries. *Reference Quarterly* 36 (Winter): 206–29.

Sager, Don, et al. 1998. Author Programming in Public Libraries. *Public Libraries* 37 (July/August): 235–41.

Saricks, Joyce G., and Nancy Brown. 1989. *Readers' Advisory Service in the Public Library,* 2d ed. Chicago: American Library Association.

Shearer, Kenneth. 1998. Readers' Advisory Services: New Attention to a Core Business of the Public Library. *North Carolina Libraries* 56 (Fall): 114–16.

Van Riel, Rachel, and Olive Fowler. 1996. Why Promote? *Public Libraries* 11: 24–25

CHAPTER 11

The Global Conversation About Books, Readers, and Reading on the Internet

Roberta S. Johnson

Readers' advisory is one of the most intimate library services, best practiced one on one, and most often satisfying when the patron knows the staff response reflects personal reading experience. That's why many people consider readers' advisory an art. The pitfall to practicing this art is the sudden sinking feeling when a patron asks for a recommendation in a genre that you've never read. Thus, the field has spawned many resources—both print and electronic (in the form of CD-ROM fiction guides)—to provide a safety net for staff, but it is the advent of the Internet and the World Wide Web that has opened the door to an unimaginably large, if slightly murky, pool of relevant information.

Since the mid-1990s, people have become well aware of the Internet as an information medium, a big filing cabinet of answers to what librarians recognize as reference questions: What's the weather in Kansas City? What's the current price of Microsoft stock? Reference librarians are spending hours on the Internet, providing answers—or the gateway to those answers—for their patrons. But what about readers' advisory? What is there of value and interest to librarians serving fiction readers? A key to this question is remembering that the Internet is a popular medium, much like television. In many ways it is just an enormous group of people talking to each other. In this global conversation a lot of people are talking about books, about fiction, about what they like to read.

In the last four years, the Internet has become a very useful tool for practicing readers' advisory, but it has also raised some interesting questions for librarians. When we have so much to look at, how do we find what we're looking for? Maybe someone across the country has the answer to my question, but how do we communicate with them? Can we find accurate information on authors that does more than echo our print sources? What are other people in the book trade—publishers, journals, libraries—offering online? And finally, what can my library and I contribute?

To get the most out of Internet resources, first ask yourself, "What are my needs?"

- Do I want to increase my knowledge of a particular genre?

- Do I need to identify particular books for patrons who have not given me much to go on?

- Am I looking for information on a particular author for a book discussion?

- Am I looking for information on forthcoming books or hard-to-find genre fiction?

- Do I need to find a particular title in a series, books on a particular theme, or books for a particular age group—teenagers, for example?

In this chapter I provide some Internet resources that answer those questions. My focus is primarily adult and young adult fiction. Most of the sites I mention also concentrate on adult fiction, but many wonderful Internet resources are primarily for children's librarians. Some of the best author sites are from writers of children's books because they understand how much fun the Internet can be. Visit *Dav Pilkey's Web Site O' Fun* (URL: http://www.pilkey.com/ [accessed December 31, 2000]) as a rib-tickling example. The *Children's Literature Web Guide* (URL: http://www.acs.ucalgary.ca/~dkbrown/index.html [accessed December 31, 2000]) is a great place to search for children's resources.

Readers' advisory librarians can use the Internet in three important ways: for answering challenging patron requests, as a source of information on authors and their works, and as a collection development resource. View the Internet as a communication tool. It puts you in touch, quickly and easily, with other librarians and fiction lovers. Emphasize electronic mailing lists. They will help you to discover and create new resources.

However, because no single Internet site has all the answers, first learn to search the Internet efficiently. My favorite search tool is Google (URL: http://www.google.com [accessed December 31, 2000]), not only for its power and speed but also for its singular lack of blinking ads, shopping come-ons, headline news, chat rooms, and electronic greeting cards. Google is my search tool of choice when I have a precise search, for example, a specific book title or a little-known author. Google is also smart enough to give you a useful return on a more general search, for example, prehistoric fiction bibliography. I also use Yahoo (URL: http://www.yahoo.com [accessed December 31, 2000]) frequently, but it is a little different from a true search engine. Yahoo is a Web directory that contains thousands and thousands of sites. It is organized with hierarchical subject headings, which makes searching through it very easy. It's good for a broad search. However, it doesn't have everything, so frequently combine Yahoo with a search engine. Google and other search engines attempt to index the entire Web. Become a smart searcher (make sure to read the "Help" section of any selected search engine), and these tools will reward you. To make digging for electronic treasure easier, here are some basic definitions.

Definitions and Differences

Web Sites

Everyone and his dog has a Web site these days, and sifting out the useful, current, and accurate ones is a task only a librarian could love. Individual sites vary in content and reliability from remarkably useful to annoyingly pointless. Sites that publishers or libraries maintain tend to be much more accurate, but they can be difficult to navigate due to elaborate graphics or confusing layout. If you are searching for an Internet site on a particular subject and lack experience, try a straightforward search tool such as Yahoo and use a simple phrase such as "horror fiction." For a more specific search, use the author's name and the book title, both in quotes, at a more powerful search engine.

Usenet Groups

Usenet is a precursor of the World Wide Web, created in 1979 at Duke University. Newsgroups are electronic bulletin boards where people exchange ideas in "threads" of commentary. The user signs on to Usenet, reads new postings, leaves a few, and logs off. Groups are divided into twelve different categories, indicated with prefixes such as *rec* for recreational or *soc* for social issues and concerns. Further divisions narrow the broad categories into specific interests, such as *rec.arts.books.hist-fiction,* for historical fiction writers and readers. Current Web browsers such as Explorer and Netscape come with built-in newsreader software for those interested in reading a particular newsgroup on a regular basis. Usenet has a very handy archival Web site called Deja.com (URL: http://x42.deja.com/usenet/ [accessed December 31, 2000]), formerly DejaNews, which collects approximately one year of postings of more than 45,000 Usenet groups. With Deja.com's Power Search, you can keyword search by title or author as well as limit your search to a specific newsgroup or subject heading. Deja.com is fun to browse for opinions on books and authors, but it is also a useful resource for oddball questions such as "How do you pronounce Ondaatje?" For example, when I was preparing for a book discussion on *The Nine Parts of Desire: The Hidden World of Islamic Women* by Geraldine Brooks, a few minutes of searching on Deja.com unearthed a feminist Islamic newsgroup that had been discussing the accuracy and intent of Brooks' nonfiction book.

Electronic Mailing Lists

The nature of the Listserv (which is a trademarked name referring to a particular kind of software for electronic mailing lists) is probably familiar to everyone who has Internet access. You sign up with a group of like-minded people in order to discuss a particular topic, and everyone's comments are e-mailed to everyone else. Some overlap exists between newsgroups and mailing lists: For example, both DorothyL and RRA-L (discussed later) are also available as Bitnet newsgroups (look for their recent postings at Deja.com). Several good directories of mailing lists are also on the Internet: Liszt (URL: http://www.liszt.com [accessed December 31, 2000]) and Tilenet (URL: http://tile.net/lists/ [accessed December 31, 2000]) are probably the most comprehensive. You can search by keyword and find lists on any subject. Unfortunately, neither Liszt nor Tilenet indexes all the available mailing lists. There are also Web sites such as EGroups.com (URL: http://www.egroups.com/ [accessed December 31, 2000]) that allow people to start their own, highly personalized lists, whether on the novels of Jan Karon or Heather Graham, without needing their own Internet server and list software. Most mailing lists archive their postings in some fashion, although the archives may be limited to subscribers or lack a search facility.

Joining a fiction mailing list can serve multiple purposes for library staff. First, it can satisfy our preoccupation and enthusiasm for a particular genre by watching authors and fans chat about forgotten classics, forthcoming hot titles, and the growing size of their "To Be Read" pile. Second, it can provide an opportunity for informal genre study for someone who doesn't normally read romances or science fiction. By joining a list devoted to that genre, the reluctant reader can become a "lurker," eavesdropping on the science fiction community discussing their picks and pans, which new author is worth reading, and which collection is the best value. Sheer exposure to names and titles will improve a staff member's recognition in the genre, raise staff comfort levels when practicing readers' advisory, and provide a helpful forum for tough patron questions. Finally, awareness of the multitude of lists and newsgroups shouldn't be confined to library staff. You might not be interested in the exhaustive Web guide to Robert Parker's Spenser novels, *Bullets and Beer* (URL: http://www.mindspring.com/~boba4/ [accessed December 31, 2000]), but there is probably a patron who would be thrilled and impressed to learn of its existence.

Here is a snapshot of six popular fiction mailing lists:

1. DorothyL

    The first, and oldest, incarnated in 1991, is DorothyL (after Dorothy L. Sayers), which is devoted to mystery fiction. It is available only in digest form, which means that it comes as a collection of messages periodically instead of one at a time. DorothyL has evolved into a collection of writers, publishers, and readers, which means discussion will occasionally focus on topics such as "What do the bestseller lists really mean?" but there is no doubt that it is a lurker's paradise.

    You may subscribe online (and learn more about the list) at the Crozet Post Office (URL: http://www.iwillfollow.com/dorothyl/ [accessed December 31, 2000]) or by sending an e-mail message to LISTSERV@LISTSERV.KENT.EDU. In the body of your message, type *subscribe DOROTHYL*. Turn off your signature file, if you have one.

    Because DorothyL is also a Bitnet newsgroup (bit.listserv.dorothyl), you can search and view postings at the Deja.com Web site. DorothyL archives are also available by e-mail at the Crozet Post Office (URL: http://www.iwillfollow.com/dorothyl/ [accessed December 31, 2000]) for list members only. Consider visiting Alec West's Mystery Vault (URL: http:// http://mysteryvault.net/ [accessed December 31, 2000]) as well for an overview and archive of mystery discussions on the Web: mailing lists, newsgroups, and newsletters.

2. Romance Readers Anonymous

    Another combination of writers and readers, RRA-L devotes its profuse conversation to romance fiction and occasionally romantic films. Among the topics discussed are characterization, subgenres such as paranormals or time travel romances, "keeper" titles, romance as portrayed in the media, and reviews of new titles. Romance fans will enjoy this warm and friendly list.

Subscribe to RRA-L by sending your message to RRA-L@ LISTSERV.KENT.EDU. In the body of your message, type *subscribe RRA-L*. Turn off your signature file, if you have one.

RRA-L is also a Bitnet newsgroup (bit.listserv.rra-l), so you can search and view postings at the Deja.com Web site without joining the list itself. The RRA-L archives are located at URL: http://listserv. kent.edu/archives/rra-l.html (accessed December 31, 2000).

3.   SF-LIT

The official sponsor of SF-LIT is the Library of Congress, and its focus is the literary discussion of science fiction, fantasy, and horror in all media including books, movies, television, and graphic novels. Simple discussion of the latest episode of *Babylon 5* is discouraged, but no topic relating to science fiction, fantasy, or horror is forbidden. This list appeals to those who want to see science fiction as literature taught in every college in the United States, but it's also a great place to identify elusive writers and stories. Witty, erudite, and truly international, the SF-LIT members give science fiction fans a good name. Sign up here to find half-remembered stories for patrons, an author's latest title, or reasons the Universal Translator should (or shouldn't) work.

Subscribe to SF-LIT by sending your message to LISTSERV@ LOC.GOV. In the body of the message, type *subscribe SF-LIT*. SF-LIT is also available as a digest. To receive the list as a daily digest, after subscribing, send the command *set SF-LIT DIGEST* to LISTSERV@LOC.GOV. The list's postings are available via the Library of Congress Web site (URL: http://www.loc.gov/cgi-bin/ lwgate/SF-LIT/ [accessed December 31, 2000]).

4.   Fiction_L

Fiction_L was created as a forum for discussion on general readers' advisory issues. This list has proved very helpful for librarians trying to locate fiction "stumpers" for patrons and has also supported lively discussions about cataloging, shelving, audiobooks on CDs, book discussions, and other important topics. Discussion is not limited to adult collections, and fiction lovers worldwide are welcome to join the discussion.

Complete information on joining the list and viewing its archives is available at the Morton Grove Public Library's Fiction_L Web page (URL: http://www.webrary.org/rs/FLmenu.html [accessed December 31, 2000]). You may also subscribe by sending an e-mail message to requests@maillist.webrary.org. In the body of your message, type *subscribe Fiction_L*.

5. PUBYAC

Youth services staff everywhere highly recommend PUBYAC, a discussion list for those concerned with the practical aspects of children's and young adult services in public libraries. Its discussions cover programming ideas, outreach, collection development, administrative considerations, job openings, and more.

Subscribe to PUBYAC at the PUBYAC Web page (URL: http://www.pallasinc.com/pubyac/ [accessed December 31, 2000]) or by sending your message to listproc@prairienet.org. In the body of your message, type *subscribe PUBYAC* and your name. Turn off your signature file, if you have one, and leave the subject line in the header blank.

6. YALSA-BK

One of several lists for young adult librarians sponsored by the Young Adult Library Services Association (YALSA), a division of the American Library Association (URL: http://www.ala.org/yalsa/professional/yalsalists.html [accessed December 31, 2000]), YALSA-BK concentrates on young adult literature, whether classic or contemporary. This list is also an opportunity for subscribers to learn what the nominees are for Best Books for Young Adults and other YALSA best books lists. YALSA-BK also works hard to include teens in the online discussion, which adds an invaluable element of genuine teen opinion.

To subscribe, send a message to listproc@ala.org. Leave the subject line blank. For the message, type *subscribe YALSA-BK* followed by your name.

Treasure Hunts

Finding a particular book for a patron who cannot remember the author or the title is the essence of good readers' advisory service. Because fiction indexing is subjective, finding a book based on a patron's description, especially an older title, can be very difficult. Even with a thorough description of the book, print and even electronic readers' advisory resources may fail, especially when the patron insists that the book is a romance novel about an artist living in Montana, and the book actually concerns an art dealer vacationing in Wyoming! Many librarians are lucky enough to belong to a readers' advisory interest group, a "network of peers," where they can quiz each other about these patron stumpers (Saricks, Mortensen, and Balcom 1997). The human brain is still the most flexible, descriptive resource, and this is where the Internet mailing lists can be incredibly valuable because they bring librarians, writers, and readers together in a thousand-or-more-member network of peers.

The genre mailing lists, such as SF-LIT, RRA-L, and DorothyL, are essentially collections of fiction lovers. You can usually count on the participants having read and, more important, remembered the book that you cannot identify. The rapid response time of these lists—I've seen questions answered in minutes on Fiction_L—makes it possible for you to answer patron questions in a very timely fashion. The mailing list unblocks that "dead end" and takes you beyond print resources.

Here's a recent example of this kind of networking. Imagine being asked, "What's that romance with Taylor in the title?" The librarian who was asked this question had no idea. But someone across the country knew.

Rosie Postelnek (R. C. Miller Memorial Library, Beaumont, TX) posted the original question to Fiction_L: "Has anyone heard of a series of romance paperbacks with Taylor in the title or series name? She says it is not Taylor County. She also says they are all written by different authors."

Christine Raap (Evergreen Park Public Library, Evergreen Park, IL) posted the following response later that morning:

Harlequin did two series with TYLER in the title. The first series was "Welcome to Tyler" and came out in about 1992–93. The second series was "Return to Tyler" and came out about 1995–1996. Both contained 12 books in the series and issued one a month. These series, Harlequin has published a number of these year-long series, are very popular in our library.

The flip side of this wonderful communication tool is human error. You can't assume accuracy no matter how vehement the respondent is. The point is that even if the information is incorrect, you usually have a lot more to go on than when you started. It's an extended version of, "Let me ask our cataloger. He reads science fiction, and I don't," except that you can now ask an e-mail question of hundreds of readers at one time.

Another question that librarians often hear is, "I heard this author speaking on *Booknotes*—or was it *NPR*?—about her new book and it sounds great. Can you find it for me?" Amazon.com (URL: http://www. amazon.com [accessed December 31, 2000]) keeps track of books and authors in newspapers, magazines, radio, and television as part of their Featured in the Media section. (From the Amazon.com home page, select "Books" and then "Featured in the Media," toward the bottom of the Books page.) Or try going directly to the source's Web site for information; for example, at Online with Oprah (URL: http://www.Oprah.com [accessed December 31, 2000]), you'll find descriptions of each of Oprah's book discussion choices.

Authors

Leading a book discussion can present a problem that the Internet can sometimes solve. I try to provide both myself and the group members with information on an author before we meet to discuss books. It's often very difficult to find information about new authors and titles. A good example was *Snow Falling on Cedars,* which everyone wanted to read, but nobody knew much about. When there are 40 million Web pages to look at, however, the chances are excellent that you will find several current biographies or interviews with the author. Searching the Internet for David Guterson information, I found interviews in two Seattle-area newspapers, neither of which I would have had access to otherwise in a small Illinois library.

A promising place to start is Yahoo's Literary Fiction Authors on the Web (URL: http://www.yahoo.com/Arts/Humanities/Literature/Genres/ Literary_Fiction/Authors/ [accessed December 31, 2000]), which lists hundreds of author pages, as well as the Yahoo sections for science fiction, fantasy, mystery, horror, and children's and young adult fiction. If you don't find what you're looking for in Yahoo, try using a search engine such as Google (URL: http://www.google.com [accessed December 31, 2000]) or Alta Vista (URL: http://www.altavista.com [accessed December 31, 2000]) to do a phrase search on the author's name or book title. This is what I did when looking for information on Chaim Potok for a book discussion of *Davita's Harp* (I typed "Davita's Harp" and "Chaim Potok" in the search field). Of course, there was plenty of information on Mr. Potok on the library's shelves, but I wondered what more recent and no doubt fascinating highlights I might be missing. These were the first two results from Alta Vista:

1. Chaim Potok at SPU—Biography
     Chaim Potok at Seattle Pacific University. SPU. Main. Life. Books. Images. Interviews Born in Brooklyn in 1929 to Polish...
         http://www.spu.edu/special/potok/life.html—size 3K—12-Dec-97 -

2. Chaim Potok: Davita's Harp: Quotes
     Davita's Harp Quotes. P. 71 Reference to the mezuzah and door harp—David Dinn and Davita. "That's a door harp....It plays music when you open and....
         http://www.lasierra.edu/~ballen/potok/Potok.davita.html—size 30K—1-Dec-97 –

At the first site, I located a Web site created for a lecture that the author had given at Seattle Pacific University in the fall of 1997. This page in turn led me to what they described as the "premium" and "exhaustive" Potok Web page, which is the second of the preceding Alta Vista hits. This example also demonstrates that information on the Internet is not always as transitory as we imagine. These sites, which I discovered in December of 1997, were still available years later.

Publishers

In 1997 libraries and enthusiastic readers were providing most of the fiction-related information on the Internet. In 1998 and 1999 we saw publishers playing catch-up in the sense that that they were putting more and more content on their pages: book discussion guides, sample chapters, author tour schedules, interviews, articles, and fan chat rooms. For example, Random House gives succinct guidelines for inviting and booking an author to speak at your library (URL: http://www.randomhouse.com/library/authortips.html [accessed December 31, 2000]). The latest trend is niche information delivered to your e-mail box, whether mystery, romance, teen fiction, or even updates on an individual author. Here are a few of the current e-mail offerings:

Del Rey Internet Newsletter: URL: http://www.randomhouse.com/delrey/drindex/ [accessed December 31, 2000]

Random House Newsletters: URL: http://www.randomhouse.com/library/notification/index.html [accessed December 31, 2000]

Murder on the Internet: URL: http://www.randomhouse.com/BB/MOTI/ [accessed December 31, 2000]

Love Letters: URL: http://www.randomhouse.com/BB/loveletters/signup.html [accessed December 31, 2000]

Penguin Putnam Club *PPI*: URL: http://www.penguinputnam.com/clubppi/index.htm [accessed December 31, 2000]

SimonSays.com Email Update: URL: http://www.simonsays.com/email_update.cfm [accessed December 31, 2000]

Time Warner Newsletter: URL: http://www.twbookmark.com/newsletter/subscribe.html [accessed December 31, 2000]

To locate a publisher's Web site, first try looking on the book's dust jacket for the URL. You can also look in Yahoo using the name of the company or visit a site such as the Publisher's Catalogues Home Page (URL: http://www.lights.com/publisher/alphabetic.html [accessed December 31, 2000]), which includes thousands of publisher's Web addresses.

Publishers quickly became aware of the proliferation of book groups. What was once a delightful online surprise is now a commonplace timesaver. There are now hundreds of book discussion guides on the Web, including classics, new fiction and nonfiction, even genre fiction. These easily printed handouts generally feature author biographies, plot summaries, discussion questions, and suggestions for further reading. Here are some of the best sources for discussion guides:

Books@Random Library: URL: http://www.randomhouse.com/library/rgg.html [accessed December 31, 2000]

HarperCollins Reader Resources: URL: http://www.harpercollins.com/readers/reader.resources.htm [accessed December 31, 2000]

HarperCollins Young Adult Reading Group Guides: URL: http://www.harperchildrens.com/rgg/outerframe.htm [accessed December 31, 2000]

Henry Holt Reading Group Guides: URL: http://www.henryholt.com/readingguides.htm [accessed December 31, 2000]

Penguin Putnam Club PPI: URL: http://www.penguinputnam.com/clubppi/index.htm [accessed December 31, 2000]

Reading Group Choices: URL: http://www.readinggroupchoices.com/ [accessed December 31, 2000]

SimonSays.com Reading Groups: URL: http://www.simonsays.com/reading_guides.html [accessed December 31, 2000]

Time Warner Books Reading Guides: URL: http://www.twbookmark.com/books/reading_guides.html [accessed December 31, 2000]

Publisher Web pages can also be excellent guides to genre fiction. An example of a useful publisher's page would definitely be Tor SF and Fantasy (URL: http://www.tor.com/tor.html [accessed December 31, 2000]). Its Web page has one of the most current and useful collections of links to science fiction and fantasy Internet sites. This is how I found the Internet Speculative Fiction Database (URL: http://www.sfsite.com/isfdb/index.html [accessed December 31, 2000]), which allows you to search for authors, titles, and series. For example, searching for Catherine Asaro returns a list of novels, short fiction, self-penned reviews of other writers, essays, and interviews. Each of these listings is hyperlinked to publication information on that individual work.

In addition, Tor SF and Fantasy features sample chapters from dozens of upcoming books in their various lines, information on author appearances, and their upcoming publishing schedule. These are standard features on most publisher sites and can be a great way to explore genres such as inspirational fiction, romance, mysteries, or speculative fiction.

Amateur guides to genre fiction have grown up, evolving from enthusiastic fan guides into complex resources for all aspects of the genre, from specialty bookstores to author tours. A site such as Useful Links for Romance Writers and Readers (URL: http://www.jaclynreding.com/links/ [accessed December 31, 2000]) offers quick access to hundreds of romance author Web pages, bestseller and awards lists, plus dozens of Web sites of interest to longtime fans or brand-new readers.

Collection Development

The Internet is useful in collection development for identifying useful readers' advisory reference works, highlighting the collection with booklists and displays, identifying all the works in a series to fill gaps, locating reviews of new genre fiction for expanding the collection, and discovering forthcoming titles well in advance of publication.

Reference Works

Every librarian faces strict budget limitations for reference tools, and it is often difficult to evaluate a readers' advisory reference source on reviews alone. However, asking the members of a mailing list what they think of a particular new (and often expensive) reference book usually results in a dozen opinions on its accuracy, usefulness, and overall value from people who actually own it. They may also suggest an alternative source. For example, I heard about *What's Next: A List of Books in Series,* compiled and published by the Kent District Library in Grand Rapids, Michigan (for information, call [616] 336-2554), from its creator, Nancy Mulder, on Fiction_L when the list was discussing new readers' advisory reference works. I use *What's Next* every day but would never have discovered it without that electronic network. Now the Kent District Library has put *What's Next* online (URL: http://www.kdl.org/libcat/whats_next.htm [accessed December 31, 2000]).

Whether you are creating a new readers' advisory department from scratch or upgrading existing services, you can poll the mailing lists for their choices for an appropriate core reference collection. People often share their favorite "miniature works" as well. For example, key training tools may include their own readers' advisory patron questionnaires, guides to giving a booktalk, or little gems such as *How to Read a Book in Five Minutes* (Sampley 1998).

You may also find the online equivalent of that genre magazine you'd like to subscribe to but can't afford. Locus Online (URL: http://www. locusmag.com [accessed December 31, 2000]) offers excerpted interviews, reviews, lists, photos of recent award winners, and publication schedules for science fiction, fantasy, and horror novels. Most of the online versions of magazines are not full text, but Romantic Times (URL: http://www.

romantictimes.com [accessed December 31, 2000]), for example, has dozens of reviews from previous issues, neatly divided by genre.

Bibliographies and Booklists

An effective way to highlight your fiction collection is the book display or the booklist, but it's not always easy to come up with three dozen novels on a single theme. Again, a well-phrased query to a mailing list (for example, "Can you suggest a few novels that pair older women with younger men?") will usually net you all the titles you could want because you're tapping into the reading history and memory of hundreds of people. Also, if someone on the list takes the time to compile all the responses and post the resulting list, it will be kept in the list archives for that moment when you realize that you deleted the file or lost the booklist master. And when your creative vein is tapped out, the mailing list members can share their successful display ideas with you.

Fiction bibliographies are also appearing more often in organized collections on the Internet, and one of the first and best sources is Book-Browser (URL: http://www.bookbrowser.com [accessed December 31, 2000]). Run by a former Indiana librarian, Janet Lawson, and her virtual partner, Cleveland librarian Cindy Orr, BookBrowser organizes books by genre, location, series, and character occupation, in addition to providing thousands of reviews, prepublication information, and author profiles. Another rapidly expanding source of reviews by theme and audience is Genrefluent (URL: http://www.genrefluent.com [accessed October 4, 2001]), from the author of the indispensable *Genreflecting*, Diana Tixier Herald (URL: http://genreflecting.com/ [accessed October 4, 2001]). Genrefluent has hundreds of recommended titles and adds more every week. Also scattered around the Web are hundreds of single bibliographies with titles such as Christian Fantasy and Science Fiction (URL: http://www.enteract.com/~mpavlac/christsf.htm [accessed October 4, 2001]) or Prehistoric Fiction Bibliography (URL: http://www.trussel.com/prehist/prehist1.htm [accessed October 4, 2001]). These Internet booklists, along with most of the titles listed at Amazon.com or Barnesandnoble.com, will often have a scanned image of the books' covers. The patron may not remember the book's exact title but might just recognize the striped face peering out of the shrubbery on the cover of *Isle of Woman* by Piers Anthony (found on the Prehistoric Fiction Bibliography). Finding a favorite search engine such as Google or HotBot, studying its Help section, and using the engine regularly will make finding these hidden gems less frustrating.

Reviews

The online booksellers do a great job of consolidating reviews for new books. Try Barnesandnoble.com to see reviews from sources such as Kirkus and Booklist as well as national newspapers and popular magazines. Best of all, you'll get a sense of what the average reader thought of a book by browsing customer comments. Keeping up with new genre fiction can be a chore, but the Internet has produced several creative solutions to that problem. Amazon.com provides a service called Amazon.com Delivers that brings reviews to you. (From the Amazon.com home page, select "Books" and then "Mystery and Thrillers." At the bottom of that page is "Amazon.com Delivers." Click on "View all categories" for a list of genres.) You fill out an online profile, selecting from categories or fiction, non-fiction, movies, and music, and Amazon.com sends you regular e-mail about new titles (with reviews!) in those categories.

The library trade journals are not standing still either. You'll want to browse Library Journal Digital's Prepub Alert (URL: http://www.libraryjournal. com/articles/books/prepubalert/prepubalertindex.asp [accessed December 31, 2000]) in order to get a jump on titles being published five months from now, as well as reviewing their Hot Picks (URL: http://www. libraryjournal.com/articles/books/hotpicks/hotpicksindex.asp [accessed December 31, 2000]) section. Publisher's Weekly offers both the PW Rights Alert (URL: http://www.publishersweekly.com/rightsalert/index.asp [accessed December 31, 2000]) and PW Religion BookLine (URL: http://lists.cahners1.com/pwreligion/pwreligion_subscribe.asp [accessed December 31, 2000]), e-mail services that deliver publishing headlines to your mailbox. Do you want to let patrons know what authors are coming to your community? Visit Publisher's Weekly's Authors on the Highway (URL: http://www.publishersweekly.com/highway/ [accessed December 31, 2000]) to see book signings listed by city, state, bookstore, author and more.

Goals for Reader's Advisory Librarians

Let's look at those "needs" questions again:

- Do you want to increase your knowledge of a particular genre? Sign up on a fiction mailing list and lurk for a few months, find genre sites with awards lists and reviews, or look for booklists on specialized themes.

- Do you want to answer tough patron questions? Tap the collective mind of Fiction_L and PUBYAC or visit Amazon's Books in the Media!

- Are you looking for information on a particular author? Look in Yahoo's author list. If the author isn't there, try the author's name in quotes in Alta Vista or Google.

- Are you looking for reviews or information on forthcoming books? Look at Library Journal Digital, Barnesandnoble.com, and Deja.com for formal reviews and reader opinions, and try Amazon.com's notification service for new books in a particular genre.

- Do you need to find a particular title in a series or a few new and recommended young adult books? Visit BookBrowser and Genrefluent.

The Library's Internet Presence

Public library staff discovered the power of the Internet for readers' advisory early on, combing the Web for fiction-related information and sharing those resources with patrons and other library staff. Sites such as Morton Grove's Webrary (URL: http://www.webrary.org/RS/RSmenu.html [accessed December 31, 2000]) and Overbooked (URL: http://freenet. vcu.edu/education/literature/bklink.html [accessed December 31, 2000]) created easy-to-use readers' advisory Web sites with dozens of well-selected links for fiction lovers. Internally, staff members recognized that their Web sites could also be easily accessed sources for their booklists and bibliographies, book discussion schedules, and discussion guides. For example, the Des Plaines Public Library has made available its collection of staff-written "Bookmark" columns from the library's newsletter (URL: http://www.desplaines.lib.il.us/readers/rs_BookmarkColumnMenu.html [accessed December 31, 2000]). The Skokie Public Library (URL: http://www.skokie.lib.il.us [accessed December 31, 2000]) has their Access database of staff recommendations on their Web site, and the Morton Grove Public Library offers their MatchBook service (URL: http://www. webrary.org/rs/matchbooksearch.html [accessed December 31, 2000]) to allow online visitors to create customized lists of new acquisitions.

But some things are still missing in this electronic network of peers. Perhaps in the near future, library staff will find time to put online their collection development policies, particularly those that address fiction collections in detail, more annotated bibliographies of both fiction and nonfiction, and guidelines to help readers' advisory librarians train staff [NoveList has some training materials], promote the collection, or deliver better service. Your library's readers' advisory department might not be more than a desk, a chair, and a helpful, knowledgeable staff person, but by making the most of the Internet, your experience and talents will cast a large shadow. Decide what is unique and wonderful about your library or your department and share it with the world.

References

Sampley, Lisa. 1998. How to Read a Book in Five Minutes. *Missouri Library World* 3, no 4: 33–34.

Saricks, Joyce G., Vivian Mortensen, and Ted Balcom. 1997. Connecting Readers' Advisors. In *Serving Readers,* ed. Ted Balcom, 34–45. Fort Atkinson, WI: Highsmith.

PART III

Envisioning an Expanded Advisory Services Role in Libraries

Introduction to Part III

The first two parts of this book represent attempts to understand the current state of advisory services in libraries, both in the more theoretical focus of Part I and the more practical focus of Part II. The third part of the book examines the future of advisory services and the possibility of extending these services both to different formats than have traditionally been the focus of advisory efforts and to diverse groups.

In Chapter 12 Robert Burgin argues that advisory services ought not to be limited to fiction and suggests that many of the lessons learned about readers' advisory services for fiction apply quite well to nonfiction. He notes that readers of recreational or discretionary nonfiction represent a substantial group of users and that the similarities between fiction and nonfiction extend to the concepts of genre and appeal that are familiar to traditional readers' advisory services. Burgin examines both traditional library tools and nontraditional tools such as Amazon.com and suggests that these tools need considerable improvement. He also suggests that an improved understanding of discretionary reading (nonfiction as well as fiction) may help us improve those tools.

In Chapter 13 Randy Pitman, the publisher/editor of *Video Librarian*, extends advisory services to include nonprint materials. He outlines a number of resources to support audiovisual advisory and then makes a spirited argument against the traditional print-centric focus of librarians. Pitman notes that we could answer many reference questions better using video or audio resources, and he urges us to embrace a wide range of avenues to education and recreation, as do our customers.

Chapter 14, by young adult librarian Angelina Benedetti, looks at how to pair teenage readers with the right books, how to market young adult collections, and how to keep kids reading in this information age. Benedetti begins by urging librarians to understand teens and the place that reading holds in their lives. She argues that librarians must be familiar with the literature published for young adults, with the books that teens read, and with their libraries' collections before they can become a successful readers' advisors for teens. Benedetti explores how to market young adult collections, how to talk with teens about reading, and how to use online resources for advisory.

In Chapter 15 Alma Dawson and Connie Van Fleet examine the future of advisory services in the even more diverse, multicultural society that librarians will be serving. They begin by discussing the meaning of "multicultural" in the context of advisory services and note that the term has many meanings and that its definition continues to evolve. They examine the trends in multicultural literature and argue that this literature has experienced a shift from cultural isolation to mainstream to genre fiction. Their exploration of multicultural genre literature is particularly interesting as is their examination of the shifts in multicultural publishing. They note that as the multicultural literature emerges, the mainstream advisory sources are beginning to include more multicultural works. Like many of the other authors in this book, Dawson and Van Fleet are aware of the general challenges of providing advisory services in libraries, and they are acutely alert to the particular challenges of providing multicultural advisory services and the importance of the extent to which librarians appreciate and commit to diversity.

Finally, St. Louis Public Library director Glen Holt provides the capstone to this book by showing how the many ideas these chapters present can motivate a single grand, practical vision. His Chapter 16 describes the St. Louis Public Library's planned Center for the Reader, a physical place "devoted to those who delight in reading, listening to, and viewing stories." In addition to the physical and material considerations of space and resources, Holt's vision includes a broad program of outreach to emphasize the value of stories and the role of the library in their provision, of training for advisors, and of research to help improve the advisory and outreach services that the Center for the Reader provides. Holt's chapter should serve not only to outline his and his staff's dream but also to inspire all librarians to examine the many ways in which we can create enriched customer-serving environments.

The first two parts of this book found cause for both concern and hope. On the one hand, there is evidence that the education of librarians does not include satisfactory training in advisory services and further evidence that, at least partly because of the lack of proper training, the advisory services in libraries are less than adequate to meet the needs of the customers. On the other, the foundations for an adequate education clearly exist, and the resources needed to do the job right clearly exist as well.

The third and final part of this book reflects the same concerns and hopes. Burgin, Pitman, Benedetti, Dawson, and Van Fleet all suggest that advisory services need to be expanded to include both neglected resource areas such as nonfiction and nonprint and neglected patron groups such as young adults and ethnic minorities. These areas clearly represent challenges for the profession. On the other hand, the same authors point to a rich variety of resources to help with the provision of services in these areas, and Holt shows that we can meet the challenges by blending the staff, material, and infrastructure resources with the lessons learned from investigations into the foundations of advisory services and studies of the ways in which we currently provide those services. All libraries have the potential, like St. Louis's Center for the Reader, to be "devoted to those who delight in reading, listening to, and viewing stories."

—R.B.

CHAPTER 12

Readers' Advisory and Nonfiction

Robert Burgin

Introduction

For Christmas my wife gave me a copy of Bill Bryson's delightful *Notes from a Small Island*, an extremely funny account of his travels in England, Wales, and Scotland. A neighbor, who is from England, had recommended the book, and as I read it, I laughed out loud on several occasions. Seeing how much I enjoyed the book, my wife was eager to read it when I finished. A few pages into it, however, she put it down and announced that she didn't enjoy that kind of humor.

Had this anecdote involved fiction (had we disagreed over Donald Westlake or Carl Hiaasen, for instance), it would have fit well into the recent discussion of readers' advisory services in libraries. But although the recent focus on readers' advisory services has been heartening, the almost exclusive focus has been on readers' advisory in fiction.

This tendency to ignore nonfiction in our considerations of readers' advisory service is unfortunate because many of our users read nonfiction for pleasure and not to meet specific information needs or to conduct research. Nevertheless, the library profession appears to have based its treatment of nonfiction on the assumptions that nonfiction readers are primarily pursuing information and that they are approaching nonfiction almost exclusively on the

213

basis of subject. In addition, many of the lessons that we have learned about readers' advisory services for fiction apply quite well to nonfiction. The picture often painted in the literature of library users struggling against information overload and poor customer service in their attempts to find appropriate fiction titles almost certainly pertains to readers of nonfiction as well.

Recreational Nonfiction Readers

The readers of recreational or discretionary nonfiction represent a large enough group to merit our attention. For example, Shearer cites data that show that 33 percent of all adult circulation in public libraries in North Carolina represents nonfiction and argues that "[s]ince much nonfiction is also recreational, the circulation of recreational books is a core business of the public library" (Shearer 1998, 114).

We do not know what percentage of nonfiction circulation in public libraries represents recreational reading (as opposed to research-related or job-related use), but a quick look at the latest 100 best-selling titles at Amazon.com (URL: http://www.amazon.com [accessed December 20, 2000]) suggests that large numbers of people read nonfiction for pleasure. Presumably, Jacques Barzun's *From Dawn to Decadence: 500 Years of Western Culture, 1500 to Present*, isn't listed among the 100 hottest-selling titles because of a sudden interest in historical research among the reading community; people are reading it because it is entertaining and interesting. Sebastian Junger's *The Perfect Storm*, about a tragic storm off the Nova Scotia coast in October 1991, is listed because it is as exciting a "read" as any adventure novel, not because thousands of Amazon shoppers are considering fishing for swordfish and need to do some career-change research. The popularity of Bill Bryson's *In a Sunburned Country* should not suggest that thousands of Americans are preparing to move to Australia and need to read about local culture there. In short, people read many nonfiction titles for their entertainment value and not to solve a problem or fulfill an information need.

As with fiction readers, librarians need to be prepared to help readers of nonfiction find titles of interest to them. Readers of Bryson's *In a Sunburned Country* may wish to read "more like that," and librarians need to consider how best to direct those readers. Does "more like that" mean more titles by Bryson (all of which are about other parts of the world), more titles about Australia (Bruce Chatwin's *The Songlines*, perhaps), or more titles by humorous travel writers (Tim Cahill comes to mind)? What Shearer calls, in the context of fiction readers' advisory, the "all-too-rare instance of probing about the emotional and psychological space occupied by the advisee" (Shearer 1996, 12) would no doubt be appropriate here.

The fact that "more like that" is a rather fuzzy notion with respect to this nonfiction title serves to highlight the similarities between nonfiction readers' advisory and fiction readers' advisory. Just as "more like that" often means more to a fiction reader than another title by the same author or another title in the same geographical or historical setting, so does "more like that" often mean more to the nonfiction reader than another title on the same subject.

Nonfiction is also similar to fiction in that genres and subgenres exist for both. Bookstores use genres instead of Dewey or LC classification numbers to arrange their collections—biographies and memoirs, business and investing, travel, and the like. Many libraries use signage to highlight these genres, and a branch of my local public library once did away with Dewey altogether and shelved entirely by nonfiction genre. Furthermore, nonfiction genres can be further broken down into subgenres, much like fiction genres. Travel, for example, can be divided into subgenres such as "The World's Great Places," "Journeys to Hell," and "Modern Masters and Young Turks," as *Outside* magazine did (Harvey et al. 1996). True crime can be divided into "Individual Cases," "Serial Killers," "Organized Crime," "Old West," "Trials," and other categories, as the online bookstore Bloodpage.com (URL: http://www.bloodpage.com [accessed December 20, 2000]) does. Amazon.com divides several nonfiction genres into subgenres. For example, "Biographies and Memoirs" is divided into "Arts and Literature," "Ethnic and National," "Historical," "Leaders," and several other categories; "Management and Leadership" is divided into twenty-three topics, including "Motivational," "Negotiating," "Organizational Change," and "Teams."

Readers' Advisory: Fiction and Nonfiction

To further explore the similarities between nonfiction and fiction from the point of view of readers' advisory services in libraries, consider Shearer's definition of the readers' advisory transaction:

> an exchange of information between two people with the purpose of one person's suggesting text for the other's later reading interest….The text suggested in the transaction is expected to meet a recreational, emotional, psychological, or educational need. Unlike a reference transaction, the successful conclusion of a readers' advisory transaction is not the provision of a fact or missing data, nor does it attempt to fill a known gap in an otherwise complete informational or knowledge framework. The success of a readers' advisory transaction is reflected in a reader discovering a book (or cassette or software) which is enjoyable, entertaining, stimulating, mind-stretching, and eye-opening; it is in the realm of the subjective. (Shearer 1996, 3)

Nothing in Shearer's definition suggests that readers' advisory pertains only to works of fiction. In fact, Shearer parenthetically notes that such a transaction might lead to the discovery of a work of music or a piece of software and uses as an example a friend's recommendation of a Scrabble software package. A perusal of any list of nonfiction best-sellers reveals that many nonfiction titles clearly meet the "recreational, emotional, psychological, or educational" needs that Shearer identifies.

Or consider Smith's suggestion that the readers' advisory transaction comprises four tasks:

1. The advisor must elicit information about the reader's interests.

2. The advisor must have developed a style of thinking about books that looks for the similarities and links between titles and not just their uniqueness.

3. The advisor must be able to establish links between titles based on the reader's interests and the advisor's knowledge of titles and readers' advisory resources.

4.   The advisor must be able to present identified titles and communicate how each title relates to the reader's interests. (Smith 1996, 103)

Clearly, the successful readers' advisor must be able to complete these four tasks with a nonfiction reader as well as with a fiction reader. What aspects of Bill Bryson's *In a Sunburned Country* did the reader enjoy? What other titles are similar in those aspects? How do we explain those similarities to the reader in a helpful manner?

Likewise, there is nothing in the Saricks and Brown prompt ("Tell me about a book you have really enjoyed") that precludes the reader's having really enjoyed a work of nonfiction. In fact, it is interesting to consider the applicability to works of nonfiction of Saricks and Brown's notion of a book's appeal, an understanding of which, according to Saricks and Brown, "is the keystone of successful readers' advisory work" (Saricks and Brown 1997, 35). Appeal is a set of elements that "take[s] us beyond the bare bones provided by subject descriptors and reveal[s] more of the [book's] essence," and Saricks and Brown outline four elements of appeal: pacing, characterization, story line, and frame (ibid., 36).

A quick look at the reader reviews that Amazon.com provides for a nonfiction title such as *The Perfect Storm* shows the utility of this notion of appeal to nonfiction. One reviewer, for instance, uses pacing and characterization to describe the title as "an absorbing, educational, fast paced adventure story which introduces you to the lives of the people of the Andrea Gail, in particular, so you get to know them, then takes you on a ride that makes it hard to put the book down." Another focuses on characterization: "[I]t makes you care about its characters; it makes you care about what they care about, and in the end, it makes you mourn their loss." A third refers to frame and pacing by pointing out "the extensive background about Gloucester, the fishing fleets, boats, technology, and the people involved. For me, each element added a richness to the drama that made the story all that more gripping….The book has an unusual structure. It cuts in and out from the present to the past, and from present to past tense and back again."

Elements of appeal may also discourage or turn away readers, a point that Saricks and Brown make quite often for fiction. The same is true with nonfiction, as is evident in the remarks of one of the reviewers of *The Perfect Storm*, who complains about "too many jumps from subject to subject" and "the mixed-up, dizzying chronology," the kind of pacing that other reviewers had praised.

These references to appeal factors are not limited to narrative nonfiction such as *The Perfect Storm*. Pacing is also referred to in one reader's review of *The Art of Happiness* by the Dalai Lama: "There is a gentle rhythm to this book—it flows from a question posed to the Dalai Lama, to his thoughtful and inspired response—followed up by Dr. Cutler's professional comments." When readers note the detailed nature of Lance Armstrong's autobiography *It's Not About the Bike* ("the intimate and graphic accounts of his chemo treatments" and "the detailed discussion of Lance's illness, treatment, and recovery"), they are referring to the element of appeal that Saricks and Brown call *frame*. When several reviewers of Bill Bryson's *In a Sunburned Country* refer to what one calls his "classical sarcasm that we have all come to love," they are referring to an element of style. Even a distinctly nonnarrative title such as Nicholas Perricone's *The Wrinkle Cure* is described by readers in terms of its appeal factors. One reader calls the book "encouraging"; another notes that the doctor "gives wonderful hope." A third calls it "easy and fun to read."

Language ("the author's use of language is evocative, unusual, thought provoking, or poetic" [Pearl 1999, xiii]), the appeal factor that Nancy Pearl used to describe works of fiction, is also important to many nonfiction readers. Laurie Lee's wonderful autobiography, *Cider with Rosie*, is called "Sensuous, breathtaking, heartstopping in its ability to pluck that which is familiar and delicious in the human experience. The poetry is Dylan Thomas made understandable." One reader says of Rachel Carson's *Silent Spring*, "Though it is gut-loaded with facts, Carson' s ingenious wording makes reading it a somewhat enjoyable experience. It seems as if the words had an almost surreal quality." A reader of the Lewis Thomas classic *The Lives of a Cell* states, "I was struck by Thomas' ability to turn a phrase, make a point, and discuss complex biological ideas in a manner that is easily understood. The writing in the book is a definite plus." Annie Dillard's *Pilgrim at Tinker Creek* is described as being "written like fine poetry."

In fact, several of the Amazon.com reviewers of nonfiction titles write about those titles as if they were describing novels. Jacques Barzun's history of western civilization, *From Dawn to Decadence*, for example, is described as "so enthralling that it moves as quickly as a short novel" by one reader and "a breathless 'page-turner' " by another. Frank McCourt's memoir, *Angela's Ashes*, "reads more like an extremely well-crafted novel of the highest order, bringing forth genuine laughter and tears," according to one reader. Another reader notes that John Berendt's *Midnight in the Garden of Good and Evil* "is the best nonfiction novel since *In Cold Blood*." Style and appeal factors are apparently as important in works of nonfiction as they are in works of fiction.

It is also possible to speculate on appeal factors that might be specific to nonfiction. For instance, does the book use examples or provide any kind of evidence to support its points? One reader of Malcolm Gladwell's *The Tipping Point* (on social psychology and fads) praises the work for being "loaded with examples and studies that make it involving, easy to read, and provide substantial evidence for many of the points therein" and for making "extensive reference to scientific literature and psychological studies to back up the points that it makes." A reader of Deepak Chopra's spiritual guide, *How to Know God*, notes that "Again and again Chopra gives examples from Indian sages of their great spiritual insight and understanding of truth." Thomas L. Friedman's exploration of economic globalization, *The Lexus and the Olive Tree*, is praised for providing "examples that bring this phenomenon to life." Of course, as with fiction, readers differ in their assessments of how well a title succeeds. One reader of Philip Evans's analysis of the Internet economy, *Blown to Bits*, notes that "They prove their points with example after example," whereas another reader of the same title suggests that "the book could use more concrete examples."

Other appeal factors might include the following:

- Reading level: Charles Givens's *More Wealth Without Risk* "covers the financial basics in simple English." Tobin Smith's *ChangeWave Investing* is "simple to read and comprehend."

- The presence of checklists: Cheryl Richardson's *Take Time for Your Life* "is loaded with many checklists, resources and to-do's." *Awaken the Giant Within*, by Tony Robbins, contains "tools and mental exercises and to-do lists....You have to practice and work on yourself."

- The presence of tests: Philip McGraw's *Relationship Rescue* contains "in-depth and rigorous questionnaires, surveys, tests, and profiles that require a 'brutally candid' mindset," according to one reader. One reader "liked the self-administered tests in [Martin Seligman's *Learned Optimism*] for checking my optimism, that of my wife, and that of my children."

- The presence of illustrations: Several readers criticized *The Perfect Storm* for not having illustrations, and a second edition of Dava Sobel's *Longitude* was recently published with the illustrations that the first edition lacked.

It is clear that something more than just subject content is at work here.

Traditional Tools

It is also instructive to examine the tools that librarians provide to the readers of nonfiction and to compare them with those that we provide to the readers of fiction.

Modern library classification, in essence, began as an attempt to solve the readers' advisory problem for nonfiction readers—or, more precisely, to put it on a self-service footing. Call number classification is a readers' advisory tool and follows from the recognition that the author's name alone is not sufficient to help the reader find appropriate material. This notion is perhaps more obvious in nonfiction than in fiction, but in the mid-1970s I worked as a cataloging assistant in a university law library that had never adopted a classification system for its monographs and had them shelved alphabetically by author.

Just as we have begun to understand that in fiction, the author is only one possible link between a title that the reader has enjoyed and "more like that," we should also realize that in nonfiction, subject classification may be only one possible link.

Consider my situation this past summer when I finished Sebastian Junger's *The Perfect Storm*. Having enjoyed this fast-paced and informative true story of a fishing boat caught in the storm of the century, I wanted to read something similar. As noted earlier, the pursuit of similar titles for nonfiction is not very different from the traditional readers' advisory question for fiction readers, and it is instructive to note that the tools that librarians and others in the "reading industry" use to help the nonfiction reader are both similar to and different from those available to the fiction reader.

First, there are the traditional library catalogs. I could, for example, look for further titles by the same author, Sebastian Junger. Unfortunately, Junger appears not to have published any other books. He has primarily published in magazines such as *Outside*, *American Heritage*, and *Men's Journal*. Perhaps some of his articles would be worth pursuing, but what about similar books?

Alternatively, I could return to the section of the library where the Junger book is shelved—974.4—and hope for another title of interest. This approach would put me in touch with other books about the history of Massachusetts, which does not seem altogether fruitful. The LC number

(QC945) leads me to other books on hurricanes—a bit better, perhaps, but still limited (as single classifications must be) to only one aspect of the original title.

Finally, I could try searching for the same subject heading that was assigned to *The Perfect Storm* (i.e., "Northeast storms—New England") . Unfortunately, at my local library system, there are no additional titles with this particular subject heading. In fact, a search of OCLC's WorldCat reveals no additional titles with that heading among the extensive holdings indexed there (over forty million records). A search of WorldCat for the more general heading "Northeast storms" reveals only a video (*Stephen King's Storm of the Century*) and a handful of technical reports (*Erosion of Nantucket Island's Eastern Shore by the Northeast Storm of December 11–13, 1992*) in addition to the original title.

It strikes me that assigning a single subject heading to *The Perfect Storm* is less than helpful, but this is what the Cataloging in Publication and my local library have done. On WorldCat, however, I note that the title has been assigned a wider range of subject headings by other librarians, including "Natural Disasters — History — New England"; "Fisheries — History — New England"; "Swordfish Fishing — History — New England"; "Fishers — Massachusetts – Gloucester"; "Hurricane Grace, 1991"; and "Gloucester (Mass.) — Social life and customs." This is somewhat better, but in every case, the reader is caught between a subject heading that is too narrow or too broad. For example, there are no additional titles for "Natural Disasters — History — New England" but over two hundred for "Natural Disasters — History" and over 3,700 for "Natural Disasters."

Nontraditional Tools

I could also take a number of nontraditional approaches in my search for titles like *The Perfect Storm*. Amazon.com, for example, lists the book and provides several options for locating further titles of interest. In the section titled "Customers who bought this book also bought," I find four other titles that were purchased by customers who bought *The Perfect Storm*: Linda Greenlaw's *The Hungry Ocean*, Jon Krakauer's *Into Thin Air*, Erik Larson's *Isaac's Storm*, and Sherry Sontag's *Blind Man's Bluff*. Having read and enjoyed Krakauer's book about another doomed journey, I can understand the linkage, even though its location (Mt. Everest) is as far from the seas off Nova Scotia as one can imagine. I had begun Larson's book some months earlier and am happy to be reminded of it. I am not familiar with Greenlaw's book, but she is mentioned in *The Perfect Storm*, where her boat was the sister ship to the doomed *Andrea Gail* that Junger focuses on. Only *Blind Man's Bluff* strikes me as out of place; its subtitle states that it is "The Untold Story of American Submarine Espionage." I recall neither submarines nor espionage in *The Perfect Storm.* But when I look at what customers who bought *Blind Man's Bluff* have also bought, I find Peter Maas's *The Terrible Hours: The Man Behind the Greatest Submarine Rescue in History.* This title interests me because of the rescue angle, and when I view its record at Amazon.com, I find Erik Larson's *Isaac's Storm* again.

Amazon.com connects authors in a similar manner, with a section titled "Customers who bought titles by Sebastian Junger also bought titles by these authors." Jon Krakauer leads the list, and Linda Greenlaw is on it, but the three other authors listed are an odd mix: J. K. Rowling (of Harry Potter fame), Frank McCourt (*Angela's Ashes*), and Arthur Golden (*Memoirs of a Geisha*). I assume that customers who bought just about anything would be likely to buy something by Rowling or McCourt, but Golden puzzles me and points out the odd combinations that sometimes result from such approaches.

Amazon.com also provides "Editorial Reviews," the first of which specifically mentions Krakauer's *Into Thin Air* and suggests that anyone who enjoyed that book will also like *The Perfect Storm.* In addition, the site contains "Customer Reviews," and there are 578 reviews for *The Perfect Storm.* A few mention other authors (Krakauer again) and other titles (*Into Thin Air* again and Cynthia Acree's *The Gulf Between Us*). As noted earlier in the discussion of appeal factors, the customer reviews can provide a great deal of detailed information about the title under consideration.

Amazon.com takes two approaches to subject classification. One is to provide a list of subject headings. Eleven headings are provided for *The Perfect Storm,* from the broad "Science" to the narrow "Halloween Nor'easter, 1991" to the vague "Specific Groups." I can search for other titles that match each subject heading, or I can check any number of subject headings and search for other titles that match all of the headings that I have checked ("Shipwrecks" and "Biography/Autobiography" retrieves nearly twenty additional titles).

Amazon.com also allows me to browse subject categories and lists five separate areas, which are shown as subject hierarchies. For example, the first category is "Science > Earth Sciences > Natural Disasters." I can search at any of the three levels in the hierarchy. When I select the full category, Amazon.com shows me a list of one hundred best-sellers on this subject, including *Isaac's Storm,* John Maclean's *Fire on the Mountain,* and John Barry's *Rising Tide: The Great Mississippi Flood of 1927 and How It Changed America.*

Barnes & Noble provides similar information at URL: http://www.barnesandnoble.com (accessed December 20, 2000). A section titled "bn.com customers who bought this book also bought" lists five titles that purchasers of *The Perfect Storm* had also bought. "Customer Reviews—An Open Forum" provides more than eighty short reviews of the title by customers. Interestingly, the section titled "More on This Subject" provides a link to "Fiction and Literature" even though *The Perfect Storm* is nonfiction. Finally, the Barnes & Noble site allows users to find other books with the keywords assigned to Junger's book, "New England" and "Northeast storms."

Other online resources for readers often include nonfiction. For example, the book discussion guides that publishers provide on their Web sites often include nonfiction titles. Among the recent reading guides of the Penguin Putnam Club PPI (URL: http://www.penguinputnam.com/clubppi/ index.htm [accessed December 20, 2000]) are nonfiction titles such as Iris Chang's description of the Japanese occupation of a Chinese city in the late 1930s, *The Rape of Nanking*; Elena Kozhina's account of how she and her mother survived the German siege of Leningrad in 1942, *Through the Burning Steppe*; Peter D. Kramer's book on relationships, *Should You Leave?*; and Judith Sills's book of psychological strategies for women, *Loving Men More, Needing Men Less*.

Finally, an approach to readers' advisory that has worked well for me in the past is to ask the subscribers of rec.arts.books, a Usenet newsgroup. Shortly after reading *The Perfect Storm*, I posted a simple request for similar titles to the newsgroup and received twenty-five replies in just two days. Most of the replies were recommendations of titles along with brief descriptions of those titles and sometimes a story about the link between the person recommending the book and the book itself (one of the persons was a former tugboat crew member). Recommended titles ranged from *Into Thin Air* (yet again) to *Mutiny on the Bounty* to Piers Paul Read's *Alive*. Interestingly, recommendations included works of fiction as well as Web sites and the URL of an archived radio interview.

Lessons for Readers' Advisory

Readers' advisory is clearly applicable to nonfiction and ought not to be left out of the increasing discussion and study of readers' advisory transactions in public libraries. Nonfiction readers are often as interested in enjoyable and entertaining reading as their fiction counterparts are. We read *Into Thin Air*, for example, because it is a fascinating story of individuals pushing their limits, not because we anticipate scaling Everest ourselves. Nonfiction reading is not always intended to find a fact or locate a piece of missing data or to fill a gap in the reader's knowledge of the world. Even when it is primarily related to information seeking, nonfiction reading may involve appeal factors that make the presentation of that information more compelling or accessible to certain readers and less so to others.

Not only is nonfiction readers' advisory possible, but it is likely that any lessons we learn from the study of why people read nonfiction titles and why they like certain kinds of nonfiction writing will be applicable to studies of fiction reading. Understanding why a reader was very fond of Peter Mayle's *A Year in Provence*, for example, but not of the follow-up, *Toujours Provence*, may help us predict whether some who liked Clyde Edgerton's *Walking Across Egypt* will also like *Killer Diller*, its sequel. It is also likely that any advances in our ability to provide better readers' advisory services to the readers of recreational nonfiction will enable us to provide improved service to the readers of recreational fiction and that "best practice" in readers' advisory transactions for nonfiction readers will help elucidate "best practice" in readers' advisory transactions for fiction readers.

Furthermore, a consideration of the problems of readers' advisory for both fiction and nonfiction ought to prove relevant to problems in related areas of library and information science and other disciplines. The central problem of the readers' advisory transaction—finding "more like that"—is, after all, the central problem of information retrieval, and attempts to understand why certain fiction and nonfiction titles appeal to certain readers are clearly pertinent to attempts to understand the slippery notion of relevance in information retrieval. For example, consider Carol Barry's work with document surrogates (bibliographic information, index terms, abstracts, and full text in some cases), in which she asked users "to circle any portion of the stimulus materials that prompted a reaction to pursue some aspect of the document" and "to circle and cross out any portion of the stimulus materials that indicated something the respondent would not pursue" (Barry 1994, 153). As Barry considers the implications of her work for future research, she wonders whether it is possible to indicate which criteria are more or less important in predicting whether users will find an item worth pursuing, whether users can predict the criteria that are important to them, whether intermediaries can elicit those criteria, and whether intermediaries can evaluate items based on users' criteria. All of these are excellent questions for readers' advisory.

It is particularly productive to look at the tools that librarians and others in the "reading industry" provide for readers of both fiction and nonfiction and to consider how to improve these tools based on our growing understanding of what we like when we like a book (nonfiction or fiction). In this context, it is important to remember, as Baker has noted, that "our regular patrons learn to use the organization systems we have provided for them, just as shoppers learn the locations of items in their favorite grocery stores. However, it does not necessarily mean that further improvements of our existing shelf arrangements are unwarranted" (Baker 1996, 128).

I saw the impact that our tools and systems have on our users one recent afternoon as I entered a bookstore behind what was obviously a father and daughter. It was the week before Mother's Day, and I assume that they were looking for a present. The father said to the daughter, "I'll ask a clerk whether they have any books of poetry about women." The daughter replied, "You can't ask that kind of question here." My first reaction was to wonder why the daughter thought that such questions were prohibited in a bookstore, but is her notion so odd given the fact that the systems that we provide to users don't support that kind of question? After all, bookstores typically have a section for poetry only—not a section for poetry written by women.

Likewise, one of the lessons we can draw from the earlier example of Sebastian Junger's *The Perfect Storm* is that although many helpful and promising tools already exist for those interested in performing readers' advisory for nonfiction, we still have much work to do in improving these tools and advisors' use of them. As I reflect on my attempt to find other titles like *The Perfect Storm*, it strikes me that my Amazon.com experience was much more useful than my experience with the traditional library tools. Not all searches on Amazon.com or other Web sites are as successful as my search, but contrast the library's traditional author, subject, and call number access with the wider range of possibilities Amazon.com presents, which includes a section titled "Customers who bought this book also bought," a section titled "Customers who bought titles by Sebastian Junger also bought titles by these authors," and editorial and reader reviews in addition to access by author and subject.

Steve Coffman has already used the contrast between Amazon.com and public libraries to suggest a number of improvements to the typical library approach (Coffman 1999). These include "fleshing out the content of the catalog records" to include to include "cover art, jacket blurbs, selections from the text, links to reviews, customer comments, author interviews and articles, and any other content that would help a person decide whether to request a particular book." Interestingly, several Online Public Access Catalog (OPAC) vendors have experimented with linking library records to pictures of the book jackets and to tables of contents. More along these lines is needed to make library catalogs truly useful to users and to readers' advisors.

It is also interesting to note that Amazon.com's use of customer purchases to link titles has parallels in two recent Internet search engines, Google and Direct Hit. Google (URL: http://www.google.com [accessed December 20, 2000]) uses the link structure of the Web to determine which sites to rank higher in response to your query; if more Web sites point to site A than point to site B, then site A ranks higher. Google's success with this method can be seen in the fact that it has recently won a number of awards, including the 2000 Webby Award for Technical Achievement, and that Yahoo recently selected it as its search engine. Direct Hit (URL: http://www.directhit.com/ [accessed December 20, 2000]) monitors which Web sites users select from the search results list and uses this information to determine which sites are more relevant to your search. Direct Hit's 1999 growth in use exceeded that of all other search engines, and in 1999 top-ranked search engine HotBot chose it to generate the first search results its users see. By contrast, existing automated library systems do nothing with information about which titles have also been checked out by patrons who checked out title X, something that could be done without violating patron confidentiality.

Even something as simple as providing more subject access points to both fiction and nonfiction requires our attention. Recall that my local library—and the book's Cataloging in Publication—assigned just one subject heading to *The Perfect Storm* (i.e., "Northeast storms – New England"). Amazon.com and a number of libraries on WorldCat assigned more headings, and we should explore ways to ensure richer subject access to our titles. After all, the stinginess with which librarians typically assign subject headings is a relic of the past, when adding a subject heading meant having to type yet another card for the catalog. In today's automated environment, additional subject headings entail much less cost.

We also need to focus on alternatives to the hierarchical subject classification systems that we have traditionally used. Hierarchical classifications tend to leave the user caught between a subject heading that is too narrow (only one title assigned to "Natural Disasters — History — New England" in WorldCat) or too broad (more than two hundred titles assigned to "Natural Disasters – History" and more than 3,700 assigned to "Natural Disasters"). Nonhierarchical networks like those represented by Amazon.com's use of customer purchases to link titles are one approach. Formal concept analysis, which results in nonhierarchical lattice structures, is another (Priss 1997).

More important, though, we need to understand how library staff members can best make use of existing tools as they assist users. In essence, readers' advisory tools such as library catalogs, Amazon.com, FICTION_L, and NoveList serve two major purposes. First, they serve as a vast external memory upon which staff and users can draw. Although well-read librarians may make the best readers' advisors, no librarian could possibly be well read enough to handle the myriad reading interests of our users, especially if nonfiction is added to the equation. Lists of fiction and nonfiction titles with rich representations of individual items and the links between them (whether based on assigned subject headings or customer purchases) are essential to the work of readers' advisors.

Note particularly the importance of the richness of how we represent individual items and contrast the richness of an Amazon.com record with the sparseness of a library catalog's record. (The typical library catalog's record reminds me of Woody Allen's summary of Tolstoy's *War and*

Peace: "It's about Russia.") If we are helping users understand why they liked a particular title and whether other titles may be of interest to them, we need to provide information as input to that process. The 578 reader reviews of *The Perfect Storm* on Amazon.com are far more helpful in this regard than the single subject heading assigned to the title by its Cataloging in Publication.

Second, and perhaps even more crucial, as library staff guide the user through what is essentially a process of exploration and discovery, we need to understand the importance of readers' advisory tools in opening this critical interaction with the user. Helping a reader understand what "more like that" means for her in a given situation or guiding a reader through the process of clarifying what he liked about a specific title is the heart of the readers' advisory process. The extent to which readers' advisory tools assist in that interaction is the extent to which they have added value to readers' advisors and the users they serve. Again, the richer and more varied the approaches the tools provide, the richer and more successful the interactions between readers' advisors and readers.

Shearer notes that "Successful readers' advisory transactions are about relating Reader A's experience with Book A to the likelihood that Reader A would value the experience of reading Book B" (Shearer 1996, 19). We can bring these about by realizing that readers' advisory services provide library staff with the opportunity to assist readers in the exploration and discovery process and by improving readers' advisory tools so that they facilitate that process. The central problem of the readers' advisory transaction—finding "more like that"—is complex, and we need all the help that we can get.

I was recently reminded of just how complex readers' advisory can be when my wife returned from a weeklong conference in Quebec. She brought with her a book that she had begun reading on the flight back, a book that she described as one of the funniest she had ever read—*Notes from a Big Country* by Bill Bryson.

References

Baker, Sharon L. 1996. A Decade's Worth of Research on Browsing Fiction Collections. In *Guiding the Reader to the Next Book*, ed. Kenneth Shearer, 127–47. New York: Neal-Schuman.

Barry, Carol. 1994. User-Defined Relevance Criteria: An Exploratory Study. *Journal of the American Society for Information Science* 45: 149–59.

Coffman, Steve. 1999. Building Earth's Largest Library: Driving into the Future. *Searcher* 7: 34–37. Also available at URL: http://www. infotoday.com/searcher/mar99/coffman.htm (accessed December 20, 2000).

Harvey, Miles, et al. 1996. The Outside Canon: A Few Great Books. *Outside* (May). Also available at URL: http://www.outsidemag.com/ magazine/0596/9605feo.html (accessed December 20, 2000).

Pearl, Nancy. 1999. *Now Read This: A Guide to Mainstream Fiction, 1978–1998*. Englewood, CO: Libraries Unlimited.

Priss, Uta. 1997. A Graphical Interface for Document Retrieval Based on Formal Concept Analysis. In *Proceedings of the Eighth Midwest Artificial Intelligence and Cognitive Science Conference*, ed. Eugene Santos, 66–70. AAAI Technical Report CF-97-01. Menlo Park, CA: American Association for Artificial Intelligence. Also available at URL: http://ezinfo.ucs.indiana.edu/~upriss/papers/maics97.ps (Accessed December 20, 2000).

Saricks, Joyce G., and Nancy Brown. 1997. *Readers' Advisory Service in the Public Library*, 2d ed. Chicago: American Library Association.

Shearer, Kenneth. 1996. The Nature of the Readers' Advisory Transaction in Adult Reading. In *Guiding the Reader to the Next Book*, ed. Kenneth Shearer, 1–20. New York: Neal-Schuman.

———. 1998. Readers' Advisory Services: New Attention to a Core Business of the Public Library. *North Carolina Libraries* 56 (Fall): 114–16.

Smith, Duncan. 1996. Librarians' Abilities to Recognize Reading Tastes. In *Guiding the Reader to the Next Book*, ed. Kenneth Shearer, 89–124. New York: Neal-Schuman.

CHAPTER 13

Viewers' Advisory: Handling Audiovisual Advisory Questions

Randy Pitman

Let me begin with an illustration of the difference between the perception and the reality of audiovisual reference/advisory questions. Back in mid-1997 we launched *Video Librarian Online*, the Web-based addendum to our print magazine, and then sat back eagerly awaiting questions and suggestions from practicing media librarians. One of the first queries came from a young lady named Chrissie, who was hosting a slumber party on a Friday night and hoped that we might suggest something suitable for a small group of 12-year-olds.

Now, if someone had e-mailed me and said, "Yo! Me and my Budweiser buddies are hosting a kegger this Friday. Can you recommend any flicks?" the answer would have been simple—*Dumb and Dumber* or the collected works of Adam Sandler conveniently bound in the "Feature Films for Idiots" boxed set. Selecting materials for young adults, however, especially preteens, is a little more difficult, regardless of the format.

I ended up suggesting to Chrissie one of my favorite young adult titles at the time, Danny DeVito's sparkling adaptation of Roald Dahl's black comedy *Matilda*, which is about a young girl saddled with the parents from hell. And then, reminding myself that this was a slumber party for 12-year-old girls, I mentioned *Romeo + Juliet* as an option, pointing out that it featured the new superstar heartthrob Leonardo DiCaprio. As a parent myself, I also felt it appropriate to point out that the title was PG-13 and suggested that Chrissie check with her parents first. A week later I received an e-mail note of thanks saying that *Romeo + Juliet* had been a very big hit with the young ladies.

Although this was not exactly what I had in mind when we launched our Web site, I quickly realized that these were the kinds of questions that real people would ask. In fact, we receive far more e-mails beginning with "Do you know the name of that TV movie where…" than we do beginning with "I'm just dying to part with $47. Could you sign me up for a subscription to *Video Librarian* right away?"

In a perfect world, of course, the only sane response to TV movie questions would be "Get a life." But we live in an imperfect world, and some of those imperfections are tax-paying patrons. "Get a life" is probably not your best response in a reference interview.

So how would you handle a typical TV-movie question? Although the issue of where to turn initially for reference queries—traditional print resources or the Web—has developed into a hot debate amongst librarians, in our scenario, it's a no-brainer. Nine times out of ten, the TV movie query comes from a person with a very short attention span who cannot recall the essential particulars—beyond the ax pile driven through the center of someone's forehead—of something they watched less than a week ago. Those few movie guides, such as *Leonard Maltin's Movie and Video Guide*, that actually cover TV are rather lacking in current information; they're also extremely poor at keyword searches. If you don't know a major director, star, or the first word of the title, you're probably out of luck.

Web Resources

Which means that it's time to don your SuperWebrarian cape and recall those inspiring words from Robert Duvall in *Apocalypse Now*: "I love the smell of reference questions in the morning…smells like…satisfied patrons."

To borrow an old English Comp 101 phrase, let's compare and contrast a few reference resources that you might use when searching the Web for answers to TV movie questions. One of your first destinations might be the All Movie Guide (URL: http://www.allmovie.com [accessed December 26, 2000]). If you take a peek under the hood of this data-baby, you'll discover information on 160,000 titles, with search capabilities for title, cast, keyword, and plotline. Unfortunately, the plotline searches are not always comprehensive. Typing in "cannibalism," for instance, brings you to two categories, "cannibalism, lifestyle of" (which inexplicably only includes *Night of the Living Dead*) and the very odd category "cannibalism, for profit" (which includes twelve entries but omits the black comedy classic *Motel Hell*). In other words, the information here is a little on the lean side.

Now let's point our browsers to the Enchilada Grande of motion picture databases, the Internet Movie Database (IMDB) (URL: http://www.imdb.com [accessed December 26, 2000]). This grandpappy (and mammy) of all movie review guides on the Web boasts an impressive 230,000 movies—200,000 of which are no doubt absolute dreck on a stick, but for research purposes, this is the one to beat. In addition to offering numerous cross-links (cast, director, reviews, etc.), IMDB makes possible a variety of keyword searches. If you click on the advanced search function, select keyword search for plot, and type in the word "cannibal," you'll bring up some fifty-three titles, including *Chew Chew Baby*, *Flesh Eating Mothers*, *I'll Be Glad When You're Dead You Rascal You*, *Rynda's Vacation Safari*, and *Redneck Zombies*, the 1987 straight-to-video effort partially made by a librarian who chose a pseudonym for the credits (and if you've seen the video, you'll certainly understand why).

Not mentioned in the IMDB list, however, is a little film called *Night of the Living Dead* (which is a pretty big omission for a film sporting a tagline like "They keep coming back in a bloodthirsty lust for HUMAN FLESH!") or *Motel Hell* or one of the darker humans-on-the-menu flicks, such as the 1989 black comedy *Parents* starring Randy Quaid. Here we come to the problem with online databases, particularly free ones: They're only as good as their original information, which is generally incomplete and often riddled with inaccuracies.

Still, the IMDB is a godsend for reference librarians. Consider, for instance, the author search. For all those questions that begin, "Can you tell me if they ever made a movie of Shakespeare's *Titus Andronicus*?" IMDB will allow you to search for "Shakespeare" under cast/crew, where you will discover that *Titus* has been filmed four times, twice in 1999. In addition to the four adaptations of *Titus*, you'll find four hundred other films based on works by the Bard, including the forthcoming *Rikki the Pig* (loosely adapted from *Richard III*), *The Secret Sex Lives of Romeo and Juliet* (1968), and the 1940 musical *The Boys from Syracuse*, based on *A Comedy of Errors*.

If you do, however, reach the point where you're watching your life trickle through your fingers while you scramble around the print and online worlds searching for the name of that guy who hosted the 1958 game show Dotto (Jack Narz), then you're ready for the Videolib listserv bunch (for instructions on subscribing, go to URL: http://www.lib.berkeley.edu/MRC/vrtlists.html [accessed December 27, 2000]). Monitored by practicing video librarians from public, academic, and school libraries, as well as video distributors, this group is, I suspect, the most video-knowledgeable collective think tank on the planet. It's not uncommon to receive several responses to queries within a matter of minutes.

Audiovisual Resources and Reference

TV movie questions should cover about 90 percent of your video-related reference questions. Actually, I'm exaggerating, but only a little bit. Video and DVD reference could play a much larger part in many libraries. In fact, writing in *Video Librarian*—some ten years ago, in our July–August 1990 issue—I asked whether students coming in to the library to use *Encyclopedia Britannica* or *World Book* for short papers on insects, foreign countries, famous leaders, and so on might be equally if not better served by audio, video, or multimedia resources on these topics.

That same year a library student in Texas made the rounds of public libraries in her state, approaching each reference desk with questions that she knew would be better addressed by video. To put it in statistical terms, the number of times the staff member directed her to the video collection is less than the number of hairs on Homer Simpson's head.

In Charlotte Brönte's *Jane Eyre*, Edward Rochester's crazy wife is generally kept under lock, key, and the moderately watchful eye of a tipsy housekeeper. Occasionally, however, Bertha Rochester escapes and—interpersonal social skills not being her strong suit—runs shrieking through the corridors, winning friends and influencing people with the decidedly non-Emily-Post-like calling cards of, say, a knife to the guts or a flame-broiled bed.

Now, gentle reader, I can see those Werner Von Braun-ish brain cogs a-turning. You're thinking that Big Bertha bears a mighty strong resemblance to a certain large bureaucratic organization that usually plods along harmlessly but every so often says or does something truly embarrassing, right? Well, those wacky folks at the American Library Association, the same schizophrenic organization that signed on to support "Turn Off TV Week" while backing A&E's *simultaneous* airing of *The Adventures of Horatio Hornblower* continue to occasionally display their print-centric colors.

Sounding like Rip Van Winkle after a helluva long nap, *American Libraries* editor Leonard Kniffel, in the December 1999 issue (and I had to do a double take on that cover to see whether it didn't really say December *1899*), informed readers (and I do mean readers) in his aptly named editorial— "Read and Learn: Two Words That Still Say It All"—that "if we ever need to summarize the mission of libraries for this entire century *and the next* [emphasis mine] in a word or two we can still do it…the word at the heart of every library is *read*" [emphasis his] (Kniffel 1999, 36).

Personally, I think we can ill afford this juvenile more-book-lover-than-thou kind of rah-rah rhetoric. Even in an imperfect world such as ours, it's not only possible but absolutely imperative that we embrace—as do our patrons—a wide range of avenues to education and recreation. What will the survival rate be for those librarians who, unable to think out of the "book" box, automatically hand a student a print copy of Martin Luther King's "I Have a Dream" speech, only to receive a puzzled look and be told, "Actually, I was looking for the original"? The *primary* version of King's speech, like many other twentieth-century events, is audiovisual based, and I assure you that tomorrow's taxpayers will quickly tire of the provincial attitudes that still pervade our profession.

Regardless of attitudes, numbers tell a different tale. I asked Carol Dunn, audiovisual librarian for the Findlay-Hancock County Public Library in Findlay, Ohio, what the circulation figures were for a medium-sized library in middle America. According to Dunn, during the month of November 1999, a total of 39,257 books was checked out from the library, compared to 34,485 audiovisual items (27,133 of which were videocassettes). She also pointed out that 50 percent of the library's video collection is "nonfiction," which, no doubt, proved extremely helpful in answering the 2,642 audiovisual reference questions the library handled that month.

Although Einstein and I come from different gene pools, my remedial math skills are sufficient to see that there is *nothing* in Findlay-Hancock's circulation figures to support Mr. Kniffel's phantom "mission." Yes, we are a nation of readers, to be sure, but we are so much more, and the best of our libraries reflect this diversity.

I believe that if librarians began directing patrons to video resources when appropriate, they would discover that the vast majority of video reference questions really aren't about TV movies. In fact, there are all kinds of questions that we answer by automatically pointing patrons toward the book stacks that we could just as easily (if not better) handle with the video format. How many librarians, for example, faced with patrons looking for instruction on improving their short game on the putting green, would automatically send them into the 200s looking for prayer books? If they were thinking outside of the book box to encompass all formats, they'd suggest Questar Video's *The Power of Prayer* as well. Seriously, though, the library that is still buying three copies of the latest golf instruction "book" needs to get off autopilot and join the rest of us in the twenty-first century.

The Limitations of Audiovisual Resources

Having said that, I think we still need to render unto Gutenberg what is Gutenberg's. To paraphrase Jane Austen, it is a truth, universally acknowledged, that tape sucks. Audiocassettes, videocassettes, John Cassavettes, they all seem—like the heart Celine Dion sings about—to go on and on and on—especially when you're trying to find a specific point. The problem is inherent in the medium. Tape is linear, and you must physically move from one location in the song or program to another; you cannot simply, à la CD, instantaneously replay "My Heart Will Go On" ad infinitum until your neighbors dial 911.

Videocassette is no different. If you've ever held a group of people captive with repeated claims of "Wait…it's right after this…no…a little further…" then you too know what it's like to get diminishing hit rates on your party invitations ("Uh…sorry, I'm…uh…sharpening my garden shears that night…I don't *think* I can get out of it…"). This maddening needle-in-a-haystack aspect of the video medium has done nothing to further its acceptance in the hearts of reference librarians. In fact, it's probably safe to say that videotape is the *worst* format imaginable for ready reference.

All that will change with the eventual acceptance of DVD and the proliferation of video and audio clip libraries on the Internet, but that's not going to happen overnight, and I've always subscribed to the school of thought that says that although future speculation is all well and good (and necessary), it doesn't actually serve patrons and/or students *today*. Except for those small handfuls of videos with time code indexes printed on the box—primarily cooking tapes—the only comprehensive time coded index I'm aware of is PBS's American History Curriculum Video Database.

In the past, students who came into either the school or public library looking for, say, reenactment footage of the Battle of Gettysburg could try their luck with the piddling thirty-second multimedia clips found on most CD-ROM encyclopedias but certainly nothing in-depth. Because Ken Burns's *The Civil War* is part of this PBS American History collection, however, those same students would be able to look up "Gettysburg" in the hard-copy index (soon to be available online also), go directly to the relevant videotape(s), and fast-forward (using the onscreen time code) to the pertinent segment—one of 35,000 indexed program segments on nearly 300 complete video programs!

So what's the catch? Price, of course. At $3,500 for the first year's subscription to the PBS American History Curriculum Video Database (it's a lease program, although the terms are pretty generous) and $3,000 for succeeding years, smaller libraries may not be able to take advantage of the collection. But for larger libraries and schools, the initial windfall of well over *$15,000 worth of fully indexed programming* with a steady stream of new titles arriving each year could be a valuable addition, especially when you keep in mind that many of the important figures and events of the twentieth century were documented on tape and film and that those media thereby constitute primary source material.

Nontheatrical Video

Beyond that, although reference resources related to video movies are plentiful both in print and online, few exist for nontheatrical video (i.e., those children's, how-to, documentary, and performance titles that distinguish the library's collection from the corner videostore's).

Consumer magazines devote little editorial space to nontheatrical video, while trade magazines for the video industry, such as *Video Store Magazine* and *Video Business,* tend to cover higher profile special interest titles as opposed to more educational programs.

In addition to vendor flyers and catalogs, the primary source of current information about nontheatrical video is found in the library trade periodicals that cover video, such as *Booklist, Library Journal, School Library Journal*, and *Video Librarian.* You might also want to consider picking up a copy of James Spencer's *Complete Guide to Special Interest Videos* (James-Robert Publishing, Scottsdale AZ; telephone 602-483-7007; $29.95), which, of course, is nowhere near complete but does list close to 13,000 nontheatrical titles in forty-two subject categories. Although the book serves as a catalog, it also includes copyright date, running time, price, and ISBN (when available) for each entry but does not mention the producer or distributor.

Beyond that, the most important video resource you can possibly have for nontheatrical reference questions is a well-balanced collection that is also fully cataloged and—optimally—searchable by subject keyword and format simultaneously. That, and a savvy librarian who knows—when a patron is looking for travel information on France—to direct that person to the relevant videos in the collection as well as the Fodor's guide. Unlike movies, unfortunately, the resources on the Web for tracking down nontheatrical video information are a bit skimpier.

On the one hand, the Web offers a stupefying amount of information only a handful of keystrokes away. Before purchasing a new DVD player this year, I spent a lot of time online researching information on brands and models. After narrowing my choices down to the Denon DVD 1500 or one of the Toshiba models, I came across a long thread on a serious audiovisual tech site regarding the pluses and minuses of various players that actual users had posted. Using the "Find" feature, I typed in "Denon DVD 1500" and brought up a post that read "Denon DVD 1500 vs. Toshiba 1200," which was one of the Toshiba players I was interested in. I grabbed pen and paper, opened the message, and read: "Eat me, dickweed."

This, of course, is the downside of Web information—a distinct absence of quality control on many sites, especially those with unmoderated messages. Still, if you're trying to find out whether someone has released a video on a particular subject, your choices today are so much broader than they were pre-Web.

Librarians can search the online catalogs of their vendors of choice, subscribe to large media databases (such as NICEM or Media Review Digest), make use of the larger resource sites geared specifically to the needs of librarians (such as the University of California at Berkeley's Media Resources Center page, URL: http://www.lib.berkeley.edu/MRC [accessed December 27, 2000], or Video Librarian Online, URL: http://www.videolibrarian.com [accessed December 27, 2000]), or post questions to the great think tank resource on aforementioned Videolib listserv.

Although it does help to be video knowledgeable when it comes to handling "Viewer Advisory" kinds of questions, I really think that a little common sense and a decent toolbox of print and online reference resources are more important than knowing that Pia Zadora made her big-screen debut in *Santa Claus Conquers the Martians*.

Of course, if you really hit a brick wall in your reference work, you can always e-mail me. Just let me know your age and how many people will be attending your slumber party.

References

Kniffel, Leonard. 1999. Read and Learn: Two Words That Still Say It All. *American Libraries* 30: 36.

CHAPTER 14

Leading the Horse to Water: Keeping Young People Reading in the Information Age

Angelina Benedetti

Our jobs as librarians present many challenges, and one of the greatest is connecting with the teens who use our libraries and convincing even more of them that they should try our services. In this age where information, and not relationships, receives the highest priority in the library and in society at large, pairing an individual young adult with the right book is fast becoming a lost art. In her book, *Hangin' out at Rocky Creek*, Evie Wilson-Lingbloom writes: "This concession to progress carries with it the danger of undermining the relationship of the librarian as intermediary between the adolescent and the book" (Wilson-Lingbloom 1994).

If your library has a staff member who works with the teens in your community, then you are lucky indeed. The majority of public libraries in the United States do not have a young adult librarian on staff. Even in cases where there is a young adult librarian on hand, serving teens in a public or school library is a juggling act, and sometimes the ball that gets dropped is on-the-floor service to our teen clients. In a public library, a youth services or young adult librarian is expected to put in many hours on a reference desk, to perform outreach to schools and community groups, to create innovative programs for teens, and to develop an exciting collection. School librarians serve even more masters, putting in time teaching, developing curricula, and overseeing computer labs. Given this reality, librarians serving teens can use the combination of a well-organized and user-friendly collection and enticing and informative displays to market their collections. This chapter discusses how to pair a teen with the right book and how to market a collection successfully so that teens can find the books they need, thus "leading the horse to water" and keeping kids reading in an information age.

Teen Readers

One the first things that I try to remember when working with teens is how complicated their lives are and how many things they are thinking about at any one time. With the pressures of school, extracurricular activities, active social lives, lessons of every sort, and just hanging out, it is lucky that they find any time to read, let alone come to a librarian for a recommendation. It is no surprise that many of the teens who come to our libraries never approach us but instead use the library independently. They may be meeting friends for homework, using our computers, and/or browsing the collection on their own. They may be nervous about approaching the desk or unsure that we will understand what they want. Teens are driven by their desire to save face and will avoid the risk of appearing "stupid" for not being able to articulate exactly what it is that they need.

This reticence does not mean that teens are not reading, even given their busy lives. A recent online survey of 3,072 teens (ages 11–18), conducted by ALA's Young Adult Library Services Association (YALSA) division and SmartGirl.com, found that 43 percent of the respondents said that they enjoyed reading for fun but did not have enough time to do so. ("'Take Time to Read' is new TRW theme" 2000) As teens grow older, their reading is more likely to be directed by their schoolwork requirements.

Just as with adults, the library is not the only place where teens look for good books. They ask their friends what they are reading. They see titles that interest them in the supermarket or local bookstore. They pick up what their parents are reading. They receive books as gifts from the well-intentioned adults in their lives. I will often begin a classroom visit by asking whether the students would like to tell me about the books that they are reading. I am constantly amazed by the variety of books that these teens are reading and surprised by how many of the books were *not* checked out from a library.

Reading for Readers' Advisory

Before a librarian can become a successful readers' advisor for teens, he or she must have some connection to the literature published for young adults, to what teens actually read, and to the library's collection. Although these three goals are fundamentally connected, one achieves them by using different strategies.

In her groundbreaking work, *The Fair Garden and the Swarm of Beasts*, Margaret Edwards (1994) described her own requirements for librarians serving young adults at the Enoch Pratt Free Library. They were to read three hundred of the titles currently appearing in *Books for the Teen Age* (New York Public Library 2000). They were to keep current, adding new titles to their repertoires. Even though this is an altogether admirable goal, it is difficult to achieve in an era when mastering databases and search engines is seen as having more immediate benefit. That said, it is still important to know the literature. If you are able to read only a handful of titles, be sure to maintain an awareness of new publications. At the end of this chapter is a list of selected resources for young adult readers' advisory. ALA's YALSA division provides excellent lists of Best Books (URL: http://www.ala.org/yalsa/booklists/bbya/2000bestbooks.html [accessed January 5, 2001]), Popular Paperbacks (URL: http://www.ala.org/yalsa/booklists/poppaper/poppaper00.html [accessed January 5, 2001]), Quick Picks (URL: http://www.ala.org/yalsa/booklists/quickpicks/2000quickpicks. html [accessed January 5, 2001]), and Best of the Best titles for teens (URL: https://members.ala.org/yalsa/membersonly/booklists/bestofbest2000.html [Password required to access]).

Although maintaining an awareness of the best and newest titles in young adult publishing is fundamental to successful readers' advisory, the reality of what teens actually read may be different from what librarians are reading *about*. The most popular titles among teen readers are less likely to appear on Best Books lists than they are on grocery store shelves. The next time you do your weekly grocery shopping, browse these shelves. Are there any new series? Movie or television tie-ins? Magazines marketed at teens? Chances are that these are the items that the teens will be looking for in your library as well. Put your snobbery aside. Some first-rate teen authors write for series on the side. It is a good idea to read at least one of every popular series in your library to discover what it is about the series that appeals to its readers. Does the series deal with hard-hitting issues? Is it more of a fantasy of what high school *should* be like? Does it leave the reader hanging at the end of each chapter? Only when you understand why a book is popular will you be able to recommend other books like it.

Finally, get to know your own collection and how teens are using it. Survey your circulation statistics and also how many times individual titles are going out. Look at your return carts frequently. Find excuses to hang out in your stacks, observing the browsing behavior of your teen patrons. If you are putting books away, they may just ask you a question, usually beginning with "Do you work here?"

Setting Up Your Collection

I work in a library system with over forty community libraries. Each of these libraries has a different way of featuring books for teen readers. Some, like my own library, have an area set aside for teens. Some interfile teen and adult books, fiction and nonfiction. Some feature homework collections. Nationwide, the differences are even more dramatic. Some libraries put their children's and teen collections together, and some feature only fiction or only hardcover titles.

Many teen readers gravitate toward the familiar. If a teen likes a particular author, he will look for books by that author. If fantasy or horror or poetry is what they crave, they will look specifically for those books to the exclusion of all others. Given this tendency, I have organized my own paperback fiction collection according to genre, with additional sections of such teen standards as CliffsNotes and graphic novels.[1] These genres are shelved together and labeled using easy-to-read genre stickers—I confess a personal bias against color-coded classification systems where the reader must consult a chart to learn that green equals science fiction and red equals romance. The shelf labels, created on a graphics program, match the stickers. Face-outs abound, highlighting titles that I have recently featured in a booktalk or of which I have multiple copies. Even in my absence, my fellow librarians can walk a teen into the area and find a historical fiction or suspense title without the need of a booklist. My colleagues appreciate the ease of this system and have less reason to call me from my few off-desk hours to assist a teen in need.

Libraries without a clearly marked "young adult collection" can still set aside display space for teens to browse titles that might interest them. These displays can feature specific genres, highlight an upcoming library program, or celebrate a time of year (for example, Women's History Month). If a particular display has been extraordinarily effective, be sure to reuse it and note the titles that were especially popular.

Take your cue from bookstore merchandising; libraries and bookstores are both in the business of selling books to readers. The best bookstores do not just set books out on display; they also allow staff to highlight favorites, write comments for the shelf browser, and hook the customer into picking up the books. In one display I wrote brief annotations for some of my favorite books and put them up side by side with the books on display. What I learned was that I needed more and more annotations as the days went on. The books would go out as quickly as I put them up.

Reaching Out

Booktalking is perhaps the single best way to bring teens into your library and get them interested in your collection. Although I will not attempt to instruct in the fine art of booktalking (many others have written at length on the subject, including Joni Bodart [1985] and Patrick Jones [1998]), I will suggest ways to extend your sales pitch into your library and make it easier for teens to find the books they need.

Teachers will often invite librarians into their classroom to recommend books on a specific topic or relating to an upcoming assignment. Capitalize on your need to do so by also creating (with the teacher's input, if possible) a booklist that you can both hand out in class and feature in your library. Make this booklist the center of a display of the titles you discussed and be sure to leave a copy of it at your reference desk for the other librarians on staff. This will make it easier for the teens to find the books (now that your excellent talk has lured them) and also make the books available for other students who may be interested or who have a similar assignment. Keep a file of all of your past talks, both to keep you from repeating your efforts and to make it easy to update your display area if no other ideas come to you in a pinch.

There are as many ways to do a booktalk as there are young adult librarians who do them. Many of my colleagues like to talk about the latest young adult books. I will do this on request. However, from a readers' advisory perspective, I find that it is better to sell a book to a large group of readers when you have more than one copy at your library. Multiple paperback copies are even better. After a day of talking to students, I have come back to find that all ten copies of a particular title have been snatched up over the course of a few days (and once after a few hours).

Note any titles that seem particularly popular with your teens. Even though I have found that a book might be very popular with one group and not with another, some titles will perennially strike a nerve and fly off the shelves. These include the following titles, which I cannot seem to keep in stock, no matter how many copies I have:

- *I Know Why the Caged Bird Sings* by Maya Angelou

- *Tangerine* by Edward Bloor

- *Ender's Game* by Orson Scott Card

- *Staying Fat for Sarah Byrnes* by Chris Crutcher

- *Catherine Called Birdy* by Karen Cushman
- *The Silver Kiss* by Annette Curtis Klause
- *The Giver* by Lois Lowry
- *Fallen Angels* by Walter Dean Myers
- *Holes* by Louis Sachar
- *The Lord of the Rings* trilogy by J. R. R. Tolkien

If you order more copies of these books, you will always have a copy available for the reader who approaches you in the library. Although a broad collection of titles is great to suit the tastes of a variety of teen readers, it pays to have a few titles that you can recommend to a wide range of kids looking for "something good."

Talking With Teen Readers

Readers' advisory for teens can be a delicate matter. As a practitioner, I still find myself learning something new every day. Every time I find myself too comfortable, a teen reader comes along and destroys my confidence entirely. What follows is my process for matching the teen reader to the right book:

1. Begin with an easy question. My favorite is, "What is the last really great book that you read?" or "Tell me about a book you liked." Just as in any reference interview, yes or no answers leave you little room to move. If the patron appears uncomfortable with such an open-ended query or responds with "I don't know," have a few closed questions ready to draw them out. "Do you like science fiction? 'Real' stories? Romance? History?" "Do you like diaries? Poetry?" "Do you prefer male or female characters?" You can also try asking about their favorite TV shows, movies, or video games.

2. Listen to everything the teen has to say. This means both what she says and how she says it. Is the reader asking for a book for her recreation or for an assignment? What is the teen's attitude? Is it eager? Timid? Angry? Passive?

3. Refine your search. I often follow my first question with "What did you like about that book?" A kid who loved Michael Crichton's *Jurassic Park* for its focus on paleontology may want a book different from the one who loved it for its suspenseful plot. Specific questions are useful when further clarifying the request. If a reader does not want anything "too scary," by all means ask what "too scary" is. If the teen is looking for a book to fulfill a classroom assignment, ask

whether there are any limits to the assignment. Does the book need to be a certain length? By a living author? If you can, take a look at the assignment itself.

4. Narrow your age range. I often ask my patron what grade he is in just to give me a point of reference. Just looking at a teen is a faulty system. So many are further along in their physical development than their chronological age would suggest. They have often been told that they are too young (to drive, to date, or to stay out late) so asking their age might set up defenses you do not want to encounter. What is his probable emotional and/or intellectual development? A good rule of thumb is that teens always want to read about characters who are older than themselves.

5. Assess the situation. Is the teen alone? With a parent? With friends? Be aware of how these factors affect the interview. Parents sometimes attempt to dominate the conversation, to suggest titles from their own childhood, to reinterpret or reiterate the question you are asking, or to set up boundaries for the teen's reading. Although I listen to what a parent is saying, I also ask my patron for verification, asking questions directly: "Did your teacher say that the book has to be a classic?" When making recommendations, I speak mostly to the teen, while being sure to make occasional eye contact with the parent. I offer a choice of two or more titles that might work and let them make their final choices together. Occasionally I have been in the uncomfortable position of being asked by a parent, in front of the teen, whether the book in question has any profanity, nudity, violence, racial stereotypes, same sex couples, magic, and so on. If I am familiar with the book, I try to answer the question truthfully.

6. Be real. Working with teens can at the same time remind you of your bygone youth and how old you really are. Respect the fact that you and your patron are not of the same generation. Using teen vernacular, even if you are sure that you have got the words right, will only make you sound like someone who is trying too hard. Being yourself, and perhaps tempering your rich vocabulary, works best. By nature, I tend to wax poetic about my favorite books. I have learned to moderate this instinct.

7. Be honest. With all of our good intentions, it is disconcerting to think that teens smell a fake a mile away. Many times a reader will ask, "Have you read this?" The best policy is to be truthful. No matter how savvy, no librarian can have read every book in the collection. Saying honestly that someone else recommended the book will have to be good enough.

8. Do not oversell. I personally have been known to kill a book by being overenthusiastic ("It is the *best* book!") or to turn a reader off by telling too much. As a teen, did you want to read a book that "your teachers just love"? Or one that you would "really learn something from"? Saying too much about a book is often a surefire way to keep a teen from reading it.

Although each and every reader is different, I have found that these techniques make it more likely that I will match the patron with an appropriate book. I always end my interviews by giving readers a choice of titles and leaving them to select the ones that best fit their needs and interests.

The Virtual Library and the Virtual Librarian

Some public libraries are experimenting with real-time online reference (including the King County [Washington] Library System), but it remains to be seen how well readers' advisory, especially for teens, can translate into an online environment. As we have seen from Internet booksellers, teens like to respond to books online, offer their opinions, and rate what they have read. Online retailers will send digest updates suggesting hot, new titles to their customers. It is a good idea to sign up for one of these if you would like to stay current in publishing trends and new titles for teens.

Just as they have adopted other online technologies into their Web sites (database searching, placing holds on materials, and checking on patron records), libraries may wish to consider this same method of recommending titles to their avid readers. Even as many of my teens graduate and move to other parts of the country, we still keep in touch and continue recommending books to each other. This kind of personal service may be hard to support on a large scale, but digital reference services may yet extend into readers' advisory.

Online booksellers can teach us other lessons as well:

1. The very best online booksellers allow for customer feedback. The number of customer reviews for a title equals the number of people who cared about the book, for good or for ill. Books that are very popular with teens will have as many as a hundred or more reviews.

2. Many online sellers and publishers' Web sites include author interviews and discussion group questions.

3. Online booksellers are in the business of selling books. Avoid recommending books based solely on their sales pitch. Although librarians working with teens will review for online sellers, publishers will also

push their products. Favorable reviews are good, but seek out other opinions as well. Was the review from a professional journal? From a teen? From an adult who works with teens?

4. Make it easy to find the information that you need. Some online booksellers are better than others when it comes to finding books for teens. (For example, Amazon.com features a "Teens" link on its books section index. These "Teens" pages list bestsellers, editor's picks, genre lists, and best books of the year.) Be sure that your library's home page makes it easy for teens to find out about new and favorite books.

Teens see the Internet as a place not only to find information but also to communicate with their peers. Whether sending e-mail to a best friend about what they will be wearing to school tomorrow or chatting with someone a world away about a favorite group, teens use the Internet as a way to reach out, often anonymously, to each other.

This use of the Internet has immediate repercussions for readers' advisory. Many libraries nationwide have put up sites that allow teens to post opinions or write reviews. Many more link to such sites. These reviews are, by and large, honest, thought provoking, and certainly worth the attention of any librarian working with teen readers. Three to look at are these:

- Teen Hoopla: An Internet Guide for Teens (URL: http://www. ala.org/teenhoopla/reviews/index.html [accessed January 10, 2001]). Maintained by YALSA, this site allows teens to nominate books for "Best Books," "Quick Picks," and other YALSA lists.

- Books Reviewed by Teens for Teens (URL: http://www.slcl.lib. mo.us/teens/bkreviews/index.html [accessed January 10, 2001]). Maintained by the St. Louis County Library and written by the teen reviewers who meet there monthly.

- Book Reviews by Adam Balutis (URL: http://www.euronet.nl/users/ jubo/balutis.html [accessed January 10, 2001]). Adam is a very cool kid who managed to find the right YA librarians and now has his own book review site.

The following libraries have posted their booklists:

- Our library (King County [Washington] Library System) has some of its teen booklists attached to its site, Teen Zone (URL: http://www.kcls.org/newya/ya.html [accessed January 10, 2001]). One of the most popular lists that we put out is MegaLit, our classics list (URL: http://www.kcls.org/kcls/megalit.html [accessed January 10, 2001]).

- Jennifer Hubert's Reading Rants lists are eclectic and very readable (URL: http://tln.lib.mi.us/~amutch/jen/ [accessed January 10, 2001]).

- New York Public Library puts many lists on its Teen Link site, Good Books: Recommended Titles for Young Adults (URL: http://www.nypl.org/branch/teen/backlist.html [accessed January 10, 2001]).

No longer do we need to reinvent the wheel. If we are looking for a list of books that might appeal to readers of a specific genre, we can find many to choose from without much effort. If your own library does not already use its Web site to recommend titles to teens or to link to sites that do, consider adding this feature. It may take time for teens to start using the site, but this resource will make it easier for librarians unfamiliar with literature for teens to make useful suggestions.

Conclusions

The dawning of the information age has resulted in a dizzying array of distractions for both teens and the librarians who serve them, yet the need to connect a teen reader with the right book is still very much a part of quality service to this important age group. By becoming familiar with our collections and the professional resources available to us as practitioners, we can better answer the question "Do you have a good book for me to read?" when it is posed. By marketing our collections and making better use of our booktalks, we can serve those teens who may be reticent about approaching us for help. By listening closely to them when they do approach us, we show our respect for them as patrons and are better able to match the right books to their needs. Finally, by seeing the online universe as a tool, and not a competitor, we are moving toward the future, making the most of the information age and not fighting its impact.

Note

1. Graphic novels have emerged as a new and popular way to tell a story. They feature a narrative told in a graphic format. The most critically acclaimed graphic novel would have to be *Maus* by Art Spiegelman, which won the Pulitzer Prize. Frank Miller re-created the comic hero in *Dark Knight Returns* (a Batman story), and Alan Moore set the genre on its ear with *Watchmen* (still my all-time favorite). In my collection, I include these more "traditional" graphic novels, as well as the *Big Book* series (e.g., *The Big Book of Urban Legends* and *The Big Book of Grimm*). The *Big Book* series, from DC Comics, looks at wacky subjects from all angles, featuring the work of several graphic novel artists in a single volume. For instance, Jan Harold Brunvand's urban legends work is featured in *The Big Book of Urban Legends,* with a story on every two pages. Graphic novels represent a huge

genre these days. The most popular titles in my collection (series such as *Sailor Moon*) all feature Japanese artists. These are in my library's YA collection because they would otherwise get lost in their Dewey number, 741.5973.

Selected Resources for Young Adult Readers' Advisory

Bodart, Joni Richards. 2000. *One Hundred World Class Thin Books: Or What to Read When Your Report Is Due Tomorrow*, rev. ed. Lanham, MD: Scarecrow Press.

Calvert, Stephen. 1997. *Best Books for Young Adult Readers*. New Providence, NJ: R. R. Bowker.

Cart, Michael. 1996. *From Romance to Realism: 50 Years of Growth and Change in Young Adult Literature*. New York: HarperCollins.

Dresang, Eliza T. 1999. *Radical Change: Books for Youth in a Digital Age*. New York: H. W. Wilson.

Estell, Doug. 2000. *Reading Lists for College-Bound Students*, 3d ed. New York: ARCO.

Herald, Diana Tixier. 1997. *Teen Genreflecting*. Englewood, CO: Libraries Unlimited.

———. 2000. *Genreflecting: A Guide to Reading Interests in genre fiction*, 5th ed. Englewood, CO: Libraries Unlimited.

Herz, Sarah K. 1996. *From Hinton to Hamlet: Building Bridges Between Young Adult Literature and the Classics*. With Don Gallo. Westport, CT: Greenwood.

Jones, Patrick. 1998. *Connecting Young Adults and Libraries*, 2d ed. New York: Neal-Schuman.

Lynn, Ruth Nadelman. 1995. *Fantasy Literature for Children and Young Adults: An Annotated Bibliography*, 4th ed. New Providence, NJ: R. R. Bowker.

Makowski, Silk. 1998. *Serious About Series: Evaluations and Annotations of Teen Fiction in Paperback Series*, ed. Dorothy Broderick. Lanham, MD: Scarecrow Press.

Outstanding Books for the College Bound: Choices for a Generation, ed. Marjorie Lewis. Chicago: American Library Association.

Rochman, Hazel. 1993. *Against Borders: Promoting Books for a Multicultural World*. Chicago: American Library Association.

Sherman, Gale, and Bette Ammon. 1993. *Rip Roaring Reads for Reluctant Teen Readers.* Englewood, CO: Libraries Unlimited.

————. 1998. *More Rip Roaring Reads for Reluctant Teen Readers.* Englewood, CO: Libraries Unlimited.

Spencer, Pam. 1999. *What Do Young Adults Read Next?* Vol. 3. Detroit: Gale.

Thomas, Rebecca L. 1996. *Connecting Cultures: A Guide to Multicultural Literature for Children.* New Providence, NJ: R. R. Bowker.

Zivrin, Stephanie. 1996. *The Best Years of Their Lives: A Resource Guide for Teenagers in Crisis*, 2d ed. Chicago: American Library Association.

References

Bodart, Joni. 1985. *Booktalk!: Booktalking and School Visiting for Young Adult Audiences.* New York: H. W. Wilson. (Bodart has written four other titles in the *Booktalk!* series.)

Edwards, Margaret A. 1994. *The Fair Garden and the Swarm of Beasts: The Library and the Young Adult.* Chicago: ALA Publications.

Jones, Patrick. 1998. *Connecting Young Adults and Libraries: A How-to-Do-It Manual.* New York: Neal-Schuman.

New York Public Library. Office of Branch Libraries. 2000. *Books for the Teen Age.* New York: New York Public Library. (Published each year by the Office of Young Adult Services of the New York Public Library. Copies are $10.00 each plus mailing and handling (1 copy, $1.00; 2–5 copies, $1.25; bulk orders, $1.50. Order from the Office of Branch Libraries, The New York Public Library, 455 Fifth Avenue, New York, NY 10016.)

"Take Time to Read" is New TRW Theme. 2000. *American Libraries* 31 (May): 8.

Wilson-Lingbloom, Evie. 1994. *Hangin' out at Rocky Creek: A Melodrama in Basic Young Adult Services.* Metuchen, NJ: Scarecrow Press.

CHAPTER 15

The Future of Readers' Advisory in a Multicultural Society

Alma Dawson and Connie Van Fleet

Introduction

Fiction reading has been recognized as having a powerful effect on psychological and physiological well-being, and public librarians have long recognized the power of the humanities in empowering and enfranchising the individual (Ross 1991, Van Fleet and Raber 1990, Nell 1988). Readers' advisory service, in which librarians link people with carefully chosen books, has enjoyed a renaissance in library practice and research. This chapter explores the future of readers' advisory services in a multicultural society.

A discussion of the future of multicultural readers' advisory must consider the following four basic elements:

- The meaning of "multicultural" in this and other contexts

- The nature and availability of multicultural literature

- The public demand for multicultural literature

- The actions of the library and information science profession

An analysis of trends and a description of the current context in each of these areas provides a baseline from which we may project a trajectory for the future of multicultural readers' advisory services.

Defining Multicultural Literature

The term *multicultural* has many meanings, and its definition continues to evolve. There is little consensus on its meaning, and current definitions vary with user and use. Some observers have even argued that the traditional notion of a "culture" is obsolete and that "for all but a tiny proportion of the North American population…the connection with an ancestral culture is now so vestigial that whether to assert or ignore it has become entirely a matter of choice" (Clausen 1997, 158). Although this is a growing body of thought, most scholars and writers continue to use the convenient term *culture* to denote a set of practices, beliefs, and value systems that is distinctive from other coexisting sets of mores. Broadly, one may define a culture in terms of religion, race (although this is an increasingly outmoded concept), sexual orientation, disability, ethnicity, or even a mode of communication (as in the culture of the Internet). However one chooses to define culture, it is clear that we live in a diverse society, and "put in its simplest terms, the ideal of multiculturalism is the laudable one that people from drastically different backgrounds should live together in harmony and respect for each other's culture" (ibid.).

Multicultural literature has been defined broadly to include "the literature about persons or groups that differ in some way (ethnically, racially, culturally, linguistically, by sexual orientation, or disabilities) from the sociopolitical Euro-American mainstream of the United States" (Corliss 1998, 4). Simply stated, literature that reflects diversity is known as multicultural literature. Discussions of multicultural literature and library and information services to diverse clienteles have focused separately and collectively on groups with low socioeconomic status (the poor or homeless); people with disabilities (physical, cognitive, or emotional); people for whom English is a second language (immigrants, members of the deaf community, or Native Americans); those with alternative sexual preferences (gay, lesbian, or bisexual people); the undereducated (people who are illiterate or low literate); and religious groups (the Amish, Jewish fundamentalist, and Christians). Most recently, multiculturalism has taken a global focus with calls for international librarianship (*American Libraries* 2000).

We recognize the value of a broad and inclusive definition of "multicultural" but will base the concept in ethnocultural terms. Even here, further restrictions will apply. Such a categorization would include not only world literature (African as well as African-American authors; Argentinian as well as Latino) but Irish-American, Polish-American, German-American, and Cajun authors as well.

In this chapter, the term *multicultural* refers collectively to people of color, in the words of Cuban-American scholar Gustavo Perez Firmat, those who "live on the hyphen" (Figueredo 1999, 23). In the United States, people of color are typically thought of in terms of America's four major nonwhite populations: Latinos (of Hispanic ancestry), African Americans (of African ancestry who are not Hispanic), Asian Americans, and Native Americans (Gonzalez 1990). One should recognize, however, that each of these four groups is diverse within itself. Latinos may be of Mexican, Puerto Rican, Cuban, or other Hispanic ancestry and may be newly immigrated or the product of ancestors settled in the southwest region of the United States before the Revolutionary War. African Americans may reflect ancestry of any one of dozens of cultures of the African diaspora and may be the descendants of slaves or free men and women of color who have lived in America for a hundred years or be the children of modern immigrants. Asian Americans represent very diverse cultures and speak different languages, including but not limited to Japanese, Vietnamese, Chinese, Filipino, or Thai. Native Americans can belong to American Indian tribes such as the Apache, Crow, Cherokee, Sioux, Choctaw, and others, who have unique religions, art, and language. This chapter primarily emphasizes literature written by members of these groups, while recognizing the contributions made by nonmembers who base their work in the culture of one of the groups.

Trends in Multicultural Literature

Generally, multicultural literatures currently exhibit a wide range of themes and formats appealing to a broad audience and a proliferation of new and productive voices. The literary history of the four groups in this study is varied, but common patterns emerge. Their individual and collective histories demonstrate a movement in themes from oppositional to reflective and a migration from cultural isolation to mainstream to genre fiction.

Impact of Social and Political Change

We may trace the explosion in the amount of work that authors of color have created in the past few decades to the civil rights movements begun in the 1960s. Castro contends that the noticeable and growing number of Latino novels, essays, short stories, and poems appearing in English is "a direct result of struggles and achievements of the social movements of the 1960s in conjunction with the influx of fresh immigrations from Cuba, Central America, and South America." (Castro 1997, 216). Hong reinforces the importance of social change, crediting the civil rights movement of the

1960s with relaxed immigration laws and the resulting influx of immigrants who "changed the landscape of a predominantly Chinese and Japanese Asian America" with energizing Asian American literature (Hong 1997, 412). Fisher recognizes the 1950s and 1960s as a time of "coming of age" for African American literature and asserts that "profound changes in the social and political worlds of the United States…brought forth a redirection toward a new aesthetic in the literature with new voices in African American literature" (Fisher 1997, 4).

Authors cite education as the key to renewed interest in Native American writings. Quoting Gerald Vizenor (Chippewa writer and professor at the University of Oklahoma), Maria Simson explains: " 'The thousands of [Native Americans] who went to college in the past two decades have created a whole new audience of Native American literature.'…At the same time, courses in Native American literature have exposed a mainstream audience to the culture's writings" (Simson 1991, 22). Loriene Roy observes that "while many in the Indian population are experiencing socioeconomic stresses, there is a growing cultural and educational renaissance underway. Indians are rediscovering or retaining their culture by establishing genealogy, reading and inventing literature, reclaiming their Native languages, and becoming involved with political and social issues" (Roy 2000, 32).

The resulting increase in educational opportunity and achievement for people of color has both stimulated the creation of works of fiction and ensured the demand for it. The prosperity of the past decade has solidified and expanded an audience with the leisure and values to seek out and enjoy a wide variety of literature.

Thematic Patterns

Multicultural literature seems to follow a general thematic pattern. As a literature develops, each theme adds to and builds on earlier themes, so that the literatures become increasingly varied and rich. Early writings tend to be grounded in a need for identity—an argument for recognition and respect. This self-definition is often phrased in terms of opposition to a dominant and unjust white society. It is an attempt to find one's place as the outsider, whether immigrant or native born. Authors move to the next phase, that of the person who balances between two cultures, the quintessential dilemma of those who live on the hyphen. This trend away from definition in terms of the other continues with an increased attention to self-reflection, to relationships within the culture itself. The growing voice of women is often credited with the adoption of more universally understood themes of families, of love, of issues common to all women—not just women of color.

The movement continues with the creation of mainstream fiction and growing popularity and awareness. As multicultural writers gain acceptance, their works become more mainstream and move to popular genre fiction. Castro (1997, 218) traces the thematic evolution of Cuban writers from protest and exile to exploring the tensions of living in two cultures while maintaining one's heritage, to "the psyche and aura of women's worlds" and family issues. Similarly, Fisher (1997, 6) recognizes the development of African-American literature from the 1970s through the 1990s as a process that paid homage to earlier themes with successful reprints of pioneering writers while expanding themes with greater emphasis "on self-reflection and interaction within the African American community." The period also saw new attention to women's issues and sexuality, including lesbianism, and the entry of multicultural literatures into the mainstream, as evidenced by book awards and large audiences. The period culminated with an "explosion of African American writers during this period in paperback romance genre" (ibid.). Castro (1997, 219) provides a concise model for multicultural literary history: "The early Chicano novels that meditated on the pre-Columbian origins of the Mexicano evolved to the immigration novel, to the coming of age novel, and [are] now moving into the mystery novel, the gay novel, and the romantic novel."

The pattern for Native American literature varies slightly. In the twentieth century, Native American people began to write novels of their contemporary life, taking up traditional themes and often incorporating tribal mythologies and legends into their work (Williams 1997, 525). Even now, "natives living within their own cultures find themselves the focus of increased attention and Natives living outside the culture are trying, in varying degrees, to recover old ways, thus attempting to reverse generations of assimilation" (Roy 1993, 73).

The result is a rich mixture of diverse forms and perspectives that appeals to a wide audience. Certainly, the addition of patterned fiction to the repertoire of multicultural writers provides a form that is intellectually accessible, widely available, and of considerable interest to multicultural audiences as well as traditional genre readers. It may be a positive sign that, freed from an unrealistically high standard and the need to prove their ability to produce "quality" literature, multicultural authors are now on a par with their counterparts. Multicultural authors may engage in creating "light" fiction. Recreational reading is available to multicultural audiences.

Rewriting Genre

The impact of new voices on traditional patterns and styles can be substantial, and increased critical attention has been given to these voices over the past decade. The growing popularity of cross-cultural detectives suggests that such ethnic awareness resonates with traditional genre readers as well as audiences who may have some interest in the specific culture represented. MacDonald and MacDonald contend that the ethnic detective assumes a traditional role:

> These non-mainstream detectives explore cultural differences—in perception, in way of life, in visions of the world—and act as links between cultures, interpreting each to each, mainstream to minority and minority to mainstream. Their function as emissaries between different groups is a natural outgrowth of the intermediary function of many traditional American hard-boiled detectives, figures who moved easily between their upper-class employers and the shadowy criminal underworld, or perhaps between the lower-middle-class police and aristocratic crime victims or criminals. Ethnicity has replaced class barriers, but the need for linking problem-solvers remains the same. (MacDonald and MacDonald 1999, 60)

Essentially, the defining pattern of the genre must be preserved, while the ethnicity of the characters and the representation of their culture must play an essential role. A mystery reader may enjoy learning about a new culture, but certain values and patterns that have traditionally defined the genre must be upheld if this genre is to appeal to the targeted audience. Authors of multicultural genre fiction—whether mystery, romance, Western, or science fiction—must constantly balance the need to represent and interpret an unfamiliar culture with the expected patterns of the literary form.

Genre patterns are not static. Through the voices of women, Native American, Hispanic, and African-American authors, the Western has been revitalized and transformed in the past decade. Although more inclusive and substantially changed, the Western is still recognized as such. African-American and Latino authors are bringing a new flavor to established lines of romances and creating new categories reflecting multicultural heroines and lifestyles.

The *Romance in Color* Web site identifies and profiles African-American romance writers, lists their works, and includes reviews and ratings of titles by a three-panel review staff. These reviews and ratings are exclusive of those that appear in the mainstream media. To date, sixty-five African-American romance writes are profiled. (URL: http://www. romanceincolor.com [accessed November 25, 2000]) This site is not an exhaustive listing of African-American romance authors. However, popular African-American romance writers include Sandra Kitt, who was first published by Harlequin. Kitt's works include *Significant Others* (Onyx, 1996), *Between Friends* (NAL, 1998), and *Close Encounters* (NAL-Signet, 2000).

BET Books has published several representative African-American romance authors and titles. These authors include Frances Ray, *Incognito* (BET/Arabesque, December 1999); Margie Walker, *Remember Me* (BET Books, September 1999); Shirley Harrison, *Under a Blue Moon* (BET Books, October 1999); and Rochelle Alers, *Just Before Dawn* (BET Books, May 2000). Ray's *Incognito* (1999) became the first Arabesque novel that BET television produced as a movie. Valerie Wilson Wesley, author of the Tamra Hayle Mystery Series, completes the representative sampling of African-American romance writers. Wesley received the ALA Black Caucus's 2000 Literary Award for genre fiction for her novel, *Ain't Nobody's Business If I Do* (Avon Books, 1999).

Landrum contends that such a transition is already underway in the realm of the mystery. Prompted by the success of women mystery writers, "the potential of the markets and distortions introduced through stereotyping, omission, and other forms of representation of minority presences," African-American, Native American, and Hispanic writers have disrupted the conventions of the mystery genre and begun to move toward realizing further possibilities in the form (Landrum 1999, 17). MacDonald and MacDonald observe:

> Current detective fiction, then, attempts to bridge the developing gap between traditional American culture and the new, much less European and/or nontraditional culture….When the detective story functions to examine, interpret, or mediate between cultures at the crossroads, the ethnic distinctions often substitute for the class distinctions of the traditional detective story, and the more tightly bound the ethnicity is to plot, character, and solution, the more effective the resultant story. (MacDonald and MacDonald 1999, 94–95)

According to Figueredo, the Latino detective writers have received favorable reviews by critics (1999, 29). The author recommends a core Latino detective collection consisting of at least the following authors:

Abella, Alex. 1991. *Killing of the Saints*. New York: Penguin Books.

Abella, Alex. 1998. *Dead of Night* New York: Simon and Schuster.

Anaya, Rudolfo. 1996. *Zia Summer*. New York: Warner Brothers.

Betterman, Richard. 1997. *Project Death*. Houston: Arte Público.

Corpi, Luchi, 1992. *Eulogy for a Brown Angel*. Houston: Arte Público.

Curtis, James Robertto. 1996. *Shangó*. Houston: Arte Público.

Garcia-Augilera, Carolina. 1998. *Bloody Secrets*. New York: Putnam.

Hinojosa, Rolando. 1998. *Ask a Policeman*. Houston: Arte Público.

Nava, Michael. 1998. *Death of Friends*. New York: Bantam.

Ramos, Manuel. 1993. *The Ballad of Rocky Ruiz*. New York: St. Martin's.

Sanchez, Thomas. 1978. *Zoot Suit Murders*. New York: Vintage.

Torres, Edwin. 1977. *Q & A*. New York: Dial.

Ybarra, Ricardo Means. 1997. *Brotherhood of Dolphins*. Houston: Arte Público.

Publishing

Just as the themes and formats of multicultural literature have developed and are the result of shifting social and political climates, the type and nature of multicultural literature published have evolved over time. The 1990s brought renewed interest in multicultural works. Scholars reflected and examined the difficult and complicated set of social, political, and economic factors in relation to the larger society (Harris 1993, 1996; Taxel 1997). Miller-Lachmann contends that the "rise of interest in multicultural publishing is a product of changing times. Demographic shifts in the United States, increasing global interdependence, and the collapse of colonial systems and empires are among the principal factors contributing to the emergence of new voices and their success in the publishing world" (Miller-Lachmann 1995a, xiv). Taking a contrasting view, Muse declares that "multicultural children's literature [indeed multicultural literature] does not exist to fill a quota or simply to provide a quantitative representation of quickly changing demographics." Rather, "many works provide greater access to literacy, encourage critical thinking and philosophical discourse, and teach valuable skills, while promoting cultural understanding" (Muse 1997, 2).

Problems and Progress

Numerous authors have documented the problems, the progress, and the milestones in multicultural literature (Larrick 1965, Bishop 1987, Kruse and Horning, 1991, Ford 1994, Reid 1994, Harris 1996, Taxel 1997, Corlis 1998, Dressman 1998, Day 1999). Larrick's (1965) study, "All White World of Children's Literature," is generally cited as a milestone in bringing about awareness in the publishing of African-American children's literature. She surveyed more than five thousand children's books for the years 1962–1964 and discovered that over the three-year period, only four-fifths of one percent of the children's trade books from sixty-three publishers told a story about African Americans. "With few exceptions, U.S. minority populations were either ignored or treated as comic relief, objects of ridicule, or blatant stereotypes by mainstream press" (Bishop 1987, 61). On the other hand, authors cite the important contributions of alternative presses (Harris 1993, Horning, 1993). For example, Harris reports that a "body of parallel literature created by African Americans for African American children existed contemporaneously with stereotyped literature. However, these authors lacked the power needed to usurp the authority of the images presented in *The Story of Little Black Sambo* and other books of that ilk" (Harris 1993, 63). Horning studied the publishing output of alternative presses in relation to that of mainstream presses for the period 1982–1992. Her findings indicated that alternative presses represent about 3 percent of the total publishing output of children's books in any given year. However, in 1991, nearly 23 percent of the total number of children's books was published by African Americans. In the same year, 45 percent of first books by African Americans was published by alternative presses (Horning 1993, 528).

Several events, including the Civil Rights Act of 1964, brought about substantial changes. In response to social pressures and consumer demands, more works by African Americans came on the market in the late 1960s and early 1970s (Kruse and Horning, 1991; Ford 1994). Day (1999) observed that books on minority themes—often hastily conceived—suddenly began appearing in the mid- and late 1960s. Most of these books were written by white authors, edited by white editors, and published by mainstream publishers. Not until the late 1970s did the children's book world begin to reflect a pluralist society. Reid's (1994) study of African-American young adult literature for the period 1964–1993 offers a model of development. Her findings indicate a steady increase in new works, coverage in major review sources, and award winners among its authors, as well as recognition of African-American young adult literature as an emerging specialization for scholarly research.

In his "Cult of Multiculturalism," Ford (1994) reported these practices in the publishing of multicultural literature, particularly publishers of children's literature: (1) publishers who take advantage of the renewed interest in books with a multicultural focus by repackaging and publishing out-of-print or outdated titles and then marketing these as multicultural; (2) priority in the publishing schedule being given to designated groups, such as Native Americans or Latinos; and (3) the emergence of major publishers and small presses who both produce quality titles.

Good Business

Recent reports indicate a change in the availability and quality of materials produced in general. Muse cautions that a closer examination of the numbers, such as those done by the Cooperative Children's Book Center (Madison, Wisconsin), indicates that the creation of works by minority authors is small in comparison to the overall publication statistics. Books with Native American themes are not necessarily produced by Native Americans. In fact, "[p]eople of color write and illustrate fewer than 7 percent of books for children and young adults" (Muse 1997, 6). As markets grow, attention to the ethnicity of editors is an aspect still requiring attention (Ford 1994).

Nevertheless, the audience for adult multicultural titles is growing and clamorous, and publishers are taking note. African-American multicultural titles are more numerous and more varied than ever before (Jacques 1995, Dahlin and Lodge 1995, Adlerstein 2000). Jacques reports on the thirty-fifth anniversary celebration of Marcus Bookstore, in which over 1,300 people attended a party with noted African-American authors. Store manager Blanche Richardson's spontaneous (and gratified) comment ("And it's not even Black History month!") is a reflection of the integral part that multicultural literature now plays in the everyday life of its audience.

Hong (1997) credits the market response of Amy Tan's *Joy Luck Club* with the increased productivity of Asian American authors and the willingness of major houses to publish their work. The bestseller status and million-dollar sale of paperback rights lent credibility to multicultural authors and demonstrated the appeal to a wide audience. Similarly, "hunger for spiritual ties has produced a renewed interest in Native American history, medicine, and religion. Thus, this has brought about a resurgence in themes relative to Native American titles" (Dahlin 1995).

The publishers of works on Latinos have reported similar results (Salas 1996). "Hispanic readers, too, are being drawn into the lucrative love triangle of writer, publisher and reader" (Adlerstein 2000, 49A). Small and alternative presses are flourishing, while large publishing houses are producing the work of mainstream authors such as Sandra Cisneros, Gary Soto, and Denise Chavez (Salas 1996). Bilingual publishers such as Arte Público and The Bilingual Press continue to expand, while general publishers incorporate multicultural categories within genre (Adlerstein 2000). For example, Kensington Publishing Corporation launched its Encanto Romances line with four bilingual titles. In a lucrative deal, it sold its Arabesque line (which features multicultural heroes) to BET Books, which plans to increase by 15 percent its catalog of new authors over the next year (ibid.).

Clearly, multicultural publishing is a profitable business. The rich and varied landscape of multicultural work stimulates readership (and sales).

Reprints of classic works by major houses sell well; new voices are greeted by an ever-expanding and enthusiastic audience. Given the publishing history and the limited attention to ethnic voices in curricula, multicultural literature, however, presents major challenges in the area of selection and reading guidance for the individual and the professional librarian, teacher, or bookstore owner.

Advisory Sources

As the multicultural literature emerges, mainstream advisory sources are including the works of peoples of color more and more. African-American, Native American, Latino, and Asian American authors and characters are included in guides to genre fiction such as Bouricius's (2000) *Romance Readers' Advisory*; Ramsdell's (1999) *Romantic Fiction*; and Fonseca and Pulliam's (1999) *Hooked on Horror*. Pearl's 1999 guide to mainstream fiction, *Now Read This*, identifies multicultural authors and characters very specifically (Cuban American, rather than Latino) and contains an exceptionally strong representation of such authors. Readers' advisors may search NoveList by cultural background of the author or character. Although Gale's *What Do I Read Next?* series focuses on the recommendation of specific similar works rather than matched subject headings, it includes books by authors of color both as primary entries and as suggested further reading, although frequently not identified as such. Specialized readers' advisory tools that focus on multicultural literatures individually and collectively are also available, and the number continues to grow. The sources provide valuable background for use with readers, particularly if they go beyond the annotated lists.

In assembling the *New Press Guide to Multicultural Resources*, Muse (1997) noted that even though the existence of materials is not a major issue, the selection of materials remains a critical challenge. The introductions and essays found in the various volumes of specialized resources assist not only the individual reader but also inform librarians, publishers, parents, and others who might need to know more about the various genres for purposes of acquisition, collection building, and reader assistance. The examples included in the list of professional resources that follows includes not only annotated lists of works but also provides historical context through extensive essays; identifies new and lesser known authors, illustrators and small presses; recommends core collections; and provides scholarly interpretations of the literature.

Several authors provide examples of specialized general guides that include annotated lists as well as essays on multicultural issues (Day 1999; Corliss 1998; Castro, Fisher, Hong, and Williams 1997; Kruse, Horning, and Schliesman 1997; Muse 1997; Miller-Lachmann 1995b; Rochman

1993). Several titles cover genre fiction specifically. For example, the works of Figueredo (1999), Muse (1997), and Woods's *Spooks, Spies and Private Eyes* (1999) provide guidance in detective fiction. The works of authors such as Whitson (1999), who provides a volume that represents Native American authors, characters, and themes, represents specific cultures. Schon's numerous works on Hispanic authors are represented in this instance by *The Best of Latino Heritage* (1997). The science fiction and fantasy genre is represented by Thomas's work, *Dark Matter* (2000). Although all essays, Lape's *West of the Border* (2000) provides an example of regional multicultural literature.

Are the specialized resources still needed now that mainstream sources are including multicultural literature? Both are currently needed as each provides unique access to the literature. More coverage of the topics from the historical and social context encourages an understanding and value of the literature. Romance fiction, for example, has new and growing African-American and Latino audiences (Adlerstein 2000) who will be guided to this literature for their personal enjoyment. The primary focus of these sources, however, is on literary form rather than authorship. These sources include some representation and recognition of multicultural voices, but ethnicity, by design, is not the key element and does not provide the primary organizing element.

Professional Response

The future of readers' advisory services in a multicultural society ultimately is in the hands of library and information science professionals. Recently conducted polls demonstrate widespread enjoyment of reading as a leisure activity. Polls indicate that the majority of Americans use the public library and that borrowing books remains a top priority (Towey 2001). The astounding success of super bookstores is further evidence of the sustained and growing importance of reading, and sales figures demonstrate the reading public's desire for multicultural literature (Fisher 1997; Jacques 1995; Adlerstein 2000). Research emerging from disciplines other than library and information science indicates the importance of reading in the lives of a great number of people and the impact it has on their psychological and physical well-being. (McCook 1993, Towey 2001, Nell 1988).

Reading is especially important to people of color. *QBR* publisher Max Rodriguez asserts that African Americans have always valued books, and Cheryl Woodruff, associate publisher with Ballantine/One World, contends that "[b]ooks reflect the truth of our experience better than any other medium at this point" (Jacques 1995, 36). McCook, in her persuasive essay, "Considerations of Theoretical Bases for Reader's Advisory Services," explores this modern-day belief in the power of books and reading in the context of "the library faith" (McCook 1993). Johnson, in his fore-word to *Sacred Fire: The QBR 100 Essential Black Books*, uses the rhetoric of the 1960s' civil rights movement to underscore the importance of the thought, analysis, and critical interpretation inherent in interacting with the printed word. "In the midst of formulaic entertainment, in a popular culture where 'dumbing down' is the rule, *reading* becomes the most radical of all enterprises" (Johnson 1999). His thesis reflects the arguments supporting the public library's role in preserving cultures, supporting social change, and making available to all the potentially enfranchising power of the hu-manities (Van Fleet and Raber 1990).

Given the value of reading and the public's demand, it is disturbing that the library and information science profession has not more widely and enthusiastically embraced the readers' advisory function. Saricks (2001) postulates five reasons for this reluctance: There are no specific, objective, or correct answers; fiction is perceived as unimportant; people don't ask for help; advisory questions are time-consuming; and staff members lack train-ing. Interestingly, the professional community has demonstrated an in-creased awareness of the importance of fiction guidance, The American Library Association and its divisions—Public Library Association (PLA) and Reference and User Services Association (RUSA) of ALA—have been particularly active in readers' advisory for adults. PLA in particular has been active in training through workshops. RUSA's activities focus on re-search conducted by its standing committees on readers' advisory and pub-lication of research, bibliographies of resources, and essays focusing on readers' advisory issues and practice. RUSA's journal, *Reference and User Services Quarterly*, began a column devoted to readers' advisory with the Winter 2000 issue. Individual librarians and educators in schools of library and information science are exploring conceptual constructs, effects, and service strategies for readers' advisory. Readers should explore other chap-ters in this volume for examples of work by the most vocal advocates in the field.

Schools of library and information science, however, seem to be lag-ging behind in the recognition of fiction guidance on a par with reference service or technological expertise. Saricks notes that "although it is now in-creasingly taught in library schools, for years no one learned about reader's advisory in library school, or even had professors who acknowledged that there was more to working with patrons, even in public libraries, than find-ing answers to factual questions" (Saricks 2001, 116). A 1999 survey found that only 14 of 56 responding schools of library and information science of-fered a course in readers' advisory services (Watson and RUSA CODES Readers' Advisory Committee 2000). Lack of attention to fiction guidance in schools of library and information science may reinforce the perceptions of those who find readers' advisory unimportant. Wiegand's (1997) well-crafted and persuasive arguments for an increased attention to reading in the curricula of our professional schools have fallen on deaf ears. McCook and Jasper observe that "It is seldom the act of reading that is studied in the curricula, but the act of using technology to organize and access materials" (McCook and Jasper 2001, 52). The extent to which schools of library and information science respond to sociological needs and professional demands may determine the future of the schools as much as the future of readers' advisory.

A further consideration in the future of readers' advisory in a multicultural society is the extent to which librarians appreciate and commit to diversity. Although such a commitment seems to be a given, it is a typical pattern for our profession to become engaged with a particular issue or cause for several years and then to shift its attention to a different arena. Just as attention to readers' advisory services was minimal until a resurgence in the past decade, focused attention to the needs of people of color has been cyclical. The volume of library and information science literature concerned with the needs of ethnic and sociocultural minorities reflects the fact that this subject occupied the forefront of professional concern and activity in the 1960s and early 1970s, followed by a fairly dormant period, with a recurrence of interest in diversity and multiculturalism in the 1990s.

The Trajectory

In an attempt to establish a sense of the future for multicultural readers' advisory services, this chapter has explored four basic elements: the meaning of *multicultural*, the nature and availability of multicultural literature, public demand for multicultural literature, and the responses of the library and information science profession.

Although some argue that American culture is becoming increasingly homogenized, it seems unlikely that the rich diversity of our society will disappear. A reaction of pride and a growing realization of the importance of a regard for history and heritage serve as a counterbalance to the natural blurring of cultural definitions that occur when people live in proximity and harmony. We have much to value and much to preserve. Awareness and appreciation do not equate with assimilation.

Multicultural literature is rich and varied. It speaks to universal themes yet preserves the unique perspectives that add depth, meaning, interest, and excitement to traditional forms. Increasingly, there is a movement to genre fiction that coexists with more serious work of the literary mainstream. Such a pattern brings multicultural literature into a parallel course with traditional publishing. It allows people of color the same scope and breadth—the same freedom to choose—that has been traditionally enjoyed by readers who are members of the dominant culture. In addition, the use of familiar forms creates a nonthreatening means of access for others to learn about, appreciate, and perhaps empathize with a different perspective. Concurrent with the increased attention to multicultural literature in mainstream and general purpose review and readers' advisory sources is a growth in focused, specialized publications.

The value we place on reading and on communicating through stories persists in an increasingly technologically oriented society. Response to multicultural literature has been positive and profitable. Small presses and mainstream publishers are publishing in increasing numbers books by people of color, books that include characters who represent diverse cultures, and books that explore multicultural themes. The literature that exists is widely available, and audiences continue to purchase and to borrow books in increasing numbers.

The professional library community is giving increased attention to readers' advisory services and concurrently to diversity issues, including equitable and appropriate services. There is a renewed emphasis on community and community building, with the public library as an integral and vital component that reflects the heritage and nature of its constituents (McCook 2000). Although schools of library and information science focus on technology and access rather than books and content, a growing number are offering courses on readers' advisory services. Fewer offer stand-alone courses on services to people of color, people with disabilities, or other component cultures of a diverse society. Still, even those that do not offer specific courses are incorporating the necessary skills, processes, and awareness into traditional courses, and we may be seeing the beginnings of a new equilibrium that balances humanist and technical values, content and process. In essence, the future of readers' advisory will depend on an understanding of the value of reading and the humanities, of communication processes and their implementation, and of the structures of literatures and their context within a given culture.

In each of the four major areas discussed in this chapter, we are seeing increased acceptance by the dominant culture of multicultural work and values and by the various ethnocultures of mainstream values and literary forms. Hong suggests:

> Asian American literature is finding a larger more encompassing audience without ethnic boundaries. Ironically, as the field of Asian American literature develops and broadens, it will ultimately outgrow itself because someday, such defined, exclusive ethnic terms as Asian American, African American, Latino or Native American will no longer be necessary in the multicultural American society of the future. And in this potentially tolerant, fluid world, even a reference guide such as this, which is much needed today, will hopefully render itself obsolete. (Hong 1997, 15)

Hong's vision of the future may well prove accurate. At this time, however, and in the foreseeable future, the trend toward cultural pride and preservation of distinct heritages will prevail. People of color will be able to choose whether they wish to identify themselves in terms that emphasize the distinctiveness of ethnic heritage or in terms that emphasize commonality and kinship with other cultures.

Conclusions

As we recognize that public libraries will be sources of inspiration as well as information and that these roles are equally valuable and deserving of our attention and expertise, so too will we need to be able to appreciate the different perspectives and choices of our patrons. It is incumbent upon librarians, therefore, not only to utilize the specialized multicultural resources at our disposal and to offer specialized services but to learn when these are appropriate. Based on the current trajectory, readers' advisory services in our multicultural society should continue to expand and grow.

References

Adlerstein, David. 2000. Multicultural Book Boom: Multicultural Romance Is Growing Literary Genre. *South Florida Business Journal* 21 (September 8): 49A.

American Libraries. 2000. Theme Issue: World Culture, World Librarianship: Making Multicultural Connections 31, no. 9 (October).

Bishop, Rudine S. 1987. Extending Multicultural Understanding Through Children's Books. In *Children's Literature in the Reading Program*, ed. Bernice E. Cullian, 60–67. Newark, DE: International Reading Association.

Bouricius, Ann. 2000. *The Romance Reader's Advisory: The Librarian's Guide to Love in the Stacks.* Chicago: American Library Association.

Castro, Rafaela G. 1997. Latino Literature. In *What Do I Read Next? Multicultural Literature*, ed. Rafaelo G. Castro, Edith Maureen Fisher, Terry Hong, and David Williams, 215–21. Detroit: Gale.

Castro, Rafaela G., Edith. M. Fisher, Terry Hong, and David Williams. 1997. *What Do I Read Next? Multicultural Literature.* Detroit: Gale.

Clausen, Christopher. 1997. Welcome to Post-Culturalism. In *Multiculturalism*, ed. Robert Emmet Long, 152–60. New York: H. W. Wilson. Reprinted from *The American Scholar* 65 (Summer 1996): 379–88.

Corliss, J. C. 1998. *Crossing Borders with Literature of Diversity.* Norwood, MA: Christopher-Gordon.

Dahlin, Robert. 1995. Native Americans Ride to the Fore: A Significant Resurgence of Interest Brings New Titles to a Once-Overlooked Arena. *Publishers Weekly* 242 (December 11): 50–52.

Dahlin, Robert, and Sally Lodge. 1995. A Roundup of African American Titles. *Publishers Weekly* 242 (December 11): 41–49.

Day, Frances Ann. 1999. *Multicultural Voices in Contemporary Literature.* Updated and revised edition. Portsmouth, NH: Heinemann.

Dressman, Mark. 1998. Toward a Literature of Difference. *Equity and Excellence in Education* 31 (December): 18–24.

Figueredo, Danilo H. 1998. Love's Labour's Not Lost: Latino Publishing. *Multicultural Review* 7, no. 3 (September): 24–33.

———. 1999. The Stuff Dreams Are Made Of: The Latino Detective Novel. *Multicultural Review* 8, no. 3 (September): 22–29.

Fisher, Edith Maureen. 1997. African-American Literature. In *What Do I Read Next? Multicultural Literature*, ed. Rafaelo G. Castro, Edith Maureen Fisher, Terry Hong, and David Williams, 1–7. Detroit: Gale.

Fonseca, Tony J., and Jane M. Pulliam. 1999. *Hooked on Horror: A Guide to Reading Interests in Horror Fiction*. Englewood, CO: Libraries Unlimited.

Ford, M. T. 1994. The Cult of Multiculturalism. *Publishers Weekly* 241 (July 18): 30–33.

Gonzalez, Roseann Duenas. 1990. When Minority Becomes Majority. The Changing Faces of English Classrooms. *College English* 79 (January): 16–23.

Harris, Violet J. 1996. Continuing Dilemmas, Debates, and Delights in Multicultural Literature. *New Advocate* 9 (Spring): 107–22.

———., ed. 1993. *Teaching Multicultural Literature in Grades K–8*. Norwood, MA: Christopher-Gordon.

Hedberg, Bo L. T. 1981. How Organizations Learn and Unlearn. In *Handbook of Organizational Design*. Vol. 1, ed. Paul C. Nystrom and William H. Starbuck, 3–27. New York: Oxford University Press.

Hong, Terry. 1997. Asian-American Literature. In *What Do I Read Next? Multicultural Literature*, ed. Rafaelo G. Castro, Edith Maureen Fisher, Terry Hong, and David Williams, 411–16. Detroit: Gale.

Horning, Kathleen T. 1993. Contributions of Alternative Press Publishers to Multicultural Literature. *Library Trends* 41 (Winter): 524–40.

Jacques, Geoffrey. 1995. A Mix of Feast and Famine for African Americans. *Publishers Weekly* 242, no. 50 (December 11): 36–40.

Johnson, Charles. 1999. Foreword. In *Sacred Fire: The QBR 100 Essential Black Books*, ed. Max Rodriguez, Angeli R. Rasbury, and Carol Taylor, xvii–xx. New York: John Wiley.

Kruse, Ginny M., and Kathleen T. Horning. 1991. *Multicultural Literature for Children and Young Adults: A Selected Listing of Books 1980–1990 by and About People of Color*. Vol. 1. Wisconsin Department of Public Instruction, Cooperative Children's Book Center. Madison, WI: University of Wisconsin.

Kruse, Ginny M., Kathleen T. Horning, and M. Schliesman. 1997. *Multicultural Literature for Children and Young Adults: A Selected Listing of Books by and About People of Color*. Vol. 2: 1991–1996. Wisconsin Department of Public Instruction, Cooperative Children's Book Center. Madison: University of Wisconsin.

Landrum, Larry. 1999. *American Mystery and Detective Novels: A Reference Guide*. Westport, CT: Greenwood.

Lape, N. G. 2000. *West of the Border: The Multicultural Literature of the Western American Frontiers*. Athens, OH: Ohio University Press.

Larrick, Nancy. 1965. The All White World of Children's Books. *Saturday Review* 48 (September 11): 63–65, 84–85.

McCook, Kathleen de la Peña. 1993. Considerations of Theoretical Bases for Reader's Advisory Services. *Collection Building* 12, no. 3/4: 7–12.

———. 2000. *A Place at the Table: Participating in Community Building*. Chicago: American Library Association.

McCook, Kathleen de la Peña, and Catherine Jasper. 2001. The Meaning of Reading: Fiction and Public Libraries. *The Acquisitions Librarian* 25: 51–60.

MacDonald, Gina, and Andrew MacDonald. 1999. Ethnic Detectives in Popular Fiction: New Directions for an American Genre. In *Diversity and Detective Fiction*, ed. Kathleen Gregory Klein, 60–113. Bowling Green, OH: Bowling Green State University Popular Press.

Miller-Lachmann, Lyn. 1995a. Publishing of Multicultural Books. In *Global Voices, Global Visions*, ed. Lyn Miller-Lachman, xiii–xxxv. New Providence: R. R. Bowker.

———. 1995b. *Global Voices, Global Visions*. New Providence: R. R. Bowker.

Muse, Daphne. 1997. *New Press Guide to Multicultural Resources for Young Readers*. New York: New Press; distributed by W. W. Norton.

Nell, Victor. 1988. *Lost in a Book: The Psychology of Reading for Pleasure*. New Haven: Yale University Press.

Pearl, Nancy. 1999. *Now Read This: A Guide to Mainstream Fiction, 1978–1998.* Englewood, CO: Libraries Unlimited.

Ramsdell, Kristen. 1999. *Romance Fiction.* Englewood, CO: Libraries Unlimited.

Reid, Edna. 1994. An Exploratory Study: Using Online Databases to Analyze the Dispersion of Contemporary African-American Young Adult Literature. In *African American Voices in Young Adult Literature: Transformation, Transition, Transformation*, ed. Karen P. Smith, 369–96. Metuchen, NJ: Scarecrow.

Rochman, Hazel. 1993. *Against Borders: Promoting Books for a Multicultural World.* Chicago: American Library Association.

Ross, Catherine Sheldrick. 1991. Readers' Advisory Service: New Directions. *Reference Quarterly* 30, no. 4 (Summer): 503–18.

Roy, Loriene. 1993. Recovering Native Identity: Developing Reader's Advisory Services for Non-Reservation Native Americans. *Collection Building* 12, no. 3/4: 76–77.

———. 2000. To Support and Model Native American Library Services. *Texas Library Journal* 76 (Spring): 32–35.

Salas, Abel M. 1996. The Word Game: Mainstream Acceptance of Hispanic American Writers. *Hispanic* 9, no. 10 (October): 18, 20, 22.

Saricks, Joyce G. 2001. Reading and the Future of the Public Library. *The Acquisitions Librarian* no. 25: 113–21.

Schon, I. 1997. *The Best of the Latino Heritage: A Guide to the Best Juvenile Books About Latino People and Cultures.* Lanham, MD: The Scarecrow Press.

Simson, Maria. 1991. Native American Fiction, Memoirs Blossom into Print. Survey of Books Being Published or Planned About Native American Culture. *Publishers Weekly* 238, no. 25 (June 7): 22.

Taxel, J. 1997. Multicultural Literature and the Politics of Reaction. *Teachers College Record* 98 (Spring): 417–48.

Thomas, Sheree, ed. 2000. *Dark Matter: A Century of Speculative Fiction from the African Diaspora.* New York: Aspect/Warner Books.

Towey, Cathleen A. 2001. Flow: The Benefits of Pleasure Reading and Tapping Reader's Interests. *The Acquisitions Librarian* no. 25: 131–40.

Van Fleet, Connie, and Douglas Raber. 1990. The Public Library as a Social/Cultural Institution: Alternative Perspectives and Changing Contexts. In *Adult Services: An Enduring Focus for Public Libraries*, ed. Kathleen M. Heim and Danny P. Wallace, 456–500. Chicago: American Library Association.

Watson, Dana, and RUSA CODES Readers' Advisory Committee. 2000. From the Committees of RUSA. Time to Turn the Page: Library Education for Readers' Advisory Services. *Reference and User Services Quarterly* 40, no. 2 (Winter). In press.

Whitson, Kathy J. 1999. *Native American Literatures: An Encyclopedia of Works, Characters, Authors, and Themes*. Santa Barbara: ABC-CLIO.

Wiegand, Wayne A. 1997. Out of Sight, Out of Mind: Why Don't We Have Any Schools of Library and Reading Studies? *Journal of Education for Library and Information Science* 38 no.1 (Fall): 314–26.

Williams, David. 1997. Native American Literature. In *What Do I Read Next? Multicultural Literature*, ed. Rafaela G. Castro, Edith Maureen Fisher, Terry Hong, and David Williams, 521–29. Detroit: Gale.

Woods, Paula, ed. 1999. *Spooks, Spies, and Private Eyes: Black Mystery, Crime, and Suspense Fiction.* New York: Doubleday.

CHAPTER 16

Conceptualizing a Center for the Reader

Glen Holt

The Transformation of Reader Culture

Three truisms underpin today's public library culture. One truism is that books are changing. Another is that readers are changing. A third is that libraries must change to deal with these shifts.

The foundation on which libraries can build is the constancy of the story. Human beings hang on to the stories of their childhood, school, work, and family. They turn to stories—whether those in the Bible or Harlequin romances—to fulfill needs in their lives. They delight in stories about others—whether they are sports or Hollywood heroes, human-interest tales about anonymous citizens, or picaresque accounts of the famous. They enjoy fantastic stories, whether fairy tales or video games. They tell true and made-up stories about themselves (Simpson 2000, Engram 1997, Eheart and Power 1995).

The Changeable Book

In the culture of writing and print, the book is the principal written transmittal tool for stories. The book, however, has never been just one thing but many. Since humankind first figured out how to put covers over skins and paper, books have changed dramatically.

- Monastic tomes and folio editions evolved to mass-produced editions and paperbacks.

- Story-related graphics changed books. Original sketches, woodblock prints, rotogravure illustrations, and computer-enhanced photographs mark graphic milestones in the transformation of the book.

- Technological innovations affected stories and the books that hold stories. The telegraph, the telephone, high-speed printing, sound recording, and radio; film, television, videotape, audiotape, compact disks, and more recently, digital imaging, recording, and transmission all created new opportunities for storytellers of every kind from biographers and historians to fantasy and fiction writers. The technology also changed the way books were created, the way stories were told, and even the stories that were created.

- The e-book is the newest literary tool. Fright-writer Stephen King has already published a manuscript exclusively as an e-book. Other best-selling authors are working e-books into their mass marketing. As I was completing the final draft of this chapter, best-selling fiction writers Patricia Cornwell, Robert Ludlum, James Patterson, Ken Follett, Ed McBain, and Brad Meltzer had either recently published electronic editions of hardback books or were about to do so. In each case, the electronic publication was scheduled in advance of the paper publication by a period ranging from two weeks to a little over a month. The e-book is taking its place as a presence in American literary life.

The Shifting Reader Culture

Social and cultural forces also have an impact on stories, reading, and books. Adults are working longer hours and have less time to engage in storytelling, story reading, or reading of any kind. In survey after survey, many persons—especially women—report a lack of time to read for fun or to go to the library just for fun. In the absence of solid reading time, many have changed the source of their stories from popular books to watching shorter and simpler stories on film and television (Sheldon 1992, Bailyn 1993, Pencavel 1998, Starling 1999).

Children's story use has shifted even more visibly. Raised in a high-tech world, today's children turn to movies rather than books, computer games rather than comic books, and playing video (story fantasy) games rather than watching television. In general, the younger the child and the more experience the child has with computing, the greater the preference for active self-customized computer interaction rather than sedate story reading or passive television watching. In all these examples, people are not turning away from stories, only moving to different forms and kinds of stories (Henry 2000, Dolliver 1999, Benton 1995).

Books in Library Story Culture

Amid all these changes, books remain dominant in the story culture of libraries. In the relatively poor city of St. Louis, which has a relatively high percentage of people with literacy problems, the St. Louis Public Library (SLPL) circulates annually seven books per capita and thirty-three books per cardholder. Over 55 percent of SLPL's circulations come from popular books, including the stories found in fiction, biography, and history. The vast majority of popular book circulation, of course, is fiction. Hence, almost all circulations are stories of one kind or another.

Another set of statistics illustrates the importance of books (and stories) for libraries. In a recent cost-benefit analysis, an SLPL research team calculated that users received between $2.50 and $5.00 in benefits for each dollar in public funds spent on providing library services. A large percentage of those benefits—more than 80 percent—came from three categories of service: books for adults, books for children, and staff help.

These benefits might be suspect except that library users in four other cost-benefit-analysis study communities—Baltimore County, Birmingham, King County (WA), and Phoenix—experienced similar or greater direct benefits from books and staff help. And, like St. Louis, the great majority of all their popular-book circulations are storybooks.

The Center for the Reader

In this rapidly shifting, still-book-centered story culture, public libraries have to build on their long heritage of change and adapt again. The St. Louis Public Library's Center for the Reader (CFR) is one such adaptation.

At this point CFR still exists only in the minds' eyes of staff. But planning for this space and the tools that will make it work already drive decisions about how SLPL will remodel and expand its main library and refocus its services. This chapter shares the staff's current conceptualization of CFR not because they have already solved every problem but so that others may consider the ideas and use them to generate other enriched reader-serving environments.

CFR will include four different elements:

- A physical place in the central library devoted to those who delight in reading, listening to, and viewing stories
- The headquarters for a broad outreach program informing both children and adults of the joys and insights they can find in stories and the value of turning to the public library as a source of such stories
- The center for extensive and more sophisticated training for advisors who work in the CFR space and throughout the system
- The locus of a research program focused on improving readers' advising and outreach. Research activities will focus on readers, their materials' selection, and the value they obtain from their reading, viewing, and listening experiences

Each of the following sections explores one CFR element.

The Center for the Reader As a Place

Space

The first requisite for a special place is adequate space. SLPL's current "popular library" occupies four thousand square feet. This unit accounts for nearly 60 percent of the central library's circulation.

The popular library has a very traditional appearance and feel. It is dominated by seven-foot stacks in a room lined with five-foot-high bays with shelves of popular books. Other display units hold videos along with audio books. More floor space is needed to provide more face-out shelving, a fully merchandised environment, and more seats.

The new Center for the Reader will double the floor space devoted to popular books and other current-story formats. As presently calculated, this space will be the library's Great Hall, the most magnificent room in the 1912 Cass-Gilbert Italianate-palace building.

SLPL staff are thinking through how to create within this space a new kind of reader/listener/viewer destination for the region. The underlying conceptualization is a magnet store that will attract those who delight in popular stories, their telling, and their discussion.

Materials

Library professionals already know that the well-organized abundance of central and regional libraries generates disproportionately higher circulation than well-stocked neighborhood and minibranches. Like region-serving grocery stores, or Barnes & Noble and Borders bookstores,

CFR will have an abundance of materials—multiple copies of thirty thousand current popular book titles and ten thousand stories in video and audio formats. This plentitude is based on three strategies:

- A healthy annual budget for popular materials. Nothing turns off a library's popular-materials users faster than a meager stock that does not meet their expectations.

- Regular, deep weeding of dead stock occupying space that ought to be filled with current titles. One of the great myths of popular-library operations is that users cannot tell the difference between older and newer stories and books. Every time SLPL staff weeds deeply, including weeding that cuts the overall size of a unit's collections, circulation increases.

- Adjacent shelving of classic materials and last copies of recent but still used materials. Although shelves of old books in popular libraries do not pass customer muster, carefully selected shelves of literary criticism, older classic literature, and single copies of recent popular materials circulate sufficiently to house them adjacent to CFR. This location will add to CFR's abundance and will encourage users to expand their reading, listening, and viewing into related areas. SLPL's central library last-copy and classic fiction holdings consist of about eighty thousand items. These volumes remain under a collection-development policy acknowledging that SLPL does not provide research collections in popular materials of any kind.

Anticipatory thematic displays catering to customer interests

Finding volumes by Alexander Kent, Lawrence Sanders, and Sinclair Lewis on the same or different trips to big libraries and big bookstores illustrates a common and much-abused shelving rule (i.e., the fewer alphabets and shelving topics, the better). Fiction and stories are generally not one thing but many. Many of these deserve themed display in categories that anticipate users.

One example is the Gütersloh (Germany) Public Library. For several years the staff of this institution has followed a popular-book marketing strategy that breaks out lots of kinds of story materials. These include both books and videos by subjects such as "at the beach," "your French vacation," and "love and sex." The mini-merchandising program is so popular that regular library users have come to expect its continually refreshed delights along with more traditional merchandising categories such as "war," "mystery," and "romance."

By and large, libraries—and large bookstores—do not lead in present-ing their merchandise to their customers. For comparison, look at super-markets with their hundreds of brand types and thousands of different brands. Such stores give enormous attention to shelving and displays be-cause they know that positioning influences purchases.

Some libraries have already learned this lesson. King County (WA), Columbus (OH), Hennepin County (MN), and Charlotte-Mecklenburg (NC) are all high-circulation library leaders that have pointed the way in customizing the organization of their popular materials to meet user needs. It is no accident, for example, that "for-rent" best-sellers are displayed just inside the main entrance at Charlotte-Mecklenburg's main library and Hennepin County's Ridgedale branch. Their shelving message is plain: The hottest books used by the library's best customers deserve the most conve-nient shelving and display location.

Virtual tools and access

Who could conceptualize a Center for the Reader without computers that allow patron-placed reserves of materials as well as access to NoveList, the Rating Zone, and other materials-advisory products like them, and Internet sites such as Barnesandnoble.com and Amazon.com?

CFR will acknowledge that virtual reference tools and virtual reading experiences are now part of American life. Libraries should use them and offer such services, including patron-placed reserves and interlibrary loans (whether mediated or not). Furthermore, staff ought to be more skillful in using these virtual tools than users are. After all, online information sites have become standard tools in the readers' advisory field.

CFR also has to be set up digitally so that it can provide stories when e-books become a way of literary life, not just a developing trend. In the near future, public libraries will buy "publication rights" to electronic "books" and encourage their in-person and virtual users to download the digitized text and pictures of the stories they want. CFR needs to be ready to participate in this growing literary phenomenon.

A look and feel beyond the bookstore formula

When professional librarians compare the treatment of popular books in big new bookstores and large libraries, bookstores usually win because of their amenities. Subjects are easier to find, the seating is often more gen-erous and comfortable, and pleasant smells drift out from the inevitable latte bar.

Libraries can have a comfortable feel without emulating the sales-promotional aspects of bookstores. The highest purpose in libraries, after all, is still books and skilled staff who give personalized help. Here are some design tools:

- More seating in relation to shelves. Librarians nearly always try to stuff too many books into too little space and/or they fail to weed sufficiently, so that books eventually crowd out seating. Popular libraries ought to have an open look and feel with higher seating-to-shelf ratios and less stock storage than other parts of the library.

- Good lighting can add texture to space as well as illuminate it. Task and side lighting appropriate for reading needs to be a CFR feature. Pleasant reading light is different from the lighting that illuminates the bottom rows of packed, spine-out book shelves. Bounce-off-the-ceiling lighting can provide appropriate stack illumination while accent and color-corrected study and reading lighting can give CFR comfortable reading, viewing, and listening lighting at a reasonable price.

- This section ought to look nicer than any other library section. It ought to delight those who use it. Furniture ought to be rearranged periodically. New furniture and displays ought to be substituted for older models on a frequent basis. In short, a library's best customers deserve high-quality design and fittings in the setting they use most.

- Electronic security makes it possible to create discrete (as opposed to lumped together and noisy) reader settings. Too many popular materials units look more like research-university reading rooms than friendly reading and selection places. The two environments should not look the same. Popular materials users do not need to be subjected to an academic study hall environment.

- As SLPL's cost-benefit analysis indicates, a well-trained, knowledgeable, enthusiastic staff is critical to the success of CFR, even when that staff consists of clerks, techs, and security officers. So many bad experiences occur in libraries because security and service staff are rooted to their places. The interrogative "May I help you find something?" is more appreciated by users when they have just entered and are not yet quite sure what question to ask or whom to ask. A few libraries have already organized a mobile in-library staff that moves about with cell phones. At SLPL, CFR staff are likely to be the equivalent of the institution's current homework helpers and technology assistants. Like these two sets of employees, the story assistants will provide one-on-one customization of service at a level where the reader requires it. Librarians and bibliographers have an important place in this setting. They are the brains of the operation. They manage its service. They answer questions that are too hard for others to handle. In these tasks they are part of the full expression of the library's customized-service culture.

CFR's muted sound, differential lighting, and multiple activities will send the message that the unit is a vital, ever-changing place; an explicitly designed personal-entertainment center that deserves use; and a physical setting that testifies to a continuing and dynamic relationship between library and user.

Focus on all forms of the story

The book-based story is the cheapest, most convenient, and easiest-to-read narrative format that currently exists. If the technology of information and story dissemination holds true, however, the storybook format and the way stories are told will continue to change as they have many previous times. In response to this recognition, CFR will be a multimedia facility. It will contain copies of stories and discussions of stories in audio, video, CD, live TV, and videoconferencing formats. CFR will also recognize that popular and/or important stories exist in music, including opera, as related story forms.

Authors ranging from Alexander Dumas and Charles Dickens to Stephen King and James Patterson have written stories that are the basis for screenplays. And who can forget the powerful and entertaining stories contained in the movie "Citizen Kane," the comic operetta "The Pirates of Penzance," and the opera "Aida"? These stand beside a work such as George Bernard Shaw's "Pygmalion," which has been retold as a movie and portrayed over and over in stage plays. CFR, therefore, will be a place to listen to, view, and read stories.

Cater to intergroup audiences

The Wizard of Oz and the Harry Potter novels cut across age, ethnic, and racial lines. So, too, does the work of contemporary novelist Toni Morrison, romance writer Danielle Steel, and mystery writer Mary Higgins Clark. The CFR staff will be trained to recognize that old and young, African-American and white, and old ethnic and new immigrant groups can all enjoy the same stories as well as different ones. In some cases, this integration can involve both new adult readers and youngsters already recognized as having reading problems. Part of the CFR style will be building relationships with people from all these groups and among members of different user groups.

Because they represent future customers, the most important part of catering to intergroup audiences is to integrate youth and young adults into the adult popular materials culture. Historically, in most large libraries, the young adult section occupies an out-of-the-way alcove. Children of younger ages are even more segregated. The Center for the Reader will acknowledge both groups by shelving youth and young adult collections in prominent units that are adjacent to and/or part of CFR and will include both groups in its programming mandate.

Organize readers' discussion groups

SLPL focus groups show that readers want to talk about their reading—with readers who read the same works, those who read the same kinds of stories, and those who read different stories entirely. Library users also want creative opportunities to discuss stories told in music and motion pictures. CFR can satisfy all of these programming needs, building one-on-one and group relationships by offering readers high-quality social/learning opportunities. One important way to build such relationships is through the organization of reading discussion groups.

Volunteers will become an important part of this process, expanding their role as storytellers, discussion leaders, and outreach visitors. Librarians will undertake such tasks as well, but their time is limited because they have to perform collection development, team coordination, and management tasks.

Offer customized services

Shopping on the Web has made library users all the more conscious of customized service. America Online and Amazon.com are just two computer-based companies that offer customized consumer services. In the former, the online user volunteers various consumer interests and, in exchange, receives AOL shopping opportunities and suggestions about Web articles and information. Amazon.com offers shopping opportunities on the basis of a profile of prior purchases. More customization is on the way as computers become ever more capable of broadcasting person's needs to the marketplace and of filling out a user's interest profile.

A Center for the Reader needs to customize its services. Personalized advice about what to read, anticipatory selection against profiles that readers have shared with libraries, and the bringing together of readers with similar interests for story discussion are all examples of library customization.

Convenient pickup and delivery are additional tools for customization. CFR will consider delivery options—even if they can be done only with fees. These might include contract delivery by taxi or a firm such as

United Parcel Service. They might include the online delivery of the full text or selected chapters of electronic publications to the library or to regular customers' homes and offices. As the largest holder of materials for a library system, CFR will have to be part of an efficient delivery system.

Operate a computerized stock-management system

For the past decade, most retail stock-management systems have had ordering and transference-between-location schemes built into their functionality. Anyone who shops at a department store has watched as a sales-clerk checks a stock item's availability at other locations either by phone or computer. Library stock management too often focuses only on a shelving-and-finding scheme, not on stock management.

A few years ago SLPL's technology services staff devised a computerized stock system that responds to multiple circulations of merchandised popular videos, audiotapes, discs, and books by initiating a computerized pull-item order at locations where the materials are not circulating. This Auto Rotate system also creates a queue list that staff can use to order more copies of very popular materials. In short, Auto Rotate manages a responsive stock-replacement system that optimizes the use of each stock item and gives library users an impression of greater abundance of material supplies than that which usually exists without such a system in place. CFR needs to have access to this sophisticated stock-management system.

Offer important public performances

Five years ago SLPL set out to build Friends' memberships. Staff and professional focus-group leaders asked current and potential Friends what benefits would most attract them to library-support memberships. They answered that lectures, photo opportunities, and book signings by well-known authors would most attract them.

Out of that finding came an initiative for the development of the SLPL Signature Series, talks and lectures by well-known writers, storytellers, and actor-performers. For the past five years, the Signature Series has featured performances by Toni Morrison, Mary Higgins Clark, Susan Sontag, Baxter Black, Stephen Ambrose, David Halberstam, Robert Pinsky, Gwendolyn Brooks, Rita Dove, and Danny Glover.

Events in the Signature Series have deepened the relationships between the library and its user-constituents. In focus groups, participants talked about particular Signature Series performances as memorable individual and/or family events.

Three generations of one family showed up to hear Mary Higgins Clark, whose books often constitute the crossover between young adult and adult reading, especially for young women. Stephen Ambrose was acclaimed by a different group who related his talk to their own amateur study of local and regional history. Danny Glover's reading of the poetry of Harlem renaissance writer Langston Hughes, accompanied by his associate Felix Justice's delivery of one of Martin Luther King's famous speeches, still serves as a notable memory for many SLPL Friends.

The events also help gain adherents. Each author attracts a different constituency. About half of the attendees have no previous relationship with the library. Hence the Signature Series serves as a mechanism to attract more Friends' members—and new library cardholders as well.

Library Outreach

CFR special events, most notably the Signature Series, are one means to promote the story, books, and library use. By their reputation, the speakers add stature to the library's reputation and often attract library users who would not come otherwise. There are still more proactive mechanisms. As they are conceptualizing CFR, staff members will organize both adults' and children's outreach services housed in that unit. Here is an outline of several strategies:

Partner with Those Who Promote Reading and Stories

Public libraries will never have enough staff and volunteers to do all the necessary outreach work. In this situation, partnerships are in order. In a city like St. Louis, where resources are few and where schools lack school libraries and most classrooms have too few computers, teacher-librarian partnerships deserve considerable effort. So do efforts to reach senior citizens.

- Materials are the basis for one important SLPL teacher-librarian partnership. One strategy is to organize book boxes for caregivers in day-care facilities as well as for parents with preschool children. Each of the boxes provides more than a dozen books, activities, puppets, and/or games on topics such as "telling time," "visiting the doctor," and "African animals."

- Another strategy is to organize book bags for teachers. In this partnership, teachers call the library and talk with staff about their conceptualization of a unit they want to teach. Staff members gather a book bag of twenty-five to forty books that the teachers can pick up and use as a classroom collection for the teaching of the topic.

- A third strategy is to train teachers, caregivers, and parents in how to prepare children to read and how to help them learn to read. The assumption is that parents want their children to be successful, but many are unsure of how and where to begin. Training in reading readiness and how to teach reading helps children learn to read and develops new and reinforces old relationships between the library and those who care for children.

- Another materials-related outreach activity to be housed in CFR is a seniors' book-delivery program. Because so many seniors are low literates, these circulations often involve low-literacy materials. They also involve large print. In this program, seniors who otherwise would lack access to books have them in abundance.

Friendly visitors

More than a century ago, settlement house founder Jane Addams described the home and institutional outreach activities of her staff and volunteers as the domain of Hull House's "friendly visitors." SLPL also has friendly visitors, and CFR will be the base of their activities.

- SLPL staff deliver materials and programs to more than two hundred day-care centers each month.

- SLPL staff deliver materials and programs to more than a hundred senior residences and nutrition sites each month.

- CFR will emphasize outreach to high school and college students who, in some cases, lack both popular materials and reference help.

- In addition, CFR staff and volunteers will reach out with programs, especially story telling, to new adult readers.

With Outreach and CFR staff working together, each aspect of outreach and customer service ought to be strengthened.

Readers' Advisory Training

For five years now, it has been apparent that the library staff we have is not the one we need. That perception is not a negative reflection on those who are currently employed. Rather, it suggests the historical weakness of SLPL's library in-service education, a problem for many other library systems as well.

That weakness is especially apparent in readers' advisory. Promoting the enjoyment of stories has never been an easy library specialty. Historically, the responsibility for this specialty fell to those individual staff members who read widely. These readers' advisory stalwarts were left pretty much to guide their replacements through enthusiasm for reading and mentoring in the use of limited tools. At every library location, these people's ability to suggest a good book and to help readers select the next best story became the foundation of much of a library's reputation and the source of many of its notable successes.

Libraries need to build on that tradition, but they also need to overcome the weaknesses that are inherent in this often-idiosyncratic "star system." Without special training, many readers' advisors often know well only one genre of literature and have minimal or no knowledge of others. Even if they were advising stars in the truest sense, a weakness still exists in the readers' advisory system. What advising strategies did staff use on days or evenings when that specialist was not on site? How did readers' advisory experts pass on their knowledge to their peers and successors? And how did any readers' advisor come to know the process by which to determine what help readers really needed and whether the staff had actually helped the customer?

Without good answers to questions like these, the need to train quality readers' advisory staff becomes central to promoting and sustaining interest in all forms of the story. These questions took on paramount importance in planning for the Center for the Reader.

For this reason SLPL became a partner with NoveList in the development of a formal curriculum that could help train readers' advisors and thereby to help provide an outstanding experience for CFR visitors. Out of this partnership has come the pilot curriculum for "Readers' Advisory 101." This course already has been piloted, and its authors are currently revising it.

The new multiunit curriculum now available from EBSCO lays out systematic strategies involved in the readers' advisory process, explores the reasons people read, helps staff understand the role of readers' advisory, and develops techniques for effectiveness in the readers' advisory transaction. In addition, there is training in content—how people can build their knowledge in fiction without reading every book and how staff can help users help themselves in selecting materials.

This training also suggests how readers' advisors may use new electronic tools to improve their advising. These include new general readers' advisory tools such as the well-known NoveList and categorical tools such as Soon's historical fiction site (URL: http://uts.cc.utexas.edu/~soon/histfiction/ [accessed January 28, 2001]) or AOL's science fiction site. For those whose readers have more esoteric tastes there is often intriguing information and customized publication and delivery at iUniverse.com (URL: http://www.iuniverse.com/ [accessed January 28, 2001]). Such tools—and dozens of others—support advisers' efforts to find the next book or story. Moreover, networked computer users have begun to use electronic tools, and they expect library staff to use the tools in sophisticated ways to improve their personal reading experience.

One other reason exists for adding a heavy readers' advisory training component to CFR operations. To cope with the general staff shortage in the knowledge sector, including the library profession, training has become an imperative. In the process, staff will have more opportunity for upward mobility while remaining librarians.

Applied Research in the Center for the Reader

In developing the SLPL/EBSCO-NoveList readers' advisory curriculum, the authors, Sterling Hayden, director of training at the St. Louis Public Library, and Duncan Smith, relied on Smith's experiences as a readers' advisor and a readers' advisory trainer at SLPL. Even before this curriculum-development project, SLPL staff recognized that they could provide better training if they knew more about how library patrons select and use popular books and stories and the role library staff readers' advisers play in helping with and/or affirming selections and use.

Research on fiction readers and library users is therefore on the CFR agenda. The following outline agenda expresses the purposes of and strategies for this research. In considering the agenda, remember that this research will focus on the library's best user-customers, its core readers who contribute the most absolute and relative circulations to a library's bottom line.

CFR research will explore general patterns of reading behavior and effective readers' advisory techniques by which knowledge of these patterns can help improve readers' advisory. Here are the topics we intend to explore:

Topic 1. How readers measure their selection successes and failures. Do readers who select by browsing do so because they enjoy the process or because they know no better way to get what they want?

Topic 2. How story selection changes throughout people's lives. How much do changing age, transformation of family structure, and shifts in economic circumstance affect what people select to read? Examples of questions are as follows:

- Are there discernible life cycles in the adult reading habit for regular readers? How do reading selections change with life cycles?

- Are the reading habits and the reading life cycles of Caucasians, African Americans, Hispanics, and Asians different? Recreational selections are quite different. How different are their reading habits?

- How do reading selections change with the rhythms of life such as family stress, vacations, or traveling?

- Do shifts in economic circumstances produce short-term or long-term shifts in story selection?

- What are the special reading and readers' advisory needs of new adult readers?

Topic 3. How child-to-adult reading patterns change. Among all the age issues, the transition from child to adult reading is one of the most important for library professionals and for the future of libraries. In that transition readers take the first steps of their lifelong reading habits. It is then as well that they consider their relationships with libraries and librarians. Some become lifelong readers. Others never voluntarily enter a library again.

- What are the most important factors affecting that transition?

- Why do many children turn away from reading as young adults and adults while others become even more avid readers?

Topic 4. How libraries turn on and turn off their best customers.

- What are the factors in retaining user loyalty and the ways that library staff/user transactions develop into rich and stable relationships?

- What roles do friendliness, openness, content knowledge, age similarity, and so on play in user perception of successful readers' advisory?

Topic 5. Reading patterns.

- Are there discernible reading patterns? How do they change? What factors do readers think cause their reading patterns to change?

- Test this hypothesis: The reading population can be distributed into three general categories—those who are content based, those who are style based, and those who are some combination of these two. In his readers' advisory training materials, Duncan Smith suggests this general division between those who read for content (what is happening in the actions of the characters and the character of the narration) and those who read for style (enjoyment because of the structure and sequence of plot and the predictability of principal characters in series).

- If there are discernible reader categories, do they require the same readers' advisory strategies or different ones?

- Assess models for making those judgments.

Topic 6. Effectiveness of virtual advisory tools.

- Of what help to which readers are virtual readers' selection tools such as Alexandria (URL: http://www.alexlit.com/ [accessed December 27, 2000]), reader-submitted reviews like those found at Amazon.com, and reader-interest profiling tools such as NoveList (URL: http://novelist.epnet.com [accessed December 27, 2000])?

- How can NoveList and other virtual reference products be improved to make them even better as self-help readers' advisory tools by which readers can help themselves find "the next best book"?

Topic 7. Development and measurement of the effectiveness of readers' advisory training protocols.

- CFR will provide a test bed for testing and refining different readers' advisory training-for-service models.

- CFR will assess the portability of training-model protocols.

A whole range of research techniques exists for studying readers' advisory and the reading experience. SLPL has already had success with the audio- or videotaping of focus groups and individual readers' advisor/user interactions. Telephone and written surveys also provide an abundance of information. More complicated are techniques such as readers' diaries of their readings and analysis (with permission) of borrower records, including self-analysis of checkout patterns. A single library cannot conduct all of these activities. Partnerships between academic researchers and libraries offer the best possibility for conducting large portions of this research agenda.

Conclusions

The successful library of the future, like the business of the future, will be built on relationships. The SLPL Center for the Reader is one tool for building and sustaining relationships with a library's best customers. That is true no matter whether the activity is developing a design for a better library-reading-and-advising environment, training staff to provide high levels of service in the library environment, or conducting research that provides the basis for improved service to users.

These are exciting times, as books become e-books, as family structures creak at the pressures they bear, and as stories keep appearing in new forms and formats. Amid these shifting sands, the library's best pathway is clear-headed adaptation to meet the story and reading needs of the institution's most consistent customer base. One such response is SLPL's Center for the Reader.

References

Bailyn, Lotte. 1993. *Breaking the Mold: Women, Men, and Time in the New Corporate World*. New York: Free Press.

Benton, Peter. 1995. Conflicting Cultures: Reflections on the Reading and Viewing of Secondary School Pupils. *Oxford Review of Education* 21 (December): 457–71.

Dolliver, Mark. 1999. Computers as Menace to the Youth of America. *Adweek* (Eastern edition) 40 (November 15): 33ff.

Eheart, Brenda Krause, and Martha Bauman Power. 1995. Adoption: Understanding the Past, Present, and Future Through Stories. *Sociological Quarterly* 36 (Winter): 197–216.

Engram, Sara. 1997. Good Stories Make Hope Possible. *Nieman Reports* 51 (Fall): 40–41.

Henry, Julie. 2000. Boys Drop Books in Favour of Computers and TV. *Educational Supplement* 4388 (August 4): 7ff.

Pencavel, John. 1998. The Market Work Behavior and Wages of Women. *Journal of Human Resources* 33 (Fall): 771–805.

Sheldon, Beth Anne. 1992. *Women, Men and Time: Gender Differences in Paid Work, Housework and Leisure*. Westport, CT: Greenwood.

Simpson, Timothy A. 2000. Streets, Sidewalks, Stores, and Stories. *Journal of Contemporary Ethnography* 29 (December): 682–717.

Starling, Kelly. 1999. Career Moms. *Ebony* 54 (July): 52–56.

Conclusions: Readers' Advisory Services Today and Tomorrow

Reading for pleasure is an extraordinary activity. The black squiggles on the white page are still as the grave, colorless as the moonlight desert; but they give the skilled reader a pleasure as acute as the touch of a loved body, as rousing, colorful, and transfiguring as anything out there in the real world. And yet, the more stirring the book, the quieter the reader; pleasure reading breeds a concentration so effortless that the reader of fiction (transported by the book to some other place and shielded by it from distractions), who is so often reviled as an escapist and denounced as the victim of a vice as pernicious as tippling in the morning should instead be the envy of every student and every teacher.

Victor Nell (1988, 1)

Renewed Emphasis on Reading for Pleasure

There is a confluence of streams of events that shape a river of promise for school and public librarians. Alone, each stream would encourage librarians to pay more attention to the role of reading for pleasure in the lives of their clients. Together they have the power to transform and reinvigorate library services. These streams are as follows:

- Bookstore chains, such as Barnes & Noble, have shaped themselves into inviting spaces offering easy browsing, comfortable reading, good coffee, story hours, and author events. Librarians recognize that libraries have competition and that they must compete successfully or lose their dominance in a market long their own.

- In the past decade, librarians have placed more attention on recreational fiction, especially genre fiction, in popular collections.

- During the past decade, the Public Library Association, the Reference and User Services Association, and state library associations have offered conference programs and workshops on readers' advisory and have performed committee work related to it.

- Publishers have seen that guidance to fiction reading is in need of new tools that move beyond standards such as *Fiction Catalog* and *The Readers' Adviser* to *Genreflecting, What Do I Read Next? Multicultural Literature, New Press Guide to Multicultural Resources for Young Readers,* and *Diversity and Detective Fiction.* An explosion of publishing of advisory tools has occurred.

- The St. Louis Public Library has created a new concept in library service, the Center for the Reader, devoted to pleasure reading, listening, and viewing. Many public libraries are creating spaces devoted to pleasure reading and clearly distinct from the library's informational services.

- Research into reading and readers—providing a basis for readers' advisory services—is being conducted both within the profession and in many other fields. The opportunities for true interdisciplinary work are growing.

- Researchers are observing and evaluating the degree of success or, more correctly, the degree of failure with which public libraries deliver advisory services . Knowing that they often do the job poorly has provided clear evidence that improvement is needed. This knowledge is a powerful motivator for positive change.

- Continuing education for readers' advisory work has increased dramatically in the past decade.

- Search engines help alleviate the memory overload characteristic in guiding readers to the next book. NoveList and Amazon.com, among others, have reinvigorated the way in which advisors interact with clients when discussing books and offering suggestions for further reading.

- Listservs such as Fiction_L and Dorothy_L have created virtual communities of librarians, authors, and readers devoted to sharing information on general fiction, mysteries, and so on.

- The gap in graduate professional education for readers' advisory, including building popular collections, has been forcefully noted and documented. The curricular implications of this deficit and the creation of new courses are receiving new attention.

- Professional journals such as *Booklist* now routinely feature genre fiction, including romance novels and inspirational fiction that would have gone unnoted earlier.

All of these developments trend in the same direction for librarians: a new emphasis on helping clients who seek to live fully and well, making the most of leisure and enhancing their quality of life. That confluence of trends is the impulse behind the *Readers' Advisor's Companion.* The trends are representative of the most recent version of what Nell calls "story hunger, the appetite that drove our ancestors to listen, rapt, to tribal storytellers, and that drives us today to theaters, and television shows, to libraries and newsstands" (Nell 1988, 3).

But what can we learn from the preceding chapters? What should we conclude as we reflect on the findings? What are the implications for public and school libraries, professional degree programs, and the research agenda that the field ought to pursue?

Just Because Something Is Fun Doesn't Mean It Isn't Serious

We now know that there are widespread weaknesses in graduate education for readers' advisory services and their delivery. Wiegand sounded a clarion call to the field to base much of its practice on the knowledge base of reading studies. If professional education programs followed his advice, much of the observed weakness in practice would be diminished. It is not a choice between the Internet or readers' advisory; rather, we must choose to provide both on an equal footing in all libraries serving K–12 students and the general public.

Knowing of Wiegand's and others' view that professional educators were not fulfilling the charge to prepare librarians to work with readers' advisory services, Shearer and Burgin surveyed offerings in library and information science graduate programs accredited by the American Library Association. The survey showed a serious neglect of readers' advisory and popular media even though fiction, alone among all pleasure reading, constitutes 60–70 percent of public library print circulation. Some graduate programs in library and information studies pay almost no attention anywhere in the curriculum to popular material collections and the promotion of their use. The remainder of the schools include some aspects. But some schools place most of the curricular attention on readers' advisory topics exclusively in their core; other schools place the topics only in electives. Both strategies leave much to be desired. Both the identification of interdisciplinary knowledge about reading by Wiegand and the course that Crowley developed—the outline appends his chapter—can help other educators teach readers' advisory services at the graduate level.

We have seen that it is not only education for readers' advisory that is inadequate. May shows us that public librarians usually fail in assisting the adult pleasure reader. Staff not infrequently treat the client asking for assistance with reluctance, disdain, or outright annoyance. May discovered that staff overlook the useful new readers' advisory tools, the Web sites are deficient with respect to pleasure reading, and a widespread absence of good customer service exists. Her work indicates that the deficiencies noted in earlier research are not isolated to one region of the country. Unobtrusive study of reference services long ago showed problems in pinpointing clients' information needs and in responding to them accurately. Similar techniques focusing on readers' advisory today uncover even grimmer evidence of unprofessional service patterns.

The situation in school media centers seems to be better. Doll notes that advisory services in school media centers are just as necessary and demanding as those in public libraries. She identifies a wealth of tools to assist the advisor and, like Saricks, urges advisors to talk with students about their enjoyment of books. It would be valuable to use unobtrusive observation techniques to see whether readers' advisory work for children in school media centers is generally performed at a higher level than advisory work for adults in public libraries. A study of readers' advisory service to young people in public libraries did provide some evidence that children's service librarians in North Carolina perform at a higher, although still unsatisfactory, level than do adult service librarians (Bracy 1996).

It is clear then that the field needs to improve readers' advisory practices at the building level. For that reason much of this book has focused on models of excellent readers' advisory practice. Saricks not only notes some of the best tools available, but she also shows how to integrate them into practice. Some readers, she notes, want to have direct assistance, but all can benefit from placing tools in proximity of use, such as locating those for mystery or science fiction or horror on or near the shelves devoted to them. In her recommendations we find the promise of creating an environment that promotes the value of reading for pleasure and encourages the discussion of the enjoyment of books.

The Internet's influence is felt in many chapters. Johnson writes on the "global conversation" about books, reading, and authors. Just as traditional business corporations are proving to be very successful in increasing their markets by using dot-com-type techniques, librarians are finding that the Internet leverages the traditional strengths of encouraging good reading. Libraries offer nonstop online access to the catalog; Web sites highlight reading suggestions; links appear to readers' advisory resources; annotated lists help browsers limit their searches; and young adults share their book enthusiasms with others on Web sites or in publications.

It is not only by working with individual readers that we promote pleasure reading. Armstrong's chapter calls to mind an ideal library with many active reading groups, author talks, and other celebrations of creative writing. Her library would offer easy browsing of genre fiction, bookmarks highlighting readers' advisory services and programs, and engaging displays. It would be an environment that subtly encourages readers to find books suited to their needs. If you ever visit a superb independent bookstore such as the Elliott Bay Book Company in Seattle or Mystery Books in Washington, D.C., you will quickly see how far most librarians need to go to create spaces that are conducive to making books irresistible.

The theme of using the strengths of automation to solve the thorny problems of delivering professional readers' advisory service is central to Smith's concerns. He is the founder of NoveList and believes that the field needs to study exemplars of advisory service provision (i.e., librarians such as Joyce Saricks) as they work with readers. The point is to develop algorithms that others can use in conjunction with computers. His ideas point to research in the areas that Wiegand believes we should stress in library education programs—reading and readers—and offer the hope of development of new, software-based tools to make readers' advisor practice and training more effective.

Everything done in readers' advisory finally rests on people enjoying the reading process. Ross and Sturm offer two very different ways to understand what goes on in the reading process. Ross starts with pleasure readers themselves. She interviews them to gain insights into the experience of reading and ways to facilitate it. Her work leads to the most elaborate analysis I have ever seen of what appeals to readers in the books they read. She identifies twenty-six characteristics of reading appeal (e.g., fast or slow paced, sexually explicit or genteel, conversational or descriptive, etc.). These, she observes, are worth keeping in mind when narrowing the field for the next book that might interest a reader.

This approach is a little like the game of Twenty Questions. Using diagnostic questions, the advisor narrows the set of books that will likely please the reader. One result of reflection on Ross's findings is that they help you to focus on the experience of reading and to identify individual preferences. You can practice by analyzing your own reactions to books that delight you and those that, unexpectedly, proved disappointing.

Sturm, taking an approach completely different from Ross's, discusses both the way we first learn to read and the later stages of reading for pleasure. His interest is in knowing the nature of the trancelike state we fall into when reading or that enjoyed by a child listening to a storyteller. Researchers, he notes, have uncovered evidence that the tedious and difficult job of learning to decode text takes place in a different part of the reader's brain from the effortless act of pleasure reading or listening to a story being read aloud. But beginning readers have so many skills to master before they can readily enter the trancelike state of the pleasure reader. Ross has written in a prize-winning study that "[e]xperienced readers find reading so easy and natural that it takes an effort of the imagination to bring to mind the problems that face apprentice readers as they confront long fictional narratives" (Ross 1995, 228). It is an effort of the imagination that all librarians must make over and over again as they practice their craft. Ross writes in the same study that "[I]t now appears that a reader learns to read, not by drills and exercises, but by reading a lot of text that is meaningful and personally rewarding" (ibid., 232).

Thinking about the work of these investigators, we may anticipate a time when brain researchers and library scientists collaborate on research into reading mastery using EEGs and PET scans. One result may be mappings of the regions of the brain and an understanding of how to hasten the transition from tedious work to pleasurable reading, a transition that many never make. One can speculate that in the future librarians will have means to assist people at various stages of accomplishment to become more adept readers. Even now it is seems clear that librarians can, through strategies such as story hours and books-on-tape, motivate beginning readers by demonstrating the pleasure they will be able to enjoy if they make the effort to master the necessary skills. Another conclusion is that encouraging pleasure reading is a socially useful endeavor.

Once people develop the complex skills they use in pleasure reading, then librarians must encourage them to exercise those skills regularly. We call ours the Information Economy; in this economy, well-honed reading skills are very valuable. Fortunately, librarians place over one billion books in Americans' hands each year. Both adult and juvenile circulation in public libraries has been trending upward over the past decade, with only minor dips occasionally along the way.[1]

The most difficult age group to interest in reading books is undoubtedly teenagers. The task of motivating them to read has never been more daunting than it is now. Benedetti offers many techniques to catch young peoples' attention. Her eight steps in talking with them about books provide a process to use with teens. Using a warm, personal approach and employing newer technologies offer promise. Paying attention to aggressive marketing techniques is emphasized. E-books, movie and television tie-ins, and superstar associations with reading are other means that may tempt teens to develop the library habit.

Increasing the lure of books for teens is one way to increase library effectiveness. For readers' advisory to be fully effective, librarians must look at their attitudes toward the reading of books they themselves would not read and do not value. In the preface is a quote from Margaret Atwood that contains a message for the librarian, "Just because something is fun doesn't mean it isn't serious." We've all known librarians who look down on plea-sure reading unless it involves books that have been deemed "literature." The Australian psychologist Victor Nell observes that the pleasure reader is often reviled as an escapist. Librarians must examine the reasons for such negative attitudes—most librarians themselves read for pleasure and should be leading the parade of those who celebrate its rewards. This nation spends billions of dollars in its schools teaching children to read and de-votes untold hours to showing them that reading can be one of the great pleasures of life. It is schizophrenic of society or anyone on the library staff to suggest that there is less value in spending time on pleasure reading than on answering informational questions.

Centering on the Client

In addition to practicing readers' advisory techniques with fiction, ad-visors' ought to include print nonfiction and audiovisual materials as part of their domain. Nonfiction, Burgin shows us, is very often just like fiction from the point of view of the reading experience. Nell agrees: "Nor does narrative nonfiction (travel, biography) seem to be in any way distinct from fiction in the effects it produces on the reader" (Nell 1988, 2). If you have read McCourt's *Angela's Ashes*, Mayle's *A Year in Provence*, Heyerdahl's *Kon-Tiki*, or McCollough's *The Johnstown Flood*, then you will need no further evidence that the power to sweep readers into another place and time is not a characteristic unique to fiction.

And just as nonfiction has the power to enthrall the reader, storytellers and dramatists have exhibited that power for millennia. Schools and public libraries have long capitalized on this fact by instituting story hours, puppet shows, and author readings. The number of people who can benefit from any one these events is limited, and the per capita costs are relatively high. Fortunately, both books-on-tape and videos allow librarians to extend the presentation of stories to every client. Pitman relates how he encountered the reality of client needs when he launched a Web-based supplement to the journal *Video Librarian Online.* The first inquiry he received was not the scholarly request he expected but instead came from a twelve-year-old who needed some good film suggestions for her slumber party. This is a perfect example of how advisors can meet people's real-life needs. Another exam-ple might involve a commuter facing ever longer and more boring com-mutes. A plentiful and regularly refreshed supply of suitable books-on-tape can transform that taxpayer's chore into a pleasure.

Audiovisual materials can add depth and richness to learning while also teaching many listeners how to become more effective readers. Lis-tening to dramas brings them vividly to life; novels that actors read can have a powerful emotional effect. Americans love movies; videos allow librarians to collect on film all kinds of stories once found only in books. For those who have never successfully mastered the skills necessary to enter the trance of pleasure reading, this is the best way to satisfy their hunger for stories.

As Pitman notes, understanding Martin Luther King's "I Have a Dream" speech is not really possible from reading it on a printed page; we must hear it. Imagine for a moment what it might do for our historical understanding to hear, or better, to see on video Lincoln's "Gettysburg Address" or Christ's "Sermon on the Mount." The utilization of audiovisual materials in libraries has vast potential.

But even if librarians expand the scope of readers' advisory service to nonfiction, audio and video, they still will not have completed the vision set out here. There are new audiences that have been neglected and new publications that can be assembled and promoted to them. The multiethnic, multicultural population in the United States is becoming more evident every day. Although it is clear that much has been done, much work still remains to offer African Americans, Asian Americans, Latinos, and Native Americans, among others, the level or depth of collecting and service that is more commonly available to middle-class white people in American libraries.

Van Fleet and Dawson make it clear that books for pleasure addressed to these audiences are being written and published, and the techniques to extend readers' advisory to all are at hand. There are major implications for collection development, client relations, and professional education. The lessons from adapting collections and services to different ethnic groups also apply to others in society who have a set of shared concerns and culture. Gays, lesbians, Christian conservatives, and homeschoolers come immediately to mind. It has been found that many libraries do not purchase the American Library Association's gay, lesbian, and bisexual book award finalists at the rate they provide other award books (Loverich and Degnan 1999). Librarians often treat inspirational fiction, which regularly features the values of Christian conservatives, as a genre not worth shelf space. They often treat romance fiction aimed at heterosexual women similarly.

Centering on the client is not, of course, centering on a presumed social norm or an agenda determined by librarians' values. Centering on the client is a healthy extension of the tradition of representing all sides of issues and promoting the freedom to read. Nell writes, "Books are the dreams we would most like to have, and like dreams, they have the power to change consciousness, turning sadness into laughter and anxious introspection to the relaxed contemplation of some other time and place" (Nell 1988, 2). The advisor in a public or school library works with unique clients and attempts to provide the right stories for them, not for someone else. The librarian must respect their freedom to dream their own dreams.

The last chapter in the book brings together everything that precedes it. Holt provides a concept of a new kind of *popular* library. Duncan Smith has been working with the staff at St. Louis Public Library to bring it into being. It is a Center for the Reader that collects not just books but also audio- and video-formatted stories. It supports the enjoyment of reading, listening, and viewing for pleasure, and its staff members are devoted to the work of advisory service, the generic version of readers' advisory. Continuing education to deepen and perfect advisory practice is built into the system. It is a bold new concept that captures our imagination. After it has been operation for several years, impartial researchers should study its effectiveness.

Holt's vision may be a wave of the future in large public library systems, but most of them will not have funds for any new branches in the foreseeable future. And, in any case, advisory services belong in every school and public library. It would be most unfortunate if a few centers for readers cleared the way for all other branch libraries to become Internet and reference centers exclusively. For librarians, the issue is to highlight *both* information service *and* advisory service. Librarians should evaluate and widely discuss various arrangements of library space that are intended to support this dual mission. Combining these two major and very different aspects of service is a challenge for every library that provides both. It is difficult to market and to arrange systems that offer different kinds of services and products.

Holt and his staff are to be commended for having the foresight to recognize that new technologies and new demographics dictate creative new approaches to the delivery of traditional library services. Let's free up our minds to invent a future that supports the imaginative lives of people as well as their intellectual needs.

At present, advisory services in libraries show new energy, imagination, and vitality. They are also far too often a pale shadow of their promise. We need to improve graduate education programs for readers' advisors. The readers of this book have an opportunity to bring about a splendid change in libraries, thus creating an opportunity to delight and inspire people. To bring it to fruition will involve knuckling down to having serious fun, working with interesting people, and spending lots of time reading for pleasure. But somebody has to do it.

—K.D.S

Note

1. By multiplying the nation's population rounded to 280 million by the 1999 figure of six circulations per capita, we arrive at approximately 1.8 billion books circulated from public libraries during 1999. Although this is merely an estimate, it provides an on-the-order-of figure worth publicizing widely (Wright 2000).

References

Bracy, Pauletta Brown. 1996. The Nature of the Readers' Advisory Transaction in Children's and Young Adult Reading. In *Guiding the Reader to the Next Book,* ed. Kenneth Shearer, 21–43. New York: Neal-Schuman.

Loverich, Patricia, and Darrah Degnan. 1999. Out on Our Shelves? Not Really. *Library Journal* 124 (June 15): 55.

Nell, Victor. 1988. *Lost in a Book: The Psychology of Reading for Pleasure*. New Haven: Yale University Press.

Ross, Catherine Sheldrick. 1995. If They Read Nancy Drew, So What?: Series Book Readers Talk Back. *Library and Information Science Research* 17, no. 3: 201–36.

Wright, Lisa A. 2000. Public Library Circ Down 1% Again as Spending Continues to Rise. *American Libraries* 31 (October): 64.

INDEX